STINIE

Andrew Rose, the son of an Aberdeenshire doctor, was
educated at Hardye's School, Dorchester, and Trinity
College, Cambridge. A former barrister, he was called to the
Bar in 1968 and appeared as junior defence Counsel in a
number of notable criminal trials at the Old Bailey in the
1970s.

He lives in South London, not far from Clapham Common.
He is unmarried. *Stinie: Murder on the Common* is his first
book, and he is currently working on a second *cause célèbre*,
the shooting of a rich Egyptian, Fahmy Dey, by his French-
born wife at London's Savoy Hotel in 1923.

STINIE

Murder on the Common

ANDREW ROSE

PENGUIN BOOKS

PENGUIN BOOKS

Published by the Penguin Group
27 Wrights Lane, London W8 5TZ, England
Viking Penguin Inc., 40 West 23rd Street, New York, New York 10010, USA
Penguin Books Australia Ltd, Ringwood, Victoria, Australia
Penguin Books Canada Ltd, 2801 John Street, Markham, Ontario, Canada L3R 1B4
Penguin Books (NZ) Ltd, 182–190 Wairau Road, Auckland 10, New Zealand

Penguin Books Ltd, Registered Offices: Harmondsworth, Middlesex, England

First published by The Bodley Head 1985
Published in Penguin Books 1989
1 3 5 7 9 10 8 6 4 2

Made and printed in Great Britain by
Richard Clay Ltd, Bungay, Suffolk

Dedication

For E.R.
In Memory

'Sir, did you ever know your Crown to fail to produce a theory? The Crown has always a theory!'

Stinie Morrison to the Home Secretary,
24 March 1913

Contents

List of Plates

Foreword

In this absorbing book the author tells the compelling and dramatic story of the Clapham Common murder on New Year's day, 1911 and the conviction of Stinie Morrison at his trial at the Old Bailey.

The victim of the murder was the Polish Jewish refugee, Leon Beron. A black silk handkerchief had been folded over his battered head to form a kind of shroud. There were two mysterious S-shaped two-inch cuts on each side of his nose. There were reports from the continent that 'anarchist' gangs made a practice of mutilating informers.

A fortnight before the murder, three unarmed City of London police officers were murdered when they surprised a gang in the act of breaking into a jeweller's shop in Houndsditch. They were led by a member of Leesma, an extreme political group. Two of the terrorist gang took refuge in No. 100 Sidney Street. This was besieged by police and Scots Guards. Characteristically, Winston Churchill, then Home Secretary, came to see the action for himself.

Early in 1909 two Latvian revolutionaries attempted an armed robbery of a wages car in Tottenham. A policeman and a small boy were shot dead during the police pursuit of the robbers. The Clapham Common murder, two years later, brought public opinion, in the words of the author, 'to the brink of hysteria over the challenge thought to be posed by anarchists.' The public outcry was quickly directed towards the immigrant community in the East End of London.

It was against this background that the trial of Stinie Morrison, himself a refugee from the Ukraine, took place. Mr Justice Oliver, later an eminent Judge but then a young barrister who took a minor part in the trial, described it as 'one of the most unsatisfactory trials I ever remember.' This book shows why. In his massive research upon it, the author had the unique advantage of access to the hitherto withheld Home Office files for the period. He also had the shorthand transcript of the proceedings. His conclusion is that although Morrison was shown to be a crook and a liar, he was wrongly convicted of murder.

The sentence of death which Mr Justice Darling passed upon him was not carried out. Although his appeal against conviction was dismissed by the Court of Appeal as was his application to the Attorney General, Sir Rufus Isaacs, for leave to appeal to the House of Lords, Morrison was reprieved, at very nearly the last moment, by the Home Secretary, Winston Churchill. The sentence of death was commuted to one of penal servitude. The ultimate horror of hanging a probably innocent man was thus avoided. Morrison died in prison after serving ten years of his sentence. He protested his innocence until the very end. It is a sombre and fascinating tale.

The Rt. Hon. Lord Elwyn-Jones P.C., C.H.
Lord Chancellor 1974–79

February, 1985

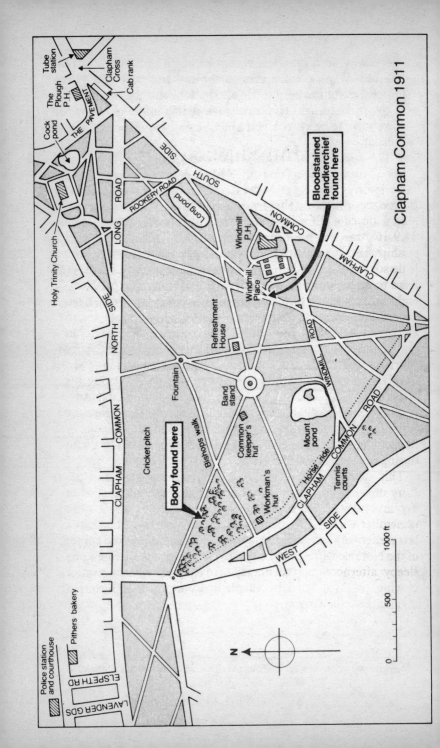

Clapham Common 1911

Tube station
The Plough P.H.
Clapham Cross
Cab rank
Cock pond
THE PAVEMENT
Holy Trinity Church
LONG ROAD
ROOKERY ROAD
Long pond
SOUTH SIDE
COMMON
Windmill P.H.
Bloodstained handkerchief found here
Windmill Place
CLAPHAM
Refreshment House
NORTH SIDE
CLAPHAM COMMON
Cricket pitch
Fountain
Bishops walk
Band stand
Common keeper's hut
Mount pond
WINDMILL ROAD
Body found here
Workman's hut
Horse ride
Tennis courts
COMMON ROAD
CLAPHAM
WEST SIDE
SIDE
Police station and courthouse
Pithers bakery
LAVENDER GDS
ELSPETH RD

N

0   500   1000 ft

Introduction

Before me, as I write these words, lies a small, battered medallion bearing the laconic inscription 'L32 Zepp Essex 24.9.16', made from the aluminium of an ill-fated German airship shot down during London's first major air raid. The little souvenir, picked up by a young soldier uncle, long dead, has a tenuous connection with this story, for among the thirty-eight victims of the raid was Chief Detective-Inspector Alfred Ward, who had played a leading role in the pursuit, arrest and conviction of Stinie* Morrison for the murder of Leon Beron on Clapham Common in the first hours of 1911. After Morrison's reprieve from the gallows (an event which Ward deeply regretted), this burly detective was able to bring his considerable influence to bear upon Home Office mandarins, helping to ensure that Stinie would not be released before the full life sentence of twenty years had been served. As it happened, Stinie Morrison achieved release, of a sort, by dying during his imprisonment.

This slender link between the soldier's keepsake and the story of Stinie Morrison was not, however, the initial spur to my investigation of this very strange affair. I cannot even remember when I first became interested: perhaps it was as a law student at Cambridge. Maybe one of the red-backed spines of the Notable British Trials[1] series caught my eye during some sleepy afternoon in the library. Anyway, it was only after moving to a flat hard by Clapham Common that I started digging away in earnest.

---

* Morrison spelt his name 'Stinie', although many sources erroneously give 'Steinie'.

Who was Stinie Morrison? An odd man, even by criminal standards. A thumping crook, with a long track record for burglary well before he came to face the capital charge of murder. His origins are obscure, lost in the vastness of the Ukraine. Perhaps aged nineteen, Stinie arrived in England during 1898, having picked up, in addition to Russian and Yiddish, a fair smattering of French and German, as well as some very dishonest habits. By the time of his trial in 1911, he had a remarkable grasp of English and could write legibly, allowing for a few misspellings and grammatical curiosities, at a time when many criminals could only indicate their signature by a cross.

He was tall, extremely well-built, possibly handsome and, despite years in jail, came to effect a manner of dress and deportment that endowed him with some little style. A professional burglar he was, but there could be no mistaking him for Bill Sykes. A hard man, with a reputation for violence and rebellion in prison, he was never convicted—if we excuse the murder rap—of any offence of violence during his brief periods of liberty. Indeed, he seems to have had a remarkable way with children, winning their confidence and treating them with genuine kindness. Stinie also had a quite astonishing appeal to women, ranging from the grubbiest streetwalker to a lady who claimed to be an Austrian baroness and who certainly was rich by any financial standards.

These features, which remove Stinie some way from the popular idea of a 'criminal type', do not themselves make for much of a readable story. It was the circumstances of Stinie's arrest and condemnation, the peculiar nature of the murder itself, that drove me onward: and the more I explored, the more fascinating it became, particularly as so many writers on this subject did not seem to have done their homework.

I came to believe that Morrison was wrongly convicted of murder. The generally accepted view is that Morrison took part in persuading Beron to forsake Whitechapel for the wastes of Clapham Common that fateful morning and that they journeyed there together, but doubt exists about the exact role Stinie played in causing Beron's death, as well as about the involvement of at least one other person in the crime. I think that Stinie Morrison, far from being a participant in the murder plot, was a tragic victim of coincidence and, on a dispassionate analysis of the evidence laid against him, the outstanding proven fact is merely a close association with the dead man in his last three weeks of life, a connection which arose from a mutual interest wholly separate from the murder conspiracy, hatched and effected by people with whom Morrison has no demonstrable connection.

I discovered a defence for Stinie, but it was a defence that, for very particular reasons, was never canvassed at the trial. It was, in all probability, a defence unknown to the little team who struggled to save Morrison from the rope and who, after his reprieve, fought vainly for his release from life imprisonment.

The English criminal trial is aimed, officially, at discovering the truth, frequently a difficult pursuit. In Morrison's case, important facts remained concealed, not merely because the defendant chose not to disclose the real circumstances of his involvement with the murdered man, but because the Crown, for its own purposes, also kept back significant truths from the court. At a time of extreme xenophobia, Stinie Morrison was a representative alien criminal whom the authorities were very anxious to see publicly condemned and they had no qualms when it came to cutting corners with this end in view.

In the face of evidence forming at best an incomplete scenario, Stinie fell foul of unhappy coincidence accompanied by an unusually large measure of bad luck. That classic example of wrongful conviction, Oscar Slater, had the misfortune to acquire a diamond brooch which, as fate would have it, resembled one stolen from the flat of a murdered woman. Unable, in effect, to prove his innocence, Slater spent nineteen years in jail for a crime he did not commit. Such victims have often been men of less than impeccable character, and for that reason less able to defend themselves from the smears of prejudice. Oscar Slater was a petty criminal, while Adolf Beck, who looked rather like the true conman in his case and was firmly identified by several defrauded women, teetered on the edge of bankruptcy and alcoholism. Stinie Morrison, with a far worse character than Slater or Beck, happened to be in the wrong places at the wrong times, his undoubted association with Beron forming the linchpin of the Crown's case against him at a hearing described by Mr Justice Oliver, in 1911 a very junior barrister, as 'one of the most unsatisfactory trials I ever remember'.

1

In the last hours of the Old Year, people made their way to St Paul's. It was Saturday night, cloudy but dry, and the crowd was in especially cheerful mood. Along Cheapside and Cannon Street they came, along Holborn and Aldgate, and up Ludgate Hill a hundred marched, to the wheezy strains of a mouth-organ. Some had travelled from far beyond the creeping boundaries of London, yet the majority came from the East End, a few minutes' walk along the City's proconsular streets. Cockney families from Bow came along for the fun, Irish labourers and their wives from Shadwell; and there were Jews, recently settled in Whitechapel, refugees from Russia, Germany and all of eastern Europe, observing with curiosity the boisterous revelries of an English New Year's Eve.

The steps of the cathedral, out of bounds, had protective railings manned by City of London police, some of whose helmets fell victim to the attentions of rumbustious youths armed with switches and bladders on sticks. The cathedral bells rang out for an hour until ten o'clock, after which the people provided their own entertainment, sang popular songs and started to jig about, helped by discordant shrieks from penny-whistles and bagpipes. Fingers got burnt on roast chestnuts and baked potatoes, while opportunist hawkers did a lively trade in paper glengarries, popular with the large number of noisy Scots. On the first floor of an office building a press photographer held up a heavy camera and the crowd smiled at his fumbling attempts to light a magnesium flare. At last he succeeded and a sea of white, upturned faces gazed out at breakfast-time readers of the *Daily Graphic* the following Monday.

Towards midnight several thousand were gathered, of

1

whom a few clustered about a silver cross and, encouraged by a shabbily-dressed clergyman, sang hymns barely audible beyond their number. Not that the prevailing spirit was entirely pagan: hats and caps were removed in a call for silent prayer a few moments before the hour struck. Solemn reflections were briskly dispelled by the loud cheering that greeted each stroke, rockets that streaked across the sky, and the blowing of sirens and whistles from the rivercraft below. It was 1911.

The style of festivities varied from place to place. In the East End they celebrated with gusto, poverty and deprivation momentarily forgotten, with residents pouring on to the streets to dance and sing. Even the lurking Whitechapel anarchists abandoned their wordy lectures and animated discussions for family parties, replete with roast goose, German sausage and imported lager beer.

Over in the West End, theatres and restaurants were packed, and the entertainment provided for the well-to-do in the great hotels was truly lavish. It was a time of flaunted wealth: a few months later, Elgar would say angrily of a fashionable audience, 'What's the matter with them?... They sit there like a lot of stuffed pigs.'[1]

If, as Elgar implied, dullness and insensitivity were endemic among the comfortably-off in London, nowhere did stolidity more approach the status of religion than in Clapham. Once an elegant Georgian village, Clapham had developed into a highly respectable Victorian suburb. The young Noël Coward moved to Southside, Clapham Common, with his family in 1913 and remembered, 'Tree-shaded roads neatly spaced with refined suburban houses, secure in small prosperity with their conservatories and stained-glass windows and croquet-lawns.'[2]

Clapham saw the New Year in modestly. On the Common, a watchman, guarding works undertaken by the Central Unemployed Body, dozed in his hut near the bandstand as midnight passed and the number of revellers walking about the paths grew gradually less. Laughter and song died away. To the north-west of the watchman's hut was the wildest part, flecked with tall scrub and thick undergrowth. *The Times* called it 'a fine stretch of the primitive common' and it was pitch dark, unilluminated either by gaslight or by electric lamp on that moonless night. At about three in the morning a man crossing the Common heard a faint cry from this area,[3] but he thought no more and walked on in the stillness.

Police Constable Joseph Mumford came on duty at six o'clock that New Year's morning and just after eight, in the grey and chilly dawn, he was patrolling along a path leading north-westwards from the bandstand. About a hundred yards beyond the watchman's hut he noticed a dark object ahead of him, to his left. Soon he could see that this was a man, lying on his back about twelve feet from the asphalt, in front of some tall bushes. It was an unlikely place for someone to be sleeping out, certainly not at this time of the year, and, as he drew nearer, Mumford saw that the man was too respectably dressed to be a vagrant, for tramps do not usually wear overcoats trimmed with astrakhan or patent-leather boots, even though the clothing and footwear were stained with mud. But the left arm, starkly outstretched, told the young constable that this was no eccentric person sleeping rough. The man was dead and had been dead for some time. He was about five feet five inches tall, stockily built and appeared to be middle-aged. Mumford had never seen him before.

A black silk handkerchief had been folded over the top of the head and tightly tucked into the collar of the overcoat beneath the chin. Blood was spattered about the top part of the coat, on the sleeves and also on what could be seen of the face, partly hidden by the handkerchief which concealed grimmer discoveries. Mumford was in no doubt that this was murder: a large pool of blood lay on the path from which a bloodstained trail curved away into the bushes for about twenty feet. This, together with the condition of the clothing and what could be seen of the face, suggested that the man had been dragged to his resting-place face downwards. Even to so young a policeman, it must already have seemed a strange death. The murderer had troubled to turn the body over and if (as was the case) he had rifled the pockets, he had carefully done up a button on the overcoat, crossed the right leg over the left and arranged the silk handkerchief so as to form a kind of shroud or cowl about the head.

Mumford acted promptly and sent for help to Cavendish Road Police Station, leaving the body as he had found it, for he had simply raised the left arm and let it drop back. He noticed a bowler-hat nearby and footprints in the moist leaf-mould and loam on which the body lay. These impressions ought to have been recorded by means of plaster casts or detailed measurements, but this was not done. It was later claimed by the officer in charge of the investigation, Divisional Detective-Inspector Ward, that there were no distinct marks and that the ground was very hard, but there was no frost on that mild night and the soil was soft enough to receive the indentations of footwear, as Mumford had observed. The failure to make a record of the marks was inexcusable, for shoe sizes could have helped identify or eliminate a suspect and possibly indicate whether more than one person had been involved in the crime. The fault probably lay with the officers, originally summoned by Mumford, tramping over the ground themselves, or letting eager sightseers do so, before senior officers arrived from Brixton to take command. This was the first blunder in the investigation of a case which was to be, in the words of the *Clapham Observer*, 'one of the most mysterious murders that has ever come to disturb the boasted respectability of Clapham',[4] an event whose repercussions echoed far beyond that genteel suburb.

2

Just over a week before New Year's Eve the scene outside St Paul's had been the reverse of joyful. At noon on 22 December 1910 a vast, hushed crowd saw three open hearses approach the west door of the cathedral, each preceded by a landau overflowing with wreaths. So many flowers lay on the three coffins that the insignia of helmet, belt and truncheon borne on each could scarcely be seen. It was an occasion of national mourning: Winston Churchill, the Home Secretary of the day, attended, and the Lord Mayor of London, with the City Sheriffs, drove down from Mansion House fully robed. King George, ruler of an empire comprising a quarter of the world's land surface and a fifth of its population, sent a titled representative from his court. After the service, a melancholy procession passed through the City, watched by thousands more, eastwards to a cemetery in Ilford, where two of the police officers were buried. The third was to be laid beside his parents in Byfleet, Surrey. Newspapers reported that the funeral was not marred by any untoward incident, poignantly noting that the young widow of one of the men had given birth to his son the day before the funeral.

The cold-blooded murder of three unarmed City of London police officers, gunned down late on the night of 16 December, had shocked the country. The outrage became known as the 'Houndsditch Murders', in which two sergeants, Robert Bentley and Charles Tucker, and a constable, Walter Choate, were killed (with two other officers seriously wounded) by a gang surprised in the act of breaking into the rear of a well-stocked jeweller's shop at 119 Houndsditch. This was no ordinary gang of burglars: the ringleader was a strikingly handsome young Lett, George Gardstein (one of his many aliases was Mouroumtzeff), who had fled Tsarist persecution to become an active member of an extreme political group known as 'Leesma' (Flame), which had anarchist and, as it later transpired, Marxist elements. The purpose of the burglary was to raise funds for political purposes, a process described by the politically committed as 'expropriation', encouraged by Proudhon's much-quoted dictum, 'La propriété est le vol,' and supported by the Bolshevik element at the 1907 conference of the Russian Social Democratic Party in Whitechapel.

The gang, perhaps seven strong, had rented premises in Exchange Buildings, which stood to the rear of the shop, and at about seven o'clock that night they started to hammer away at an intervening wall. On a Friday, the eve of the Jewish sabbath, not many people were about in the gaslit Whitechapel streets and it was very windy, causing much noise from rattling shutters and squeaking signboards. If the burglars hoped the noise they were making would go unnoticed, they were wholly mistaken, because their neighbours at length became sufficiently alarmed to send for the police. A number of officers soon arrived on the scene, including two sergeants, Bentley and Bryant, who called at the house. The door opened, they spoke to someone, probably Gardstein, and went in. Seconds later, shots were fired, Bentley fell dead and, although the badly-wounded Bryant was able to stagger out of the house, another officer, Sergeant Tucker, was killed in the ensuing gunfire and PC Woodhams was shot in the thigh. Constable Choate, a heavily-built officer, bravely grappled with Gardstein but was repeatedly shot and, in falling, dragged Gardstein down with him. As an ironic result, Gardstein was then shot in the back by one of his own gang.

The slaughter enabled the group to escape and the stricken Gardstein was helped away by two of his gang. Among their number was Jacob Peters who, then twenty-four, was to become Deputy Head of Lenin's infamous 'Cheka', ancestor of today's KGB and a man responsible for countless deaths and acts of torture before he, too, was liquidated in Stalin's purges during the 1930s. Another member of the gang, though not in the escorting party, was a twenty-seven-year-old former medical student, Peter Piatkov, who had probably been imprisoned in Russia after the 1905 disturbances. A revolutionary well-known to the French authorities, he lived for a while in Marseilles, coming to London late in 1910. Piatkov had worked for a while as a housepainter and it was as 'Peter the Painter' that he gained notoriety in the press.

The two men brought their leader across Whitechapel to 59 Grove Street, off Commercial Road, which had been an operational base for the gang since early November. The men made off, leaving Gardstein with two women, Luba Milstein and Rose Trassjonsky, who watched helplessly as their leader, desperately ill and groaning with pain, refused to be taken to the London Hospital, a short distance away in Whitechapel Road. Eventually the distraught women ran to a doctor's surgery, from where a locum, Dr Scanlon, hurried over to see Gardstein who was lying fully clothed on a bed. He was plainly near death and persisted in his refusal to go to hospital, so that there was little Scanlon could do other than seeking to relieve the terrible pain. The end was not long delayed. In the room, to Scanlon's horror, lay a Mannlichen pistol, large amounts of revolutionary literature and, among the tools of burglary, several sticks of dynamite.

The police presence at 59 Grove Street included Detective-Inspector Frederick Wensley and Detective-Sergeant Benjamin Leeson, both of H Division Metropolitan Police, two men who were to play significant roles in the investigation of the Clapham crime, but on 17 December their thoughts were directed to the dead man, the contents of his room and to Rose Trassjonsky, the terrified, half-demented woman, who had kept vigil over her lover's body until the police arrived.

Her companion, Luba Milstein, was arrested soon afterwards and a massive hue and cry was raised for the other members of the team. On 22 December the City of London police offered a reward of £500 for information leading to arrest. *The Times* wrote that, 'officers disguised as shoeblacks, as Jewish pedlars and as street hawkers have been in the streets from early morning until late at night'.[1] A vast amount of information, prompted by the enormous reward, was received by police: Wensley, for example, was sent numerous letters, sometimes five or six a day, by an eccentric police constable, George Greaves. Greaves lodged in New Road, Whitechapel and relayed a great deal of gossip which had come to the ears of his Jewish landlord, Lazarus Zavitski, but Wensley thought it all valueless and eventually had to send a subordinate to see Greaves and order him to stop writing. A paid informer, Nicolai Tomacoff, helped arrest Peters and another gang member, Osip Federof. These, and a third, Yourka Duboff, were charged on Christmas Day 1910 with participation in the murders but there was no let up in the search for others involved in the crime.

Respectable people were very alarmed, especially after the political nature of the offence became apparent. Anarchists and socialists seemed to be having it all their own way and there was a feeling that foreign rivals, such as the German Emperor, were fomenting trouble in Britain. Earlier that year serious rioting had broken out in South Wales and units of the

Metropolitan Police, and even troops, had been sent down from London on the orders of Winston Churchill. Just before the New Year, the Scottish miners in conference at Ayr were demanding a wage of no less than eight shillings for eight hours' work, supporting their militant comrades in South Wales and vigorously condemning parliament as capitalistic and anti-working class. Moreover, the Houndsditch outrage was not the first act of terrorism in London, for early in 1909 two Latvian revolutionaries had staged an armed robbery—an almost unknown crime in those days—of a wages car outside a factory in Tottenham High Road. Passers-by set upon the robbers, who fired several shots and made off, chased by a large crowd who did not appreciate the danger, for the terrorists were very well armed. During the pursuit a policeman and a small boy were shot dead and, in bizarre sequence, a Chingford-bound tram, a milk-float and a greengrocer's horse-drawn van were hijacked without, however, enabling the men to escape. One of the robbers, Paul Hefeld, became exhausted and shot himself in the head, urging the other to escape but he, too, turned his gun on himself in the children's bedroom of a cottage where he had gone to ground. Hefeld survived for a time, terribly injured. Although he could speak, he remained silent almost to the last and his true identity was never established.

The limelight of publicity shone fiercely on the East End of London and its newer inhabitants. The Houndsditch killings, coupled with the memory of those dramatic events in 1909, brought public opinion to the brink of hysteria over the challenge thought to be posed by 'anarchists' (as all extreme left-wing groups were then termed) and the presence, particularly in Whitechapel, of alien immigrants in large numbers. Xenophobia beset the land. Early in 1911, the *East London Observer* commented:

It is doubtful if there is more than a score of English families living within a radius of 500 yards of [Sidney Street]. Certainly there is not a single English tradesman there; the public houses are tenanted by Jews and foreigners, and foreign drinks are almost solely consumed.[2]

A Stepney councillor was reported in the *Morning Leader* of 12 January 1911, as saying that 'the borough had been inundated by a swarm of people fitly described as the scum of Central Europe'. Even responsible newspapers, such as *The Times*, surrendered to the prevailing mood. A column headed 'The Alien Immigrant',[3] written shortly after the Houndsditch murders, alleged that, 'the average immigrant is unsanitary in his habits: he is personally unclean,' and, in a leading article condemning both the Houndsditch and Tottenham incidents, the Thunderer proclaimed:

> Now the British criminal never does a thing like that. Burglars very rarely use firearms at all ... A savage delight in the taking of life is the mark of the modern Anarchist criminal. We have our own ruffians, but we do not breed that type here and we do not want them.[4]

This strongly felt public opinion was all too apparent while the authorities were making their inquiries into the mysterious death on Clapham Common. The *South-Western Star* spoke out bravely, if ungrammatically, for the man on the Clapham omnibus:

> Why should people who have murders to do invade a select neighbourhood like Clapham? Above all, why should alien Jews come here? We sincerely hope that neither Clapham nor Battersea is about to be overrun by undesirables as other parts of London has [sic] been.[5]

3

The body was moved to Battersea mortuary, where it was stripped, washed and propped up on a bench to be photographed by a police cameraman. The head had been terribly battered and a huge wound, horseshoe in shape, gaped open on the right side of the forehead, on which, as well as on the scalp, there were marks of other injuries. The horseshoe wound represented the effect of the fatal blow, delivered by a blunt instrument with massive force, splintering the skull. A post-mortem was held on 3 January, at which the pathologist, Dr Freyberger, noticed that other injuries had been caused by a knife at least five inches long. The man had been stabbed three times in the chest when he was already dead. Most curiously of all, the face had been slashed about: five cuts on the right side and two on the left. Most of the cuts seemed to have been made at random, but on either side of the nose, starting from an almost equal point, there lay the tracks of two cuts, entirely symmetrical in shape and length. The two-inch long cuts were described as 'S-shaped', like the holes on either side of a violin, but they did not show very clearly in photographs of the corpse. Dr Freyberger explained that rigor mortis was then present and the muscles of the face were drawn, causing a flattening of the skin, which resumed its fullness after rigor had passed off. The authorities attached as little importance as possible to these marks but they certainly impressed the pathologist. At the inquest, Dr Freyberger observed that the slashings must have been part of a very deliberate attack, saying, 'I have never seen anything of the kind before. They are very extraordinary marks quite unconnected with death.' This opinion was shared by Dr Joseph Needham, then Divisional Police Surgeon at Balham, who told the coroner, 'The symmetry of the marks on the face is very extraordinary, like two S's, one on each side of the face. They could not have been produced accidentally. No mere coincidence could have produced them.'

'Some sign, do you think?' asked the coroner.

'Yes, I think there is a meaning to them', also commenting that for a murderer to stop to inflict such injuries seemed remarkable.[1] Dr Needham stuck to his opinions when interviewed by a journalist the following day,[2] for the police were already expressing the view that the medical men had gone too far. The authorities were very anxious to treat this murder as a straightforward killing in the course of robbery despite the unusual circumstances of the death. Dr Needham would not be budged, 'I adhere to the statement made before the coroner,' he said, 'a statement which was based on the most careful examination and measurements...' The police said that they had not noticed anything significant about the face when they took possession of the body but Needham pointed out that they were in no position to make a full examination and such details as the S-marks could only have been discovered in the mortuary.

Journalists had plenty of scope to exercise their talent for imagination. The mysterious slashings were variously related to *The Sign of Four* by Sir Arthur Conan Doyle, to Wilkie Collins' *The Woman in White*, while the whole affair was aptly likened to a 'shilling shocker' by the *Daily Graphic*. Grisly reports flooded in from all over Europe confirming the practice of branding, scarring and otherwise mutilating actual or suspected informers, often involving use of the letter S, which might stand for 'Szpieg', 'Spic', 'Schlosser' and a regular gamut of obscure words broadly representing the Judas syndrome.

Nevertheless, police derived some support for their theory from the solitary halfpenny which was all that remained of any cash the dead man might have had on him. Divisional Detective-Inspector Alfred Ward was in no doubt about the matter. A heavily-built man, with a round, fleshy face and black walrus moustache, he looked every inch the typical Edwardian detective. Seeing him stride across the Common to the scene of the crime on that New Year's morning, no passer-by could have mistaken Ward's occupation. A wing-collar and sober tie protruded above the massive, belted raincoat and the whole ensemble was crowned by a regulation black bowler-hat. A most determined man had arrived to take charge of the case, as the inexperienced Cavendish Road officers were soon to know.

Ward was attached to W Division of the Metropolitan Police and his base was Brixton Police Station. At that time there was poor liaison between the various divisions, which meant that many criminals went about their work unknown and unpunished, but Ward realised that he would have to call in men

11

with experience of a very different part of London, for the dead man was of Jewish appearance and there were not many from that community in Clapham, although a home for aged Jews had been established in Nightingale Lane, just off the Common. The deceased, though looking older than his forty-seven years, did not qualify by what remained of his original appearance for a place in that institution and Ward had to look further afield. He sought the advice of the Assistant Head of the Criminal Investigation Department, a tall, elegant Old Etonian, Sir Melville MacNaghten, who had qualified himself for this important post at the Yard by spending several years as a tea-planter in India. MacNaghten journeyed to Clapham Common to see things for himself and told Ward to do something which the latter already had in mind, which was to seek the help of H Division officers, whose manor included White-chapel.

It was no easy matter to identify the body. A drab notebook was found in his clothing containing a number of French and Polish names, mostly those of women, accompanied by entries recording weekly payments, some as little as sixpence and a few with the ominous words 'in arrears' alongside them. This little rent book, besides suggesting a man of property, also disclosed a small tallyman's business in which moneys were loaned out for the purchase of goods (usually clothing) and repaid, with interest, in weekly instalments. In reality, the dead man had probably been receiving other payments from women in respect of far less respectable activities and had advanced loans to finance operations well removed from the purchasing of skirts and flannelette underwear. But on New Year's Day, the most important clue to identity was an envelope, found in an inside pocket, which bore the address 'Mr Israel Iglazer, 16 Coke Street' and the scrawled word 'boots'.[3]

Ward, accompanied by Sergeant 'Boxer' Hawkins, made for Leman Street Police Station, situated midway between the Tower of London and Commercial Road. Here he found his man: Detective-Inspector Frederick Wensley. Wensley, sporting a luxuriant waxed moustache, was less bulky than his Brixton colleague and his face had a solemn aspect, causing one writer to compare him to a sorrowful elephant. Whatever the shortcomings of his appearance, Wensley ('Weasel' to the underworld) was an experienced, resourceful and ambitious officer, who had already seen twenty years' service in White-chapel and who had played a leading part in several murder inquiries. Like many other policemen, he was a keen Free-mason and later achieved senior rank at Scotland Yard, where he was instrumental, with others, in forming the Flying Squad. When he retired in 1929, journalists dubbed him 'The Most Famous Detective in England'.

Wensley knew his ground well and seems to have had an exceptional memory for detail but he was unpopular with the Whitechapel immigrants, who suspected him of corruption. Probably he knew rather less about the ways of the immigrants than he tried to make out. He was a tough detective, brought up in a tough school, and adopted an unusually aggressive manner with suspects, even for those robust times. A luckless burglar[5] wrote that Wensley was undoubtedly the most menacing officer he had ever come across, 'It was no use playing about with him,' he recalled ruefully. On one occasion a prosecuting barrister[6] rebuked Wensley for unnecessarily blackening the character of a prisoner in court and a heated argument ensued, which did not add to the dignity of the judicial process and illustrates Wensley's ruthless determination.

On New Year's Day, Wensley already had his hands full with the Houndsditch inquiry and had been on duty nearly twelve hours when Ward, an old friend, arrived at midday. 'Fred,' said Ward, 'I've come along for your help. There was a murder on Clapham Common last night and we think the man who was killed was one of your Yiddish friends.' Wensley gave the envelope bearing the Coke Street address to Detective-Sergeant Leeson, who set out accompanied by a uniformed sergeant. When they arrived at No. 16, in the heart of the Whitechapel ghetto, the signs were not very encouraging but the intrepid pair persisted and, by early evening, they had identified the dead man as Leon Beron, who had been living with his brother David in a room on the second floor at 133 Jubilee Street. A third brother, Solomon, was an occasional

13

visitor. No one was in occupation when the police gained entry to the room by forcing a strong padlock. It was to be a waiting game. Leeson telephoned Wensley at Arbour Square Police Station and both men met at Leman Street from where, after a brief conference, Ward, Wensley and Leeson left together in a taxi—no police cars in those days—and headed back to Beron's house. The room in which the brothers lived was filthy and a large quantity of used clothing, some of which was evidently soiled, was stored there. Under the bed, the officers found a large black box containing a number of papers* and a photograph which Wensley immediately recognized as that of Leon Beron, the murdered man. Wensley had known of this man for four or five years. He had no legitimate occupation, yet he was always in funds, was well dressed by the standards of a desperately poor community and had a great passion for gold, jewellery and women. Beron was often to be seen in the Whitechapel streets early in the morning returning from one of the many brothels in the area. The rent book showed that he was a landlord but the property he owned consisted of slum housing in Russell Court, St George's-in-the-East, and the rents, when paid, brought in less than ten shillings a week and, additionally, the houses were mortgaged, so that this man of property could not have supported his lifestyle on that source of income alone. Not that he was an unpopular landlord: he would sometimes allow his tenants a respite if they got into difficulties with the rent and did not trouble them about their business. He may have taken a cut from the earnings of prostitutes living in some of the nine houses in Russell Court, although that income never reached the pages of any rent book. People who were not his tenants had no reason to find him an attractive personality. He was miserly in his habits and, outside a small circle of intimates, taciturn in manner, with good reason not to tell the public too much about his activities, although an ostentatious display of gold and jewellery had already landed him in trouble. In broad daylight, some two or three years before his death, he had been set about by two men in Watney Street, off Commerical Road, and robbed of a gold

---

* Said to include pornographic literature and photographs (G. Logan, *Wilful Murder*).

14

chain, a £5 piece and other moneys but, as will be seen, it is possible that the attack may have had some other motivation than robbery.

In that poor, crowded community there would have been some who suspected this affluent man of playing a double game, acting not only as crook but as a paid police informer, either to the British police or to the agents of a foreign power. The Tsarist secret police (the Ochrana) had sent agents to keep an eye on the activities of Whitechapel revolutionaries since the middle of the nineteenth century but there is no evidence that Leon Beron was a spy for the Ochrana—for one thing, he spoke no Russian. To Ward and Wensley, though, Beron was potentially a dangerous subject. Far better to have press and public believe that the dead man was a harmless eccentric, a man children used to call the 'Mad Landlord', or, as Wensley later described him, a 'quaint little Jew'.[7] All sorts of complications might arise if the truth, or even a hint of it, emerged and the occurrences of the next few days were to confirm this view, which became, in effect, official policy.

In the early hours of 2 January, Leeson and his brother officer were rewarded for their dreary vigil by the sound of footsteps on the stairs leading to Beron's room. At David Beron's entry the officers leapt from a hiding-place and shone their lamps on to the man's face. It was totally impassive. He was taken to Leman Street for questioning but David was well below average intelligence and police accepted that he had not seen Leon since Friday, when David had gone to a friend's house to help organize a wedding. David occasionally worked in a jeweller's shop in Whitechapel Road and, in contrast to his late brother, was very shabbily dressed and seemed on the verge of destitution. Nevertheless Leon obliged him to pay ninepence a week towards the rent of 2s. 9d.

Solomon Beron arrived at 133 Jubilee Street just after nine o'clock that morning. He wore smarter clothes than his brother David and was very strange in manner, though he satisfied the police about his movements after several hours of interrogation. He told the officers that he had started to worry about Leon after his failure to appear for Sunday morning prayers at Jubilee Street, a regular meeting for the three brothers. He had a room at Rowton House, a rather up-market lodging-house in Whitechapel, for which he paid sevenpence a night and had been living there for nearly a year. Solomon, a slight figure with almost Asiatic looks, provided the police with most of the scanty information available about his mysterious family.[8]

On 17 April 1863, Leon Beron was born at Guvalki in Poland, then ruled by the Tsar. Of Leon's mother nothing is known, but his father Mordecai, or Max, Beron had been born in 1839, probably in the same area, and Leon was the first child of the family. The early 1860s were unhappy years for Polish Jewry, for the nationalistic rioting in Poland at that time gave the authorities every excuse for anti-Semitic persecution, some Jews being active in the campaign against Russian rule.

Among the revolutionaries, suspected or actual informers were summarily dealt with and members of one secret revolutionary committee became known as 'Stiletczski' because of the stiletto daggers carried by them, occasionally wielded to terrible effect. A young Englishman named Farndell,[9] later a modern-languages lecturer in London, saw the body of a murdered man lying in the street opposite the palace of the Russian governor in Warsaw. Scored on each cheek was the letter 'S', which was taken to stand for 'Szpieg' (Spy) or 'Szpic' (Informer). This kind of mutilation was not an isolated act and Farndell learnt of a case in Lodz, where a body was found with signs cut into each temple.

For Max Beron, and those of his religion, the temptation to leave Poland was very strong and in 1864 the family moved to France where David, Solomon and three daughters were born. In later years Mr Beron senior claimed to have had an upholstery business in Paris, though a daughter said that he was an iron-bedstead manufacturer. Leon, however, though he may have started life as an upholsterer, became a locksmith and married a Frenchwoman, Adele, by whom he had a daughter, Jane.

In March 1894 the Beron family, with the exception of one daughter, moved to the East End of London. By this time Leon's mother was dead and the reason for the move is unknown, although they may have been disturbed by the wave

1 Stinie Morrison in January 1911.

2 Clapham Common, New Year's morning 1911. Leon Beron's body, as PC
Mumford found it: a strange death.

3 Solomon Beron gives evidence.

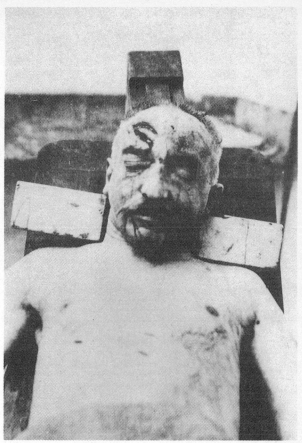

4 Leon Beron's body showing the horse-shoe wound to the forehead: the S-shaped mutilations on either side of the nose do not show up very clearly, but Dr Freyberger, the pathologist, explained why.

5 *Above* From left to right, Divisional
Detective-Inspector Ward, Detective-
Inspector Wensley, Detective-
Sergeant Dessent and Detective-
Sergeant Brogden, outside the
entrance to the Old Bailey on the last
day of Stinie's trial.
6 *Left* Alfred Stephens in March
1911.

of anarchist violence which swept over France and other parts of Europe from the later 1880s, culminating in the assassination of the French President, Carnot, in June 1894. The family reputedly brought with them a small fortune, the equivalent of £26,000 amassed, they said, from the upholstery business, although Leon's activities as a locksmith, coupled with his subsequent behaviour in England, suggest a criminal connection which may have contributed some unlawful revenue to the family coffers.

From their arrival in London neither Max nor Leon had any legitimate employment. David's mental condition precluded him from all but the most modest work, though Solomon returned to Paris in the early 1900s and worked as a representative for his sister's drapery business. Even Solomon was never regularly employed and by 1911 was describing himself, with perfect sincerity, as 'an independent gentleman'. Max and Leon were never on good terms and quarrels over the family's resources widened the breach, since Max's unwise speculation resulted in mortgage foreclosure and the loss of all the money. Penniless, Max was forced to seek help from the Home for Aged Jews in Nightingale Lane, off Clapham Common, and was duly admitted in October 1908. Leon neither visited nor corresponded with him.

Another reason for the disharmony between father and son arose from Leon's promiscuity. He was always a womanizer and even after marriage to Adele sought the company of prostitutes. After arriving in England, Leon and Adele went to lodge at 46 Brick Lane, the home of Philip Deitch. There, in 1898, they made the acquaintance of their landlord's daughter-in-law, Nellie, and husband Sam. In 1900, Adele began to show the symptoms of insanity which caused her to be committed to Colney Hatch, the famous asylum in Friern Barnet. The cause of her mental illness was physical, not psychological. She had contracted syphilis, probably years before as a result of her husband's infidelities, and developed general paralysis of the insane. She died in May 1902. Leon seems to have been luckier than his wife for he never showed any obvious sign of the disease although, shortly before his murder, a neighbour noted his peculiar gait, with a strange swing about it, which may have been an early indication of locomotor ataxy, a lack of muscular co-ordination that sometimes appears in syphilitic patients. Perhaps his daughter never forgave Leon, for she remained in Paris, living with her mother's relations. His spinster sister, Jane Beron, claimed his net estate in England, valued at £95. He left no will.

During the 1900s Leon may have been involved, as receiver and/or financial backer, in a series of burglaries. Such activities explain how Leon was able to lead a comfortable existence, despite the squalor of his room in Jubilee Street, and to afford sexual adventures with the many prostitutes who plied their trade in the brothels which then existed all over Whitechapel, many doubling as unlicensed drinking and gambling dens. In about 1905 he lived for a short while with an Englishwoman who styled herself 'Mrs Beron'[10] and he even went so far as to pay £16 to a local jeweller for a lady's gold watch and chain, which he presented to his mistress. She does not seem to have been very grateful for the gift because, soon after, she left for America and returned only briefly to Whitechapel, leaving Leon to his nocturnal prowlings.

During the day, however, Leon liked to relax in a kosher restaurant. Whitechapel was studded with these little eating houses, run on continental lines and whose customers lingered long over cups of lemon tea, gossiping, reading newspapers in Russian, German or Yiddish, smoking and playing chess. After his mistress had departed for the New World, Leon used to go almost every day to the Warsaw Restaurant at 32 Osborne Street. There he would sit from lunchtime until midnight, occasionally leaving for an hour or so to conduct business in more private surroundings. On Saturday nights he would collect the Russell Court rents and afterwards change the silver he had been paid for gold, a task which the good-natured restaurateur, Alex Snelwar, was pleased to perform. He rarely spent more than 1s. 3d. on his food and spoke only to selected customers, some of whom, in that cosmopolitan meeting-place, were undoubtedly criminals themselves or connected with the underworld. Early in December 1910 Leon made the acquaintance of a professional burglar, a relationship which was very definitely not to the latter's advantage.

4

On the morning of 17 September 1910, a tall, well-built man of about thirty stepped through the wicket-gate of Dartmoor Prison, that grim fortress set in the moorland landscape of Devon. He wore a suit that had not seen the light of day for nearly five years and which reeked of camphor. He was of striking appearance, over six feet tall, with an intelligent expression in the deep-set dark eyes. The stone-breaking he had done, under the watchful gaze of mounted warders, had left him the legacy of a deep tan, but years of prison life had etched noticeable lines about his mouth and his face had a drawn, sunken look. Some people described him as handsome but, if he could be so regarded, the good looks were rather coarse and the eyes liable to seem shifty; but his forehead was broad and clear, the hair dark and curly and his nose prominent and well-moulded. He was by no means the 'criminal type' of popular imagination.

The man never gave consistent accounts of his background and lived his short life of freedom under a variety of assumed names, eventually settling on Stinie Morrison, by which he is best known. He liked to pretend that he was an Australian, born in Sydney, or that he had been a cowboy or a professional actor. Sometimes, rather nearer the mark, he made himself out to be a dealer in precious stones. Only once, when trying to persuade the Home Office into an early release from a long sentence, did he provide credible details about himself.[1] He was born, he thought, in 1879 at a remote township, Korsovsk, in the Ukraine, where most likely his family, poor Jews, had been obliged to live by Imperial ukase well away from popular towns. No detail is known about any relations.

His real name may have been Alex Petropavloff and in his teens he left Russia, perhaps to escape the harsh conditions in which he had been raised or to avoid three years' conscription in the Tsar's army or, more likely, to escape punishment for some juvenile offence. He travelled to Germany and on to France where he spent some time in Paris. He had a remarkable ear for language and, unfortunately, a strong disposition to commit crime. His dishonest career was probably well under way when he arrived, a youth of nineteen, in England during 1898.

Stinie was soon in trouble. He stole some ledgers from an employer and for this first offence in England received a sentence of a month's hard labour from the magistrate at Worship Street Police Court in December 1898. He called himself Moses Tagger but when he next appeared before a magistrates' court, only a month after his release, he used the name Morris Stein. He was charged with being 'a suspected person found on enclosed premises', which meant that he was suspected of being about to commit a burglary. For this second offence he received two months' hard labour. Three months of freedom were followed by yet another appearance in the dock but this time in the grander atmosphere of North London Quarter Sessions, where he saw barristers and judges in wig and gown. Stinie was rapidly heading for the first division of crime, but for this burglary the judge imposed a lenient sentence—six months' hard labour—warning him of the consequences of further malefaction. 'Morris Jagger' paid little attention to the judge's remarks, spending perhaps two and a half months at liberty until, in mid-April 1900, his White-chapel room was raided and a large quantity of tobacco and cigars was found, proceeds of a shop burglary that he had probably committed. For receiving stolen property Stinie, 'Morris Stein' again, got fifteen months' hard labour. This frequent use of aliases, always popular with criminals, was particularly useful in the days before the development of finger-print identification. There was always the hope that one or more of your convictions would not appear on your 'form sheet' when you came before a court for sentence and in those times of poor communication between the London police divisions, you might live under another name outside the area in which you were last arrested and, for a while at least, escape the attention of the authorities.

Released from prison early in the summer of 1901, Stinie played a leading role in a gang of German and Russian burglars active in the eastern suburbs of London. Within weeks of his release, in the early hours of 24 July, Stinie and another young criminal, Wolf Kennought, were spotted by police while carrying off the loot from a domestic break-in at Dowgate House, Cambridge Park, Wanstead. Although they put up strong resistance, they were both arrested and Stinie made his first appearance in the columns of *The Times* by dint of his debut at the Old Bailey. Kennought received eighteen months' hard labour for his part but Stinie, the same age as his confederate, had a far worse record and was punished by five years' penal servitude. In March 1905 he was petitioning the Home Secretary for an early release but his behaviour in prison was noted as being only 'fair' and he had forfeited fifty-five days' remission by misconduct, 'perhaps deservedly' as he admitted. He asked to be allowed to return to Russia or perhaps go to Canada but the response was negative until, on 5 August 1905, he was let out as a convict on licence, which involved reporting monthly to the police and notifying any change of address during a stated period known as a 'ticket of leave'. Failure to comply with the licence conditions was an offence, one which Stinie would later commit. In 1905 he seems to have complied with the regulations but, unfortunately, failed to keep away from crime. He was, by now, a highly experienced, if rather unlucky, criminal in a network of fellow-thieves and receivers at home and abroad. He made the acquaintance of Max Frank, alias 'Frenchy', a Lithuanian Jew, who had a jeweller's business, with post office attached, in Walworth Road, near Elephant and Castle in south London. Frank was a receiver of stolen property and allowed prostitutes to live above his shop. Stinie, whose striking looks and charming manner secured all manner of sexual success with women, was happy to use the services of whores when he was in funds and it may have been as a result of such a liaison that he met Frank, for he already dealt with another receiver at this time, one Woolf, who had a shop in Kennington Lane. Stinie knew a third receiver, a pimp

21

like Frank called Barnett Rotto who fronted as a grocer at 18 Charlotte Street, near Tottenham Court Road, an area with a large immigrant colony.

While he was making his way to England, Stinie worked in continental bakeries and, from time to time during the long spells of imprisonment, practised his skills as a breadmaker in prison kitchens. By 1905, however, Stinie was sufficiently up in the ways of the world to affect, while at liberty to do so, a style of dress and manner quite inappropriate to the humble status of baker. He was fond of wearing good clothes and jewellery, affecting a wide-brimmed hat and breeches at this period, which he wore to emphasize his supposed colonial background in Australia. This affectation might not have impressed a shrewd observer but among the immigrants, where he spent most of his time, he struck quite a dash and many believed the exciting stories of ranching life which he attributed to himself.

On 14 January 1906 this pleasant interlude was abruptly halted. PC Page, patrolling his beat in Maida Vale, saw Stinie 'loitering about in a suspicious manner' in the small hours of the morning. Stinie came quietly (perhaps the constable's physique had something to do with this) and was found to be in possession of housebreaking implements. Further inquiries revealed burglaries in Carlton Hill, Abbey Road and Hamilton Terrace, all the homes of wealthy St John's Wood residents. In all, about £170 worth of property had been stolen, usually by means of forcing a basement window. At the police station he was vigorously interrogated about the other members of his gang but Stinie refused to grass, saying, 'I'd rather suffer ten years than give anyone away,' an example of honour among thieves[2] which he followed, with one notable exception, until the day of his death.

In the event, he got five years' penal servitude, plus a year and eighty-three days resulting from the breach of licence from his previous sentence. He was sent to Dartmoor and took his punishment badly. Always a moody prisoner, Stinie was sometimes very bad-tempered but after a spell of good behaviour he was assigned to the prison bakehouse, work familiar to him and regarded as something of a privilege by the prisoners. Unfortunately, Stinie took a violent dislike to another inmate who worked alongside him at the kneading trough. There was a scuffle and the man was knocked to the ground. The result was two days' bread and water; the sentence pronounced by the Governor, Basil Thomson.[3]

Another incident brought graver consequences. Work at the quarries sorted out the weak from the strong and Stinie, one of the toughest inmates, at a peak of fitness in his mid-twenties, quickly achieved ascendancy over contemporaries to become 'Cock of the Quarry'. The introduction of a rival into the working-party one hot summer's day caused a fight in which the pretender was knocked to the ground. Stinie compounded his offence by laying out a warder who had, as he thought, shied a stone during the rumpus. The warder, bleeding from his fall, lay on the ground while a tremendous struggle took place to subdue the enraged Stinie, who at one point brandished the fallen officer's truncheon at the Deputy Governor. The panel of visiting magistrates was unimpressed by Stinie's plaint that the other prisoner had used a contemptuous expression in Yiddish ('schnorrer'), thus provoking the fight.

He was sentenced to twenty strokes of the 'cat' and three months in chains, on bread and water. A warder later remembered the chilling spectacle:[4] 'Morrison was . . . led along with a strong escort to where a bright nickel-plated triangle stood, its base stood in sockets on the ground. He was stripped, a tiny jacket placed over him to cover the lungs and the rest of him left naked.' After the medical officer had taken his pulse, Stinie's hands were strapped together and fastened to the apex of the triangle, his chained feet being drawn apart. After a 'terrible groan' at the first stroke, he made no sound for the rest of his ordeal. When, at last, the beatings ceased, he shouted, 'Twenty-five to one. Judges and doctors and governors and screws. All trying to make an innocent man squeal. Well keep on trying!' The warder added that he had never seen a flogging received so stoically. But the scars, bodily and mental, inflicted by this institutionalized brutality, would remain with Stinie all his days.

In better times, Stinie worked in the farm party and became a noted sight near the prison in Princetown as his tall figure, in the arrowed tunic and breeches of the convict, led teams of

Clydesdale horses through the streets to their working-places in the fields. By August 1909 he had settled down and his conduct was assessed as 'good'.

He was eventually released in September 1910, but on a fresh licence, which ran until March 1912. Before he left prison he told the Anglican chaplain[5] (Stinie was listed as 'non-denominational' at this time) that he wanted to get a job and avoid prison life. Stinie decided to look for work as a baker. As soon as he got to London he made for Whitechapel, met a Mrs Marks and persuaded her (women seem to have been easily persuaded by Stinie) to let him lodge at her home, 26 Grove Street, a road notorious as a haunt of criminals, prostitutes and revolutionaries, including, later, the Houndsditch gang.

Next morning he went over to Charlotte Street to see Barnett Rotto, the supposed grocer. On the face of it, Stinie was returning to his old ways and could hardly have made a worse start, yet there is no doubt that Stinie, a hardened criminal if ever there was one, was for once making an effort to find honest employment.

Rotto recommended a Jewish baker, Rosen, who had a shop in Golden Square, Soho. Rosen made the offer of a job starting in a few days' time but Stinie was dismayed by the prospects. 'I did not stop with them,' he said, 'because they are Jewish people ... they have not got standing hours. Some Jews expect you to work nineteen hours out of every twenty-four right off and they expect you to go out with a barrow after you have done your work all night as a baker.'[6]

This was, of course, a crude generalization but there were some very unscrupulous employers around. In February 1911, an inquest[7] heard about the death of a fifty-year-old foreman baker in Southwark, who had regularly worked a thirteen-hour day for a pittance. On hearing that the man had died of heart failure, being 'thin, delicate and pale', a coroner's juryman took the employer to task for this blatant exploitation. The dead man, he said, had worked for fourpence an hour, 'Are these good wages for a foreman baker?'

The man had not been paid by the hour, rejoined the employer calmly, 'He was set a task. My bakehouse comes up to the requirements of the law.'

Baking bread held no terrors for Stinie, who bought a copy of the *Daily Chronicle* four days after his release and scanned a column headed 'Situations for Men Vacant'. There he read this entry:

> BAKER. Wanted young man. Age 24;
> make dough. Mould. 213 Lavender
> Hill, S.W.

The same day Stinie caught a train from Waterloo to Clapham Junction, walked up Lavender Hill and found number 213, Pithers Bakery, opposite the Shakespeare Theatre* and a few yards from Lavender Hill Police Station. Undeterred by that proximity, Stinie went into the little shop and met the baker, Tom Pithers, and his talkative wife, who was intrigued by the new applicant.[8] Stinie told them that he was an Australian and had lived in France a good deal, adding, for good measure, that his father still lived there. The absence of references was explained by these long spells of residence abroad but he could ask a friend who lived near Tottenham Court Road to speak for him. Quite what the Pithers would have made of Barnett Rotto will never be known because the baker and his wife were already so impressed with the man's bearing and intelligent manner that the job was his. Indeed when Stinie told them he had worked in the East End six years before but that his employer had moved, Mrs Pithers observed that, even if he was still there, a reference six years old wouldn't be much good and Stinie was offered the job.

'He spoke excellently,' she remembered, 'like a well-educated man. In fact he didn't seem like a common man at all.' But they did notice peculiarities in his speech, including a Dickensian habit of substituting 'w's' for 'v's': 'You could tell he wasn't English,' said Mrs Pithers.

The new employee, who lived above the shop, proved to be an excellent worker. 'I'm not used to English methods,' he told Tom, 'since I've worked mostly in Australia or on the conti-

---

* The Shakespeare Theatre, opened in 1896, was an imposing structure standing next door to Battersea Town Hall. It was demolished in 1956.

nent.' Pithers undertook to teach him and his pupil was a fast and willing learner.

'You only had to tell him a thing once and he knew it. He was first-rate with the fancy bread and I should think he had worked at it on the continent.'

Stinie was soon promoted to the post of a second hand but Pithers found him too indulgent with the workmen to be left in charge.

'I'm not going to be strict on anybody,' declared Stinie, with bitter memories of a harsher discipline, 'and if you want somebody who'll inform against the men you'll have to get somebody else to take the job.' That apart, Stinie gave every satisfaction to his employer and, like every baker's assistant, had to work hard. He started at midnight, worked until about nine in the morning, came on duty again at six in the afternoon and made dough until eight, when he took a few hours' sleep before the next shift. He was paid twelve shillings a week with board and lodging.

After a month, Stinie did the morning bread-round, delivering loaves to the substantial Victorian terraces in Elspeth Road and Altenburg Gardens, opposite the north-west part of Clapham Common. The Pithers noticed that he had no friends in the district and rarely had a letter.

'He was a very quiet, well-behaved man. He was always in early and was a teetotaller, I should think,' said Tom Pithers.

When asked if Stinie was ever quarrelsome, the baker's wife said firmly, 'Oh dear, no. You could say he was most gentlemanly. He used to play with the children and he was so gentle with them. No woman could have been more gentle.'

But there were some people in Lavender Hill who did not appreciate Morrison's presence in the neighbourhood. As a convict on licence, he had already reported, as he was bound to do once a month, to Leman Street Police and duly informed the authorities of his new address in south London. The fact of an ex-convict living and working across the road, albeit legitimately, must have been a source of great anxiety and irritation to the local police. Stinie soon felt pressure from that source when uniformed constables started to call at the bakehouse, ostensibly to warm bottles of cold tea which they carried to refresh themselves in the small hours of a chilly autumn beat. A complaint to his employer brought no result. One day, perhaps of his own accord or as a result of a broad hint from some local CID officer that he should get off the manor, Stinie decided that it was time to go. But he did not walk out on the job. On Monday, 7 November, about six weeks after he had started work at the bakery, he told Pithers that he had been sent a telegram from France telling him that his father was ill. Naturally he wanted to go as soon as he could but he promised to stay for a week rather than cause inconvenience. By Wednesday a replacement had been found and Stinie left Lavender Hill, saying with a grin, 'You'll keep my job for me, won't you?' He looked in at the shop towards the end of November and chatted to Mrs Pithers for a while, until she caught her husband's eye winking at her to cut it short.

This brief episode undoubtedly represented a genuine effort to live an honest life, a thing as difficult as it is rare for an habitual criminal* such as Stinie to do. He had tried hard to go straight but pressures not only from the local police but from his own nature were too much. Stinie returned to White-chapel, where familiar patterns quickly re-asserted them-selves. As if to mark this change of attitude, he failed to notify police of his change of address and lived in a variety of lodgings, moving frequently. He had, to be sure, never totally severed himself from his old haunts while breadmaking in Clapham. He had visited Rotto's shop in Charlotte Street several times, perhaps amusing himself with the whores always to be found there and would travel to the East End, where one day he met Mrs Cinnamon in the street and proudly told her of his employment in Lavender Hill. But now the days of sweating in a bakery for twelve shillings a week were over for good. There were easier ways of making money, much more money, and Stinie knew them all.

---

* There seems to be no reported evidence of any major domestic burglaries—Stinie's speciality—in either the Lavender Hill or Clapham Common area during his time at Pithers bakery.

5

He was back among his own people. Stinie ate out in the little kosher restaurants of Whitechapel, initially favouring Cohen's in Fieldgate Street, near the famous bell-foundry where Great Tom and Big Ben were cast and whose elegant Georgian premises, built in 1738, may yet be seen, facing Whitechapel Road. The Cohen family were much impressed by the smart appearance of the new customer, in contrast to the largely working-class clientele of the restaurant. Stinie told them, shamelessly, that he had studied singing in Italy for several years and was now an actor, an assertion supported by the make-up he occasionally wore, giving his cheeks a glossy appearance. This did not surprise the restaurant proprietors who were well aware of the Yiddish theatre in Fieldgate Street. Hebrew characters above the entrance proclaimed it the 'East London Palace' and it was a popular attraction in all sections of the ghetto community. It comprised a long hall sloping down to a stage, and the cheapest seats were threepence, so all but the completely destitute could afford to go. The acting, though mostly amateur, was of a high standard and performances were often sold out. A typical programme boasted sentimental ballads, recitations, fiddlers and short plays usually with a moral theme set in eastern Europe, reviving memories of village life far away from the streets of London. The Palace was not the only Hebrew theatre and many clubs organized similar entertainments. Whether Stinie performed on stage in Fieldgate Street is not known but he was certainly fond of Yiddish theatricals and took part in several of them that winter, as the greasepaint demonstrated. He particularly looked forward to the dance which often followed and the opportunity of meeting pretty girls who might be persuaded to walk out with him.

But financial problems were pressing. Stinie, fond of the good life, could never resist the temptation to gamble at 'spielers', or illegal gaming-houses, which abounded in Whitechapel. The little money saved from his work at the bakery was rapidly running out and ways had to be found of raising cash. It was not long before economic necessity prompted a scheme but Stinie needed help from others. He had known Hugo Pool for many years, almost since landing in England: Pool may have been a member of the gang in which Stinie played a leading role during the summer of 1901 and, once back in Whitechapel, Stinie renewed the acquaintance. Variously known as Pool, Paul or Povl, Hugo was known to the underworld as Shonkey, and at thirty-five years of age he was squat and ugly with a ginger moustache and a ruddy complexion. Probably of German origin, he had met, and bedded, a provincial girl, Ethel Clayton, in 1910. Ethel was then eighteen, quite pretty, and of extremely low intelligence. She was born in Huntingdon but after her father had died in 1908 the mother re-married and abandoned her children. Poor Ethel drifted to London and, like so many other penniless girls, had to take to the streets to live. She and Pool, a convicted thief, lived first at 116 Grove Street, later moving to 2 Hardinge Street, not far from Arbour Square. There she continued to operate as a prostitute, Pool living off her earnings. Now and again she would bring a tipsy sailor, flush with money after a voyage, back to their room, enabling Pool to roll the victim and steal his cash. The hapless matelot would be dumped in the street, where drunken sailors were a commonplace, and like as not would be unable to remember where he had been robbed. Pool treated Ethel very badly, frequently beating her, and for a time in 1910 she left him. She agreed to return if he would treat her better, which he promised to do, but he never reformed and Ethel endured hard times until he eventually deserted her late in 1911.

A third member of the team was recruited, Maurice Robinowitz, a well-known forger enjoying a spell at large that November. It was decided to defraud a London bank.[1] The mode of operation was relatively simple: a bill for £300, payable to bearer, was forged, the signature ('F. Barnes') being copied from a genuine cheque. The bill was presented at the Holloway branch of the London & South-Western Bank at 12.45 p.m. on 30 November, possibly by Stinie himself or by a fourth man while Stinie waited outside. The bank paid over the £300 in £10 notes and one £20 note. The gang moved quickly and by two o'clock that afternoon Pool was in Cook's Ludgate Circus branch changing the £10 notes (£280 in all) into 7,000 gold French francs. At precisely the same time, Robinowitz, a shabbily dressed man of forty-five wearing a 'slouch' felt hat, changed the £20 note into gold francs at the Cheapside branch of Cook's. In those days, cashiers were liable to record the serial numbers of any banknotes paid out as these were comparatively rare and, since passing the notes might lead to detection, it was essential to turn them into anonymous gold as soon as possible. These gold francs could later be changed into notes, a process which would not itself attract attention in an age of plentiful gold coinage provided that the sum in each transaction was not too large. Stinie said that the gold was exchanged at various West End branches of Cook's, but a subsequent claim to have netted the entire £300 for himself was untrue. There would have been at the least a three-way split and Stinie's share may have been as low as £60, a figure which he quoted to an intimate shortly after the coup.

£60 should have been enough to be going on with but on the very day of the fraud Stinie bought a gold watch and chain, invested in a variety of garments and spent about £22 during the spree. He was also losing heavily on the gaming-tables. There had to be another job.

About the beginning of December, he moved to 5 Grove Street, not so very far from where the Houndsditch conspiracy was being plotted, and took a ground-floor front room for a fortnight. Stinie forsook Cohen's for the Warsaw, the little restaurant in Osborne Street frequented by Leon Beron. As at Cohen's, the advent of Stinie caused a mild sensation among the regulars. His bottle-green overcoat was admired, as was his smart appearance and the quite remarkable variety of his suits. He now claimed to have lived in Paris, Berlin, St Petersburg and South Africa, as a traveller in jewellery. Once he showed the proprietor's wife a tin box which, as he would have it, contained diamonds but her inquisitive request for the detail of Stinie's occupation was firmly resisted. 'That's my business,' he said.[2]

The habitues of the Warsaw restaurant were, legitimately or otherwise, interested keenly in gold and jewellery and Stinie was immediately rendered an object of the greatest attention, an interest dramatically heightened when Stinie acquired a six-chambered Browning revolver and cartridges, bought, so he said, for seven or eight shillings at a stall in Aldgate, an unlikely source even in those days of lax firearms control. At the Warsaw Stinie made no secret of owning a pistol. After *The Great Train Robbery* had appeared in 1903, scores of cowboy films had been shown in Edwardian picture-houses. Several of the Warsaw's patrons enjoyed the 'flickers', whose silent screen obviated the language barrier and Stinie lent colour to his supposed ranching days by pulling out his gun quite openly in the restaurant, where it was probably seen by a police informant.

As December wore on, Stinie struck up an intimacy with Leon Beron and the two men would often be seen deep in conversation over the lemon tea. One Thursday night, 29 December, they paid a visit to the Hardinge Street brothel. Perhaps the picturesquely-named 'Fat Nancy' was in residence: certainly Ethel Clayton was there, wisely staying indoors because 'a sailor I had brought in was robbed of £7 by Pool and he was on the look out for me to do me in'.[3] She heard the three men, Stinie, Beron and Pool, talking volubly and earnestly in Yiddish, which she could not understand. Leon returned to his miserable room even later than usual, which so irritated his sleepy brother David that Leon had to promise to come in earlier in future. Neither brother realized that Leon's mortal future was now a matter of hours.

At midday on the 31st, Beron's landlady, Mrs Miller, saw her strange tenant for the last time, padlocking the door to his room. Always particular, he tried the lock several times before satisfying himself that all was secure before going downstairs into the street. He took his customary frugal lunch at the

31

Warsaw, afterwards visiting his slum properties near St George's-in-the-East, where he collected the modest weekly rent.[4]

Shortly after seven that evening Stinie and Leon were seen going into the little cafe. The proprietor's pretty ten-year-old daughter, Becky Snelwar, jumped up as they entered. Stinie, as the Pithers had noticed, was fond of children and he always made a fuss of Becky, bringing her a small present from time to time. After he had taken off his overcoat, Becky helped extricate a bulky brown-paper parcel from the depths of a capacious pocket. 'What have you got in there?' asked the little girl excitedly. It was a flute, he said, and Becky, who thought that flutes were things fairies played, asked for a tune. Stinie wisely demurred and the package was handed for safekeeping to the half-mad waiter, Joe Mintz, with whom Stinie had had a difference that morning. Mintz scowled as he put the parcel in the cigarette cupboard behind the counter. The restaurant was full, perhaps thirty customers visible through the uncurtained windows, and Stinie was seen to be speaking at some length to Leon before both men finally left at about a quarter to twelve. In the course of the evening each left the cafe separately for a short while: Solomon Beron remembered seeing Leon standing alone in Fieldgate Street at about 10.45, outside Cohen's restaurant. Leon would not speak to his brother. Solomon thought that it was because Leon had taken too much drink.

The two men may have decided to see the New Year in by patronizing one or more of the neighbouring brothels, for they were seen together at various times and places until perhaps one o'clock, when they parted company somewhere in the maze of little streets between the Whitechapel and Commercial Roads. Amid the noisy, tipsy crowd thronging the streets, many returning from the revelry around St Paul's, they agreed to meet the following morning at the Warsaw. Some time after Stinie's current landlady bolted the door behind her lodger, Leon Beron acquired another male companion.

6

At about two o'clock on New Year's morning, a hansom cab was meandering down Mile End Road eastwards to the City. Edward Hayman, the cabdriver, was in his forties, thickset, with dark hair and a bushy black moustache. He lived in Lower Kennington Lane, south of the river, and was at that time working nights, which usually meant that the cab would be drawn by an old or tired horse. As his cab made its way back into Whitechapel, Hayman saw in the yellow gloom of the gaslamps another hansom ahead of him, slowly moving away from two men standing on the pavement. One was short and stoutish, the other tall.

Just beyond the junction with Sidney Street, Hayman caught up with the other cab, whose driver, he thought, had very likely refused a fare.

'What! Is it too far for you?' he shouted, but the other driver, whose identity was never discovered, ignored him and drove off. Hayman quickly turned the hansom round and went back to the pair, who were by this time walking eastwards, in the direction of Bow. Strangely, neither man made any effort to hail the cab and it was left to the cabdriver to solicit a fare, which he did by asking, 'Cab, gentlemen?'

The taller man said, 'We want to go to Lavender Hill,' and, if Hayman is to be believed, mentioned the Shakespeare Theatre. 'How much do you want?' said the man: unlike taxi-cabdrivers, the hansom-cabdriver had to bargain for his fare. 'Say five shillings?' said the man. Hayman nodded and the smaller man, who was supposed to be Beron, got in first. He kept his head down and did not speak, so Hayman had very little opportunity of observing him. There was nothing unusual about picking up a fare at this point in the Mile End

Road. Hayman would have taken no more notice of this trans-action than of the hundreds of other fares carried throughout the year. Furthermore, the design of the hansom, which seated the driver at the rear of the vehicle on a raised platform, pre-vented any view of passengers during the journey. There was therefore no question of Hayman being able to identify either the smaller man, whom he saw very briefly, or his taller com-panion: apart from a short conversation before the journey, and the instruction to stop, there was precious little time or op-portunity to study his appearance or note his voice. Hayman never mentioned any peculiarities of speech on the part of the taller man, for example, such as had impressed the Pithers when they first met Stinie.

The cab plodded on over London Bridge, down Borough High Street and on to Vauxhall and Wandsworth Road and eventually to Lavender Hill. Although the cab had passed the Shakespeare Theatre, Hayman apparently made no inquiry of his passengers and stopped only when the little trapdoor in the roof of their compartment was pushed up and a voice said, 'Stop.' Hayman drew up a few yards to the Clapham Junction side of Lavender Gardens, some way beyond the Theatre, and the two men got down from the cab. The tall man paid the fare and Hayman drove down Lavender Hill towards the cab-rank outside Clapham Junction station. He was there about ten minutes but did not see the pair again. They had paused at the corner of Lavender Gardens and were still there when they dis-appeared from his view.

Lavender Gardens is not the nearest public road to the part of Clapham Common where Leon's body was found and it is necessary to walk the length of it from Lavender Hill to get anywhere near the Common. If Hayman's account, which is totally uncorroborated, is correct, the men may have intended visiting a house in the region of Lavender Gardens. Otherwise, Clapham Common Northside, a major thoroughfare easily reached from Wandsworth Road or Lavender Hill, would have been a more convenient setting-down point for a direct excur-sion to the Common and it would have been easy to delay making any move to that dark corner until the cab and its driver were out of sight. Perhaps most significantly of all, if

Stinie Morrison was indeed the taller man, he was taking an enormous risk by being set down at the junction of Lavender Hill and Lavender Gardens, for the corner was directly opposite Lavender Hill Police Station where Stinie and his criminal background were only too well known. Police stations do not keep office hours and patrolling officers would be about at all times, quite apart from the possibility that someone might be looking out into the street.

There were no witnesses to the final journey, no one remembered seeing two men head for the recesses of that blackest part of the Common. Leon was totally unprepared for the massive, crushing blow to his forehead, rendering the temporary darkness of the grisly meeting-place a permanent nightfall for the victim.

7

Stinie got up just before nine on New Year's morning and had a splash under the pump in the back yard. Unbolting the front door, he walked the short distance to the public baths in Sidney Square, where he could enjoy the luxury of a hot tub. Once back in his room, he changed into a smart green suit, in which he received Mrs Zimmerman when she brought her lodger his usual cup of milk and a biscuit. The 'bed', made up on the sofa, had obviously been slept in she thought as she straightened the sheet. Stinie gave her three shillings for his week's rent, sevenpence for his milk and asked his landlady if she would deal with his laundry, as Sunday was the day for the weekly change of underclothing. He would use two or three collars a week and one or two shirts, and was probably thought of as a fastidious dresser.

Then he made a break with his recent pattern of behaviour by taking his breakfast not at the Warsaw but back at Cohen's in Fieldgate Street. He explained this change, plausibly enough, by reference to Mintz's sullen laziness the previous morning and, if he were indeed the murderer of Leon Beron, he did something very strange, for he returned to the Warsaw, looking in at about eleven o'clock.[1] He left without speaking to anyone and, after depositing his Browning pistol and cartridges in the left luggage office at St Mary's Station (now closed) in Whitechapel Road, he made for Max Frank's house in Lambeth. There he persuaded Max to change £10 worth of sovereigns for banknotes, a transaction which, for once, was unlikely to have been dishonest at a time when banknotes were easily traceable. Gold reigned supreme as the medium of dishonesty.

At Max's house, in the face of some opposition from Mrs Frank, Stinie made arrangements to move in with Florrie Dellow, a prostitute and one of a motley collection of lodgers at 116 York Road. Florrie, perhaps twenty-two, had come to London from rural Lincolnshire, her head filled by cheap magazine stories of the glamorous lifestyles of all manner of gilded celebrities, and tried to earn a living on the stage. Florrie never became a Gaiety Girl and marriage to a good-for-nothing called Dellow was the only alternative to starvation. After he left her, in 1908, she drifted into prostitution and earned quite a reasonable living. She could afford to pay one of the other lodgers to cook and wash for her. She was much taken with Stinie.

Next day the mysterious crime was headline news, luridly billed ('Man Slain on Clapham Common'—'Foreign Jew from the East End'—'Vendetta Suggested'—'Stabbed to the Heart'), with the Whitechapel connection strongly emphasized. Stinie, an avid reader of newspapers, was soon aware that his companion had been killed. Perhaps it was just as well that he did not re-visit the Warsaw, for Solomon Beron, released after several hours at Leman Street Police Station, had convinced himself of Morrison's guilt, probably providing police with an early clue to the identity of the 'mysterious stranger' in the restaurant. Nobody seems to have known Morrison's name, or indeed to have known him by any name at all, but there were many who could supply a good description of Leon's erstwhile companion. Once back at the restaurant,

Solomon joined in the eager gossip about the murder, incautiously mentioning that he was likely to inherit Leon's slum housing,[2] an expectation which was not to be realized. People began to recall all sorts of things, putting sinister interpretations on a variety of memories.

Customers tried to remember when they had last seen the pair, all the time spurred on by Solomon constantly reminding them that the tall stranger was at the bottom of the mystery. Stinie's Russian origins, too, were suspect, for within the Jewish community there were cultural sub-divisions and the newly-arrived were painfully aware of their own backgrounds. 'The Polish Jews tended to look down on the Dutch Jews, the Lithuanian Jews on the Polish Jews, while the German Jews looked down on everyone else...'[3] The clientele of the Warsaw, as the name implied, were mostly Polish Jews, with some from Germany, and hostility would easily be aroused towards Stinie, a 'Russified' Jew, once the accusing finger was levelled at him.

This was not long in coming. Crime reporters were hot on the trail and, remarkably, the staid ultra-Tory *Morning Post* scooped the lot by providing detail from the Warsaw as early as the morning of the 3rd. The voices of the Snelwars and several regular customers are plainly recognizable, as is the figure of Stinie himself, 'tall, slim and carried himself well', a man with a smart green overcoat and a distinctly sophisticated air.

By late on that Monday night, Stinie was beginning to emerge as a prime suspect, especially when the *Convict Register* was produced, showing that he had failed to notify any change of address and had last been heard of working near Clapham Common.

Meanwhile, developments were occurring south of the river. On 2 January one Arthur Turner, a motor-cabdriver, gave Ward a statement[4] which, initially, seemed a major breakthrough, referring to a noisy threesome picked up at London Bridge Station on New Year's Eve. One of the passengers, said to resemble Beron, asked Turner if he knew Clapham Common, but the party travelled only as far as the Horns, an enormous Victorian red-brick gin-palace, then standing at the corner of Kennington Road and Kennington Park Road, premises with a lively, cosmopolitan and thoroughly disreputable clientele. The other two fares were 'a foreigner', with a suitably sinister curly black moustache, and a woman, flashily dressed in blue, with a white squirrel muff and gloves, who was heard to remark, 'You can't fuck me for a shilling,' to 'Beron', said to have been the worse for drink.

Ward was not impressed. Turner had put the start of this Rabelaisian journey at 10 p.m. when, without doubt, Leon was in or around the Warsaw, over a mile from London Bridge and the description of 'Beron' corresponded a little too closely with published material. Cabdrivers, unhappily, had a poor reputation for truthfulness and some were associated with professional criminals.

Doubts about Turner's claims do not rob the Horns of its importance, for among the drivers, pimps, racing-men and other shady characters was one man who would play a major part in Morrison's ultimate fate. On the Monday night, the crowd of regular drinkers at closing-time (12.30 a.m. in those days) contained a stocky man of about thirty, with a bushy, unkempt moustache and a rather down-at-heel appearance. Alfred Stephens was very much at home in this unsavoury company, possibly supplementing his meagre income by acting as a paid police informer, and had recently moved into the home of Lawrence Rappolt,[5] a petty crook. Stephens was a hansom-cabdriver and hard up, a state of affairs induced partly by gambling, for there were plenty of 'runners' willing to take illegal bets in the Horns, and partly by the low wages of hansom-cabmen, even less than the thirty shillings a week commanded by their motorized colleagues, who thought themselves poorly paid. By 1911, the horse-drawn hansom was already obsolete, an elegant survivor from the days of Victoria. Seven years before, only two licensed motor-cabs had spluttered around the London streets but now more than seven thousand of them plied for hire and the hansom could not compete. Stephens, whose shabbiness reflected the decline in fortune of the vehicle he drove, was plainly in poor health; hours spent sitting on top of his cab in all weathers, in the terrible London fogs, had affected his lungs and he spoke in a husky, bronchial voice, at times barely audible, coughing frequently. Before Christmas this miserable character had slipped out of his lodgings in Chapter Road, Kennington, owing £2 back rent, and took refuge in the Rowton House at Elephant and Castle until Rappolt offered him a room. His new host had a bad record for violence (he once nearly bit through a man's finger) and associated, as Stephens well knew, with race-course thieves who then operated in notorious 'race-gangs' all over the Home Counties and notably in Brighton. Once, while in prison at Warwick, Rappolt had made the acquaintance of Max Frank and was well aware of Stinie Morrison's reputation, as were several other Horns regulars.

That night there had been a good deal of talk about the fatal morning and interest was aroused when Stephens was heard to say that he was on the rank at Clapham Cross, at the eastern extremity of the Common. 'I took up a man just after the last tram left for Tooting,' he said, 'but it was a poor night. I'd hoped to get a fare or two from St Paul's, but I only took twelve shillings all told.' His audience, mostly cabdrivers themselves, murmured sympathy: poor old Alf, always a bit of a loser . . . [6]

Before the month was out, loser or not, Alfred Stephens would tell a very elaborate tale about the events of New Year's morning, a far remove from the brief and sorrowful story vouchsafed to his friends over a pint or two in the Horns.

8

Not long after Stephens and his pot-house cronies had ambled unsteadily home, the small hours of 3 January witnessed unusual activity in Whitechapel. Along Commercial Road, filtering through the side streets, came strong detachments of uniformed police, accompanied by plain-clothes officers, conspicuous among whom were Wensley and Leeson. A massive police presence discreetly surrounded an early nineteenth-century terrace house, No. 100 Sidney Street, where, according to reliable information, two armed members of the Houndsditch gang had taken refuge. Groups of officers were deployed strategically in the houses opposite, in neighbouring alley-ways and yards, and on the roof of Mann & Crossman's brewery, which overlooked the suspect property. It was a cold, windy night, with intermittent squally showers of sleet and rain, making it difficult to evacuate the irritable, frightened tenants but, at last, the legitimate occupants of No. 100 were silently removed.

In the yellowy gaslight, just before dawn, police knocked loudly at the front door and, for good measure, threw gravel at the first-floor front windows of the room in which the fugitives were thought to be hiding. At once several shots rang out and Leeson fell to the ground, struck in the chest, and melodramatically announced that he was dying,* which, in the event, he was not. Another bullet passed harmlessly through a detective's hat. Police withdrew and regrouped, awaiting the arrival of the Metropolitan Commissioner, Sir Edward Henry, and other senior officers, including the unmistakably debonair figure of Sir Melville MacNaghten. The police were armed with outdated pistols and their ineffectual response to the superior fire power of the trapped men, who made full use of their automatic Mauser revolvers, impelled the authorities to send for troops, notably the Scots Guards stationed nearby at the Tower. Winston Churchill, at the Home Office, was telephoned retrospectively for his approval, which was not long withheld. Once the military had taken up position, a regular battle, watched by a huge crowd, raged between the soldiers and the two gang members, who had barricaded the first-floor windows with furniture and bedding. In all, some five hundred rounds of ammunition were discharged at the house in the course of the siege.

Churchill's pugnacious spirit, coupled with a love of the limelight, overcame prudence and he could not resist hurrying down to Sidney Street to see the action for himself. The

---

* 'Mr Wensley, I am dying. They've shot me through the heart. Give my love to the children. Bury me at Putney.' See, inter alia, *Daily Mail* (Continental edition) 14 January 1911.

denouement was not long in coming, for shortly after one o'clock a thin column of smoke wound its way upwards from the attic windows, a harbinger of doom for the two gunmen. The house was soon ablaze, probably due to the fracture of a gas-pipe by a rifleman's bullet, but firemen were shot at as they approached the rear of the property and Churchill, in a controversial gesture, directly commanded a junior fire officer not to put the fire out. He may have been repeating a police directive, but two days later, in a letter to the Prime Minister, he wrote: 'I thought it better to let the house burn rather than spend good British lives in rescuing those ferocious rascals...'[1] In the event, two charred bodies were found in the ruins, one of which seemed to have been killed by gunfire and the other possibly suffocated by smoke.

The ensuing public outcry was immediate, forceful and firmly directed towards the immigrant community. Feelings of outrage, engendered by the Houndsditch killings, fuelled by the extraordinary episode on Clapham Common and the stirring events in Sidney Street, were expressed at all levels of society. Within two days of the siege the King was informing Churchill of his hope that 'these outrages by foreigners will lead you to consider whether the Aliens Act could not be amended so as to prevent London from being infested by men and women whose presence would not be tolerated in any other country...'[2] The *Morning Post*, after a token nod to the majority of law-abiding settlers, compared alien criminals to typhoid bacilli,[3] writing that the little alleys and courts off Brick Lane contained 'aliens of the worst type—violent, cruel and dirty, and only to be described as pests ... ignorant and filthy in their habits'. An even more inflammatory tone could be detected in the popular press. An *East London Observer* correspondent alleged that the Jews 'are entirely one when they combine against the nation whom they honour with their very unwelcome presence. I don't call the Jews a nation; I prefer Gibbon's expression, "The enemies of the human race".'[4]

There were ructions, too, at a borough council meeting in Stepney, when one councillor stridently claimed that 'for the last fifteen or twenty years this borough has been inundated by a swarm of people fitly described as the scum of Central

Europe'.[5] Even Anglican clergymen were not immune from the prevailing hysteria. An East End vicar[6] protested at being obliged to read the burial service over the bodies of the two men who had perished in the siege (not that there was much left of them for burial anyway) and a local councillor, supporting him, demanded that the 'usual coffin supplied to the respected dead of this parish' ought not to be used, but rather some kind of cardboard eggbox. This ludicrous proposal was ruled out of order by the Chairman of the St George's-in-the-East Board of Guardians who added, comfortingly, that the men had not died in the parish and, as their remains lay in the City Mortuary, the Board could not be compelled to bury them. Hostility towards foreigners was further exacerbated by the brazenly hostile tone of the German press, whose comments were widely reported in England. References to the 'tragi-comedy' of Houndsditch and Sidney Street were gleefully printed in Berlin. The English police had been warned about these characters, they said, but thought they could handle them without bloodshed. Was it really necessary for the 'Minister of the Interior' to lead an immense force of police and military, not against an invading army, but against two miserable scoundrels? 'We organize such matters better in Germany,' added the Berlin *Lokalenzeiger*, with infuriating smugness.[7]

The graphic detail of the Sidney Street siege was splurged over the pages of every newspaper in the succeeding days, though by no means to the exclusion of the Clapham crime. At an early stage, police were discounting any connection between the two events but this did not prevent speculation, some of it exceedingly wide of the mark. The discovery of a woman's wig in the debris at Sidney Street brought to mind a preposterous story, surely put about as a joke, that a man answering Beron's description had been seen sitting on a park bench on Clapham Common that New Year's Eve, while not far away strode a monstrous woman, broad-shouldered and of substantial build, whom some anonymous observer had suspected to be a man in drag. The very time of the supposed sighting—nine o'clock—was enough to render the tale at once absurd, but the *Daily Chronicle* was not put off. 'That the affair has some connection with the Houndsditch murder,' it declared gravely, in the light of this apocalyptic vision, 'seems almost certain.'[8]

Amid the purple passages and the lurid sensationalism, one event passed off in the starkest simplicity. The poor, battered remains of Leon Beron were laid to rest in a plain deal coffin at the Jewish cemetery in East Ham. A small band of detectives, in plain clothes, kept watch during the brief ceremony conducted by a rabbi of the United Synagogue. Solomon and David were the only mourners that wet and windy afternoon, standing by the bare graveside with not a single flower or wreath to be seen. Each threw three spadefuls of earth on to the coffin, in accordance with Jewish custom, before leaving the scene.[9] The plot is unmarked by headstone or plaque and can only be identified from the keeper's records. Leon Beron, a man of mystery in his lifetime, keeps his secrets with him in the grave.

9

The principal object of Messrs Ward and Wensley's attentions that first week of 1911 was commuting spasmodically between Lambeth and Whitechapel. According to his own account, Stinie had been a good deal east of Sidney Street on the day before the siege, even venturing into a 'Christian coffee shop' somewhere off Bow Road. He was, undoubtedly, again in Whitechapel on the 4th and does not seem to have been lying low, skulking about, as might be expected from someone burdened with the guilty knowledge of a murder. Nevertheless, the net was inexorably closing around him and, by about the 5th, news had already begun to leak through to the press that the police had a suspect in mind whom they particularly wanted to interview. Ward had been up most of the night of the 4th/5th working on the case when information came to hand that Stinie had been lodging with Annie Zimmerman until New Year's Day and might be returning to Newark Street for his laundry.

At a high-level conference later that day, chaired by Sir Melville MacNaghten, it was decided to place observing officers in a room opposite the Newark Street house and to list Morrison as an ex-convict wanted for failing to notify a change of address. A notice to this effect was duly published in the following day's Police Informations, under the misleading title, 'Wanted for Petty Offences', though it added, ominously, 'Carries firearms and may attempt to use them'. This oblique approach reflected the lack of hard evidence, a scarcity which prompted the authorities to circularize cab-ranks and commercial stables. A large notice,[1] boldly printed and specifically addressed to cabmen, offered a reward of £1 to any driver who

> between midnight and 6.00 a.m. 1st January 1911 took up at the neighbourhood of the East End two men, and drove them to Clapham Common; also if any driver picked up one or two men in the neighbourhood of South Side, Clapham Common, or Clapham High Street, between 2.00 a.m. and 6.00 a.m., 1st inst., going in direction of London . . . The Reward will be paid to the driver or to any other person who first furnishes the address at which the person above described [sic] was set down.

Oddly, no reference is made to the large rank outside Clapham Junction Station, roughly equidistant in an opposite direction from the scene of the murder to the rank in Clapham High Street.

The wording indicates that the police had already formed a theory about the murder. Late-night sightings of Beron and Morrison together explain the reference to the outward-bound journey of two men but Ward and Wensley were both of the opinion that the murder was most probably the work of a pair, hence 'one or two men' who might have been picked up travelling away from the Common. Hugo Pool, a known associate of Stinie, was probably pulled in for questioning on the 4th, as some newspaper reports suggest. In the event, Pool was no help to the police and he was released.[2] A week later he was seen again and made a written statement, which did not impli-cate Stinie in the murder but did confirm that he was a frequent visitor to 2 Hardinge Street and had brought Beron along on the 29th.

The fact that a reward notice had to be displayed shows that the police had little faith in the public spirit, let alone truthful-ness, of cabdrivers for, apart from Turner's dubious story, there had been a complete dearth of information from this source. The £1 offered was an attractive proposition, especially to the poorer-paid hansom-cabdrivers, to whom this sum could represent well over half a week's wages, and it was not long before two characters rose to the bait and approached the police. They were Hayman and Stephens. A motor-cabdriver, Alfred Castling had called at Brixton Police Station on the 4th. Ward was sufficiently impressed by Castling's unsigned statement (which, unlike Turner's version, could be made to correspond more closely with the time of Beron's death and other incontrovertible evidence) to dispatch an officer on the 9th to the Hanover Arms, near the rank,* and flush out Castling, drinking there with his cabdriver cronies. Castling willingly signed his statement, resting the paper against the pub's outside wall in the lamplight, a curiously casual way of gathering evidence in a murder inquiry.

Meanwhile, confidential police information began to fall into the hands of the press. The very day after surveillance was mounted on 91 Newark Street, the *Morning Post* could note that the police had been 'maintaining close observation on certain premises in the East End' and promise that an arrest was in the offing. Also on the 6th, the *Evening News* referred to a man 'known to have been in the company of Beron on the night of the murder and whose Christian name . . . commences with the letter S'.[3] Next day, the *Morning Post* took this a stage further by speculating that the murderer had inflicted the S-shaped mutilations 'in order to prove to his confederates that he had committed the act . . . There is authority for stating,'

---

* Less than 300 yards from the 'Horns', favourite haunt of Alfred Stephens and within easy walking distance of Edward Hayman's home off Lower Kennington Lane.

the article continued, 'that search is now being made for a man whose name ... begins not with the letter "S", but with the letter "M".' This is confused but there is no doubt that it came from a source within the police, for the report specifies that no one from the Warsaw restaurant (and the *Morning Post* reporter had spoken to the proprietor and several regulars) could put a name to the 'mysterious stranger'.

On the 8th, the Sunday papers were hot on the scent, *The People* writing, rather oddly, that 'S is the initial of the assassin himself, who has a propensity for signing his own name and is left-handed.' Why a propensity to sign one's own name should bear some hidden, dark significance was unexplained, but Stinie was indeed left-handed, as the police—and, it should be said, some of the Warsaw personnel—were well aware. From the official side, such leakages were most undesirable and they would also serve to prejudice Morrison's position in due course. Ward, virtually besieged by the press since New Year's Day, stoutly denied that he was responsible, but it is now clear that at least one of his subordinates was willing, for whatever reason, to oblige news-hungry journalists.

The press had been alerted, the public expectant, and police were ready to move at any time. The only rogue factor lay in Stinie himself. When would he fall into the trap?

10

Detective Harry Jeffery was bored. This was the third morning he and Jim Bellinger had been keeping watch on 91 Newark Street and there was still no sign of the elusive ticket-of-leave man. No one, of course, had officially told these junior officers that they were really looking out for the Clapham Common murder suspect but they knew, just the same. They only had to look in the daily papers to find that out.

Shortly after 9.00 a.m., Jeffery dug his colleague in the ribs and gestured to his left. From their room they could see a tall, distinctive figure, dressed in a well-cut, long overcoat, walking along Newark Street towards them on the opposite side. It was Stinie—Morris Stein to his observers—carrying a Gladstone bag, brown-paper parcel and a smart walking-stick. He stayed in No. 91 a short while, during which Annie Zimmerman hurried over to the Japanese Laundry for Stinie's washing, only to be told that it would not be ready until late afternoon. Stinie, who had been amusing the Zimmerman children, said he would call back. He walked off in the direction in which he had come followed, at a suitable distance, by Jeffery and Bellinger, roughly dressed in plain clothes and who slouched along, hands in pockets, trying to look like East End ruffians, always keeping their quarry within view. Presently, Stinie called at a house in Parfitt Street and stayed there for about seven minutes, while Jeffery managed to get to a phone and breathlessly gabbled out a message to Wensley's eccentric correspondent, Constable Greaves, on switchboard duty at Leman Street. Over at Brixton, Ward was delighted to receive the staccato communication: 'P.C. C.I.D. Jeffery H Division to D.D. Inspector Ward W.D. Please come to Leman Street at once.'

Stinie was trailed the short distance to Cohen's restaurant in Fieldgate Street. There, the proprietors, knowing nothing of the impending drama, were pleasantly surprised by the return of their distinguished-looking customer, said to be 'quite a gentleman, apparently an Englishman'.[1] Fried eggs, coffee and rolls were ordered and, hanging up his coat and bowler-hat by the door, Stinie settled down in the tiny dining-room to read a newspaper (alleged, by one sinister report, to be the Berliner *Tagblatt*).[2] Once or twice he glanced out at the gloomy, mist-laden morning but showed no sign of concern, even when a plain-clothes detective briefly put his head round the door to see exactly where the target was sitting.

Suddenly the door banged back against Stinie's chair and the little restaurant was filled with police, the ample figure of Sergeant Brogden in the van. 'Armed detectives,' noted the press, 'looking more like loafers than anything else.'[3] The suspect's arms were pinioned behind his back as Wensley, with grim relish, commanded, 'Stein, I want you!'

Brogden, clumsily groping for hidden weaponry, caused

47

Stinie to yell out, 'Don't get putting anything in my pockets,' later said by the police to have been an 'entirely unnecessary request', but the technique of planting evidence is as old as the Force itself and Stinie was acutely aware of this danger. His fears on this occasion were to prove groundless. 'All right, I'll come,' he said, in calm response to Brogden's abrupt demand, and he was led quietly away, pursued by the irate form of Mrs Cohen loudly complaining about the bill for breakfast. An officer said she was not to worry, being careful not to commit the Police Fund to the expense, and it was left to Stinie himself to settle the debt some six weeks later, graciously sending a shilling with a covering note addressed from his cell at Brixton Prison.[4]

The Whitechapel streets had been sparsely peopled this foggy Sunday morning but word of the arrest somehow got round and, well before Leman Street could be reached, a huge crowd, estimated by police at between three and four thousand, was following the little group, much to Wensley's apprehension. Stinie was frogmarched along, bitterly resenting the inquisitive behaviour of people, some of whom peered rudely into his face.

'Have another look! Have another look!' he snapped angrily. Curiosity was rampant. Who was the tall man? He was too well-dressed to be an ordinary crook. Was he the Clapham Common murder suspect or was he one of the Houndsditch terrorists? Was he both? They shouted to the captive in Yiddish and German, French and Russian, asking him what it was all about or venting their own theories on the matter. The dread word 'murder' must, surely, have been bandied about amid this polyglot mayhem, for Stinie, furious now, turned towards Wensley. 'You've made a big blunder,' he shouted, 'this isn't the first one, but it's the biggest blunder you've ever made.'

Wensley would always maintain that none of the arresting officers had been told directly that Stinie was a murder suspect but, as has been seen, there is no doubt that they were all aware of the real position. Bellinger, in fact, had been sent down from Brixton specially to take part in the observation. Yet it would be claimed that Stinie had volunteered incriminating remarks on the subject of murder before any mention of Beron's fate had been made. If true, this was a classic 'penny dreadful' confession, where the suspect conveniently blurts out, unprompted, matters which only the perpetrator of the crime would know. Perhaps Wensley thought that this adolescent approach would impress a jury, for he certainly gave instructions that the murder should not, in the first instance, be mentioned.

Stinie was brought into the station charge-room where he was solemnly told that he had been arrested for failing to live at a registered address, a fiction duly recorded in the Occurrence Book. Before long, he was demanding to be allowed to make a written statement. 'This is a serious matter,' he said, 'and I want to clear myself.' Wensley eventually re-appeared, to be confronted by Stinie. 'You have accused me of serious crime. You have accused me of murder,' he said excitedly. Wensley, hiding his delight, made impassive reply that he had done no such thing, but Morrison persisted, adding, 'You said you wanted me for a serious crime and that it was for murder and I want to make a statement.'

Wensley seems to have overlooked the possibility that a chance remark from someone in the crowd en route to Leman Street had put ideas into Stinie's head as, indeed, might the dramatic circumstances of the arrest itself.

Stinie made his statement, which was typed out, with a little help here and there, at his dictation. He gave York Road, Lambeth as his address and said:

I have sent for Divisional Detective Ward and Wensley and desire to make a voluntary statement in consequence of my having been arrested this morning under the suspicion of murder—Mr Wensley having told me this. I am an Australian, born in Sydney, brought up in England. I am a confectioner and baker, and now a traveller in common jewellery. During the month of September I obtained a situation as a journeyman baker at 213 Lavender Hill. I should think I was there about ten weeks altogether. I was sleeping there during the whole of that time. I left of my own accord, having saved up about £4. I then commenced to travel in cheap jewellery. I went to reside at No. 5 Grove Street, E., and remained there for two weeks. I bought the cheap jewellery from various persons; you will find the receipt for some of it in my bag. On leaving Grove Street I went to reside at No. 91 Newark Street. I remained there until last Sunday, the 1st, and then went to live with a girl named Florrie at 116 York Road, and have continued to live with her up till the present time. Last night I stayed with a friend named Mrs Cinnamon, who lives in a building off Grove Street—the number is 32, and is next to a grocer's shop—as I was too late to return to my lodgings. This is my voluntary statement and all I wish to say.[5]

Significantly, this account is in no way a direct alibi to the Clapham Common murder. Perhaps Stinie was unsure whether the police were holding him for this offence, for the Houndsditch murders or for some recent killing which had not yet been reported in the newspapers. Hardly had the ink dried on Stinie's statement than Ward and Brogden were off to York Road, arriving at about noon. They made straight for Florrie's room, where they found Florrie chatting to Mrs Hall, another lodger. Ward burst in, perspiring considerably from the effort of running up the stairs, and jerked his thumb towards Florrie's visitor. 'Out!' he barked, causing the terrified woman to flee, and he locked the door behind her. 'Are you a foreigner?' asked Ward sharply, whereupon, barely pausing to register Florrie's robust denial, he and his fellow officer proceeded to take the room apart. Floorboards were prized up, drawers and cupboards cleaned out, their contents scattered, and the mattress was turned over and flung on one side of the room. Even Florrie's purse was closely searched for incriminating material. In the event, the sole discovery of any importance was the cloakroom ticket for the pistol, which Stinie had slipped into the lining of a bowler-hat. Perhaps, when he made his statement, Stinie had overlooked the possibility that this might be found, or simply thought that the gun was the least of his troubles, for he had never made any use of it. An officer was hastily dispatched to St Mary's Station to see what the ticket would bring forth and, after releasing Florrie, Ward found

Max Frank hovering uneasily at the back of the house and told him to come along to Brixton Police Station. He was allowed to go after making a written statement; Ward may not have been aware at this stage that Max was a convicted receiver. At any rate, he quite failed to search the rest of the Frank home and, in particular, the jeweller's shop at Southwark Bridge Road. Time was of the essence if there was to be any hope of tracing Leon's watch and chain, yet it was not until the next day, possibly at Wensley's prompting, that police raided the shop and seized over a dozen movements, none of which could be related to Beron's watch. Max was pulled in again for questioning. This time Ward was fully briefed about Max's career (he had been released the previous June after serving fifteen months for receiving jewellery) and grilled him for several hours about his relationship with Stinie, but in the end Ward had insufficient material to charge Frank with any offence in connection with the death of Beron and he was released early on the evening of the 9th.

By that time, Stinie had been formally charged with murder. The afternoon of his arrest had seen Sir Melville MacNaghten shimmer into Leman Street Police Station and offer his languid congratulations to Ward and Wensley. Stinie, doing his best to sleep amid the noisy surroundings of a police cell, was rudely awoken at midnight by Brogden, who brusquely ordered him to strip. Dressed only in his pants and socks, the prisoner was thrown a couple of blankets for warmth in the chilly night ahead.

In the morning, Ward returned some of Stinie's clothing, pointing out some bloodstaining on the collar, cuff and sleeves of the shirt he had been wearing at the time of his arrest. Stinie was notoriously liable to sudden attacks of nosebleeding, a fact already well-known by the authorities at Dartmoor but, instead of telling Ward this, he angrily went on the defensive, 'That isn't blood at all. That is mud that I got yesterday.' But there was blood on the clothing—his own blood. A murderer would have been very foolish to go about the streets of London wearing a bloodstained shirt, for a week after the crime, but blood had been found.

Stinie was duly charged with murder, after which he was

placed on an identification parade, the opposite of modern procedure. Twelve men were 'recruited' from passers-by. Predictably, Ward described the stand-ins as 'equally as well-built as he and as well-dressed', but the chances of getting such a collection together from the Leman Street area in those days seems remote. An assortment of witnesses assembled at the police station: Alex Snelwar and some of the Warsaw's regulars, Mrs Deitch (with whom Leon and his wife had lodged in the late nineties: she claimed to have seen Stinie and Leon together early on New Year's morning), a clerk from the left luggage office and the cabdriver Castling. All were put together in one room, providing them a splendid opportunity to gossip about this one sensational experience in their otherwise unremarkable lives. Several of the Warsaw contingent, now firmly in Solomon Beron's camp, were eager to canvass the idea of Stinie's guilt and their familiarity with his appearance put them in a very good position to prompt likely waverers such as Castling and Mrs Deitch, neither of whom had had a good look at the man they said was Stinie. It is not always possible, of course, to stop witnesses talking among themselves but this herding together was in blatant disregard of fair investigative procedure and, with hindsight, considerably weakens the force not only of the Castling–Deitch identifications but also of the generality of evidence given by the other witnesses.

Stinie, now Ward's prize, was moved to Brixton Police Station soon after the parade had been dispersed and, late in the afternoon, as the light was fading, was taken to South West London Police Court in Lavender Hill, a stone's throw from Pithers' bakery where he had spent those few weeks of honest work in the autumn. There was no mystery about the court appearance, for the press was, as ever, well-informed about the latest developments. News of the arrest was flashed by Exchange Telegraph to Fleet Street shortly after one o'clock and Monday's papers all reported that a man had been detained in connection with the Clapham murder.

At half-past three, Stinie entered the wrought-iron dock in the centre of the panelled, gaslit courtroom. Reporters were present in force but the public gallery was less than half full as

Stinie, bowler-hat in hand, stood before the magistrate, the Hon. John de Grey, a man well into middle age with the choleric looks of an Indian Army colonel. There was an audible murmur in court, for the accused man did not conform to the 'criminal type' so beloved of journalists and such primitive criminologists as Cesare Lombroso. The *South-Western Star* commented that 'his aspect was one which would not cause suspicion anywhere', describing the face as 'refined and intellectual, the high, broad forehead being particularly striking. The dark eyes were well recessed and the eyebrows pleasingly arched. The nose, though prominent and curved, was not that of the Jew's, being more delicately modelled, and it indicated a love of refinement which is not usually associated with the Hebrew character ... The face had nothing harsh or forbidding, but, on the contrary, it was expressive of softness and gentleness of manner and might have belonged to a reticent philanthropist.'[6]

Dressed in the long, bottle-green overcoat, Stinie sported a soberly blue tie and high, turned-down starched collar, above a well-cut suit and smartly polished boots. A large gold signet-ring was conspicuous upon his right little finger. His bearing was calm and steady, a godsend to the numerous photographers, obliged to take what shots they could with long exposures in the dim gaslight. Photography in court was not forbidden, though flashlight was unthinkable, and cameras were propped on every available ledge and shelf.

Stinie listened with no visible sign of concern as Ward, 'coldly official', recited the facts of Beron's death and Stinie's arrest. When de Grey asked Stinie if he had any questions, it became obvious that the prisoner wanted to make a declaration from the dock. 'I should like to say what I have to say to you,' requested Stinie but he was told firmly that all he might do at that stage was to ask questions of Ward. Desperate strain showed in Stinie's high-pitched and fruitless plaint, 'Cannot I have anything to say at all? Am I going to be tried without being heard?' He was duly remanded to Brixton until the 17th but, before the prison van jogged away from the court building, had sufficiently recovered his composure to ask an astonished warder if he had such a thing as a cigar on him.

11

A week later, Stinie again appeared at Lavender Hill court, brought over in a closed cab at eight o'clock to avoid the large crowd that would gather in the hope of glimpsing the well-dressed alien. This time, in addition to the familiar overcoat, Stinie was seen to be wearing a smart pair of lemon-coloured gloves, but his equanimity suffered a severe jolt when he realized that the prosecution's case was now in the hands of Richard Muir, for the Director of Public Prosecutions had taken over the case from the police. Muir, the senior of only two principal prosecuting, or 'treasury', counsel at the Old Bailey, was then fifty-three and at the peak of his fame, a portly man of medium height, whose fleshy face was liable to flush with anger if his forensic path were crossed by witness, defendant or judge alike. With a background untypical of his contemporary lawyers, this son of a Glasgow ship-broker, a Scotsman very much on the make, had received a sound commercial education rather than following the road to public school, to Oxford or Cambridge, trodden by the majority of barristers. He helped support himself in early, penurious days at the Bar by working as a parliamentary reporter for *The Times* and always had a ready eye for the press gallery in court.

His was a driving, burning ambition to succeed, to win his cases and carve as many notches on the gun as possible. A teetotaller, he never smoked, living for his work, and would often stay in his chambers until midnight, 'getting together a case that would be absolutely impregnable', as his biographer noted.[1] Meticulous preparation involving multicoloured crayons and a card-index system was characteristic of this prosecuting monomaniac, who was unpopular among easy-going, clubbable colleagues. Contemporaries remembered him as a man with a heart of stone who, all too easily, became convinced of the guilt of those he prosecuted, a very dangerous development when associated with the undoubted power of the man as advocate. 'He went out for the triumph of his side,' wrote one author,[2] and, rather than being a prototype of the modern Crown prosecutor, Muir was one of the last of the old school of Newgate advocacy, all the more deadly for his fierce application and minute attention to detail. 'It was said of Sir Richard Muir ... that the lucidity of his argument and the clarity with which he stated the facts ... wove a net so tightly round the prisoner ... that he could never afterwards escape from it.'[3] The process was greatly helped by the careful diction and melodious voice of a man who once dreamt, like so many others at the Bar, of becoming an actor.

With this relentless scalp-hunter on his trail, Stinie's thoughts in the crowded courtroom may have echoed those of the hapless Crippen when told that Muir was to prosecute him. 'I wish it had been anybody else but him. I fear the worst.'[4]

Muir carefully set out the Crown's case against Morrison. Stinie listened impassively, clutching a bowler-hat in his left hand while the other rested on his right hip as he stood, head cocked slightly on one side, throughout the long court day. His self-control snapped only once when Muir, harping on the mention of the word 'murder' at Leman Street Police Station, had bluntly asked, 'How could he know it, unless he had knowledge of the fact that he was the murderer?'

'That's a lie!' shouted Stinie, in a vain protest across the court. 'I was charged with murder in the restaurant.' A stocky figure of middle height, attired in frock-coat and striped trousers, emerged from the lawyers' benches and made for the dock. Stinie was no longer facing a capital charge unaided, for he had obtained the services, as yet unpaid, of a Fleet Street solicitor, who had briefed counsel to represent Stinie in court. At that time there were great names at the Bar—Edward Carson, Marshall Hall and F. E. Smith—and so sensational a case as the Clapham Common murder must have caught the eye of many an aspiring, able barrister. So there was surprise when it emerged that Stinie Morrison was to be defended by Edward Abinger, at fifty-two still junior counsel, never to take silk, who had pursued an undistinguished career at the Central Criminal Court for over twenty years and who might, with justification, be described as an Old Bailey hack.

The defence solicitor, Claude Lumley, disliked and distrusted by police, was an eager but inefficient character, whose failure to organize his own affairs led to bankruptcy in 1921 and whose judgement seems to have been remarkably weak. Why he chose Abinger is not known but religion may have played a part in the selection, for Abinger was born Edward Abrahams, the son of a Jewish solicitor.[5] After school, where he met Rufus Isaacs, a brilliant advocate appointed Solicitor-General in 1910, Abinger went abroad for his university studies at Jena in Germany. His background was as dissimilar from that of the contemporary lawyer as was Muir's, but there is no true comparison between the two men. Abinger's was a neurotic, excitable and garrulous personality, temperamentally unsuited to practise as an advocate. Narrowly escaping death in a steamship disaster in 1899, he became an insomniac, virtually addicted to veronal. Occasional success in cross-examination was all too often lost in a welter of irrelevance which infuriated judges and left juries hopelessly confused. In the Morrison case, the most dangerous aspect of the man was a profoundly held belief in his client's innocence, an emotional commitment as damaging in its way as was Muir's settled conviction of guilt. Both men lacked the necessary professional detachment from the issue of the case but Muir was by far the more skilful advocate and, for good measure, had the big battalions of authority on his side.

Abinger asked de Grey if the money found on Stinie might be released to help pay for his defence, adding, optimistically, that 'he supposed there was no question of larceny'. The total sum, about £14, included the incriminating £5 notes and the application was refused. A few days later, Stinie petitioned the Home Office for the money, adding pathetically, 'They have also taken away my coat from me. It is very cold and I could do with my coat to wear.'

A departmental memorandum illustrates the working of the official mind: 'Assuming he is guilty, this money is almost certainly proceeds of the crime,' observed the writer, who conceded reluctantly, 'the practice has been in favour of allowing the prisoner to employ such moneys for his defence'. With a characteristic speed, the sum of £14.4s.1d. was handed to Stinie a fortnight later, by which time he was wearing a prison-issue overcoat, not quite of the cut and style to which he had accustomed himself since leaving Dartmoor.

12

The humdrum world of Lavender Hill Police Court carried on in the intervals between Stinie's remand appearances, its cases reported only in the finely-printed columns of local newspapers. Justice was summary, the punishments often savage. A group of unemployed youths had been fending off starvation by the surprisingly easy means of importuning older men for homosexual activity on Clapham Common.[1] There appears to have been no shortage of 'toffs in top hats' willing to pay for their pleasures, but one sixteen-year-old had the misfortune to accost a plain-clothes police sergeant, making an 'abominable proposition' to him late one night. That the boy was educationally subnormal weighed not at all with de Grey. 'True,' he said, 'he may be dull in intelligence, but that doesn't justify these practices.' The maximum sentence, three months' hard labour, was imposed, the magistrate regretting that he could not give more.

A similar sentence was meted out to a second youth, despite an excellent character, by Frederick Mead, the other stipendiary magistrate at Lavender Hill, a man whose reputation for severity in sexual cases was notorious. 'The lash would be a proper punishment,' he declared to the luckless youth, who was plainly terrified. 'This horrible thing must be put an end to and I intend to impose the highest punishment I can.'

Another boy received the tariff after unsuccessfully pleading to the arresting officer, 'I won't do it again if you let me go this time. The last gentleman only gave me tuppence.'

Perhaps the most striking example of judicial cruelty involved a totally limbless man, William Goy,[2] who had broken the law by allowing himself to be placed in a box resting on the shafts of a barrel-organ in Clapham High Street. Beside him was a notice which read:

> Ladies and Gentlemen. I am an
> Englishman born without arms and
> legs. This is my only means of
> earning a living.

He was arrested and charged under the 1824 Vagrancy Act with 'wandering abroad and endeavouring by the exposure of his deformities to gain alms' and had to be lifted into the dock to make his appearance before the Hon. John de Grey.

'I think it's very hard,' said Goy, who readily admitted his crime, 'I was only trying to get a few halfpennies. If I'm stopped, all the other cripples should be stopped. One man goes on his hands and knees and hops like a frog, but no notice is taken of him.' His voice trailed. 'I don't spend my money on drink like other men.' The magistrate, wholly unimpressed, was concerned only to know why Goy had not been brought in before.

The arresting officer had a compassionate nature and evaded the question by replying, 'I was in plain clothes—and it wasn't on our ground.'

But de Grey was determined that the public should not be offended by the sight of a limbless cripple on display in the Metropolis. 'It is not decent,' he declared, 'for him to display his deformities in public streets,' and, turning to Goy, he added, 'There is not the slightest necessity for you to starve. Other people go into the workhouse and you can go there too. I think it is quite right that you should be prevented from going about the streets as it is not nice to see a person in your unfortunate position.' Goy was fined five shillings, or five days' imprisonment in default, and warned that if he came before the court again 'the punishment will be severe'.

Stinie, a reluctant celebrity, returned to court on 24 January, minus his overcoat, though the newspapers were as anxious as ever to report any sartorial progress, even to the extent of noting his 'patent-leather shoes with large lace bows and fancy coloured socks'. These regular remand appearances formed part of the committal proceedings before the investigating magistrate and dragged on throughout January and February. Much of the evidence was tedious and repetitive. One afternoon the *Daily Chronicle*'s reporter could hardly keep himself awake in the stuffy court. The two warders guarding Stinie took turns to sit down and a young solicitor's clerk slumbered peacefully and undisturbed for fully half an hour. Only Stinie remained watchful, standing upright and virtually motionless in the dock. 'He might have been an artist's model posing for a portrait.'[3]

But there was a parallel inquiry taking place from which Stinie was debarred—the inquest, adjourned from 5 January. It was hardly surprising, then, that Lumley stood up on the morning of the 30th and asked for the inquest to be adjourned until after the police court proceedings were over, a reasonable request which in 1926 was given the force of law. But the Battersea coroner was not a man ahead of his time and proved unhelpful.[4] 'I do not think it would facilitate the inquiry,' he snapped, adding irritably, 'I am anxious to get rid of it as soon as possible.' The outcome, to the coroner at least, was evidently predetermined.

Amongst the predictable testimony came some evidence which set pens scurrying over shorthand notebooks, the words of a man summoned to attend by the coroner, a man whom neither prosecution nor defence was at all eager to call as witness, a man whose arrival was keenly awaited by Richard Muir. The object of so much attention was Max Frank, who must have known that he could be accused of being the receiver of the murdered man's watch and chain as well as an 'accessory after the fact' by exchanging two five-pound notes for stolen gold at the behest of Stinie Morrison on New Year's Day.

As Frank was solemnly sworn on the Old Testament, Muir looked on with pleasurable anticipation.[5] Free from the constraints imposed by the rules of evidence in a criminal trial, he pressed his advantage to the full and mercilessly cross-examined his victim, maximizing prejudicial effect against the absent Morrison. Muir knew that detailed reports of the questioning would appear throughout the country in the daily press, amongst whose readership would be the twelve men destined to occupy the jury-box at Stinie's trial.

Frank agreed that Stinie had called on him on New Year's Day and had changed gold for two five-pound notes but (and it may have been the truth) he would not admit to more.

MUIR: Have you any idea why he came to see you on this Sunday morning?
FRANK: He said he wanted to change his lodging...
MUIR: Did he give any reason for his dissatisfaction?
FRANK: He said it was too far.
MUIR: Have you any better reason why he should come to you on the morning of January 1st?
FRANK: No.

Having established the witness's evasiveness on that point, Muir changed tack.

MUIR: How much gold did he have?
FRANK: I did not hear what you said.

But Max had heard the question well enough and wanted time to think, for the wrong answer might land him in the dock with Stinie, but Muir was well aware of that trick.

MUIR: Answer the question, now. Behave yourself, sir.
FRANK: How much gold?
MUIR: Answer the question.
FRANK: £10 in notes.
MUIR: How much gold had he got?
FRANK: I did not count his gold...
MUIR: How much?
FRANK: I could not say. He had a good bit.
MUIR: About how much?
FRANK: I could not say. He might have had £15 or £20—or he might have had more—or less.

This told very heavily against Stinie. What was he doing by visiting this shifty character on the day of the murder, apparently flush with money? But for Muir it was not quite enough. He knew that in England the fact that a man consorts with criminals does not of itself prove that he is guilty of crime. Nevertheless the prejudicial effect of showing association with undesirables may be enormous and Muir, enabled by the coroner's inquest to do what he could not do in a criminal trial, played his ace by demonstrating that Stinie had been visiting not just a shady, evasive man but a professional receiver, someone who would be willing to fence stolen property no questions asked.

MUIR: Did he not know you as a receiver of stolen jewellery?
FRANK: I do not think so. How could he know?

This, on any reading, was a palpable lie, and Max was to pay for it.

MUIR: Are you not a notorious receiver of stolen jewellery?
FRANK: I am not receiving now. . .
MUIR: How many times have you been charged with receiving stolen jewellery?

Frank vainly appealed to the coroner, who told him he must answer the question.

FRANK: Twice.
MUIR: How many times have you been charged with receiving stolen jewellery? I did not ask you how many times you have been convicted.

This was really unfair, for Muir was pressing the witness to include details of cases in which he was acquitted or where charges had been dropped.

FRANK: Three times.
MUIR: Four times, sir.
FRANK: Very likely, four.
MUIR: And you have sworn in the box that you knew nothing about stolen jewellery?
FRANK: I was convicted before and I paid for it.

Muir moved in for the kill.

MUIR: What did you give him those two £5 notes for?

FRANK: For sovereigns.

MUIR: Are these the notes?

FRANK: Yes, sir.

MUIR: Did not you give him those two £5 notes for Beron's jewellery?

FRANK: I did not, sir.

The episode proved an invaluable means of bringing home a far stronger case than could possibly be put over at the trial. As for Max, thus destroyed, he went home to York Road an unhappy and confused man, promptly penning a letter of deeply felt complaint which he posted to the Home Office:

> Allow me to make a complaint, the way I was showen up and abused by Mr Muir KC. am I a re[ce]iver? am I a notorious? how many times was I charged and how many times have I been convicted? ... I should like to know your Highness if I did wrong some time ago I have Paid my penalty for it ... I get now an honest living and carry on a Resp. business ... Since it became knowing in the paper I can not get a customer to enter my shop and therefore I am a Ruined man again and there is plenty of crowd standing outside my shop and looking ...

The coroner's summing up seems to have been a cursory affair, containing a number of unjustified assumptions. 'He said that there was very little to dwell upon on the medical evidence,' reported the *Morning Post*. The S-shaped marks were 'quite slight and had nothing to do with the cause of death'. The jury's task, he had said, was 'simply a question of the identity of the murderer ... They had a complete chain of evidence which seemed to indicate a prima facie case.'

Given this clear lead, the jury were out only five minutes before the foreman rose to declare, 'We find that Leon Beron was murdered and in our opinion it is a case of wilful murder against Stinie Morrison.'

13

Amid the forensic alarms and excursions, one prosecution witness had become, with reason, a very worried man. Alf Stephens, the cabdriver, was sufficiently concerned to present himself before de Grey in mid-February.[1] Arrest warrants were duly issued, though never executed, against four men who, Stephens alleged, had threatened him while he was at the Fenchurch Street station rank on 3 February. Why this application had to wait over a week to be made is not clear. One of the quartet, apparently, was a member of a race-gang but—a curious feature—when Stephens saw him on a later occasion the police were not summoned. In the event, no further trouble befell him from this source and it may be true that Stinie was receiving help from friends, particularly in view of Muir's dark assertion that the men were of 'Jewish appearance'.

It was Stephens' long-standing friendship with Rappolt that bore the most serious consequences. The pair had known each other for over twelve years (Rappolt had once been a cabdriver) and Stephens knew all about his friend's violent criminal past and association with race-gangs. Perhaps Rappolt already scented a copper's nark before 15 January when Stephens carelessly let slip that he had just come from Brixton Police Station where he had been speaking 'about giving evidence'—Stephens' own words. The cabdriver's tongue, loosened by drink, brought a sudden coolness to the public bar that night.[2]

'You oughtn't to have gone and done that,' said Rappolt. 'Them coppers is a load of blackguards and liars. They've done me no good in my time and you,' he said, prodding a stubby forefinger at Stephens, 'you ought to be fucked for telling them.'

Stephens was in no immediate danger—this was just a warning—and, before he left, there was some conversation about Stinie, whose reputation had spread well south of the river.

The session broke up in good spirits. Perhaps Rappolt and his cronies thought that Stephens had been warned off providing evidence for the police but Stephens may have been more deeply involved with the law than he was prepared to admit, even when in drink. An informer is often spurred to help police if he has himself committed serious crime, knowing that if he does not provide the requisite co-operation, the axe may fall on him. At any rate, before the week was out, Stephens had been over to Leman Street and, after seeing Stinie's photo in the papers, had selected him on an identification parade. Stephens seems to have kept quiet about attending the parade for, on the following Sunday night, Rappolt was warning him not to pick Morrison out. But, after the press had reported Stephens' evidence on the 30th, there could be no doubt that he had become a major prosecution witness. Regulars at the Horns noted the discrepancy between the sad story he had told on the morrow of New Year's Day and Stephens' testimony in court. The more acute may also have discerned inconsistencies in timing.

Nevertheless, Stephens continued to use the Horns as his local and it was not until a week after the application for warrants against the Fenchurch Street heavies that any harm befell him. Perhaps, as Rappolt averred, Stephens had become too friendly with Annie, Rappolt's mistress, and this brought matters to a head but at all events an ambush was set up in the path of Stephens' unsteady route home in the small hours of 21 February. Rappolt and three others were waiting for him and Stephens, felled to the ground by a punch in the face, was repeatedly kicked to cries of 'Copper's nark' and 'Clapham Common perjurer', the latter a distortion of the phrase 'Clapham Common murderer' current in the newspapers. The injuries were not in themselves serious but Stephens, whatever his romantic aspirations, was a chronic bronchitic and took the experience badly, seeking refuge in the protective custody of a police cell.

The Rappolt case fell like ripe fruit into the prosecution's lap. Stephens' assailants had been arrested shortly after the incident and, in some haste, committal proceedings began at Lambeth on 22 February, Muir attending as prosecutor. He began by an oblique suggestion that Stinie was behind it all. Stephens was in poor health, he said, and 'seemed to have been selected by some persons, whose interest in the matter was not difficult to understand, for terrorising'. He then referred to the supposedly Jewish appearance of the men at Fenchurch Street (an incident which had nothing to do with the Rappolt case), presumably to strengthen the prejudice against Stinie. Muir then gave an account of what Stephens would say, which in the event differed from the evidence and suggests that Stephens had altered his story between making his police statement and giving his testimony in court.

What Stephens did—and it was very damaging to Stinie—was to bring out the conversation in the Horns, with references to Stinie's past and his connection with Max Frank. The episode had no relevance to the real issue—whether Stephens had been assaulted by four men on 21 February—but Muir, to his disgrace, took no steps to prevent this sensitive material coming out, encouraging Stephens to give the fullest detail.

Not all the papers carried the story as told in the committal proceedings. Some may have failed to appreciate its importance; others may have behaved with a sensibility to the basic principles of fair play and justice. Unhappily, at least three dailies reported Stephens' evidence: *The Times*, the *Daily Chronicle* and the *Daily News*, each in broadly similar terms.[3] *The Times* wrote:

> Woolf, a jeweller of Kennington Lane, told Stevens [sic] that he knew Morrison well and that the tale he told about being in Australia was all 'madam'. He told Stevens that Morrison had been imprisoned twice and that he had had two 'five years'. He also spoke about a man called Frenchie, who had done business with Morrison. Rappolt had said 'I know Frenchie. We were in Warwick Gaol together.'

The account goes on to identify 'Frenchie' with Max Frank.

There can be little doubt that someone on Morrison's jury—

65

if not several of the membership—must have read at least one of these accounts before coming to court. From the Rappolt affair the news emerged, loud and clear, that Stinie had a criminal record, and a bad one at that.

The trial of the four accused opened just a week before that of Morrison. Only two of the defendants were represented by counsel, both white-wigged juniors, no match for the Muir steamroller. Stephens repeated his allegations and Rappolt, with two others, was easily convicted, each man receiving a term of imprisonment with hard labour for the assault. Muir's heavy-handed probing of Rappolt's murky background caused an unexpected moment of light relief.[4]

RAPPOLT: I think that ends my career, don't it? (Laughter)
MUIR: Oh no! In July, were you not arrested on the Brighton Racecourse for obstructing the police, who were endeavouring to secure a welsher?
RAPPOLT: Yes, but I was not convicted. The Chief Constable let me out and it's a pity there are not more like him. (Laughter)

Muir seems to have exploited the earlier proceedings quite deliberately to ensure that Stinie's jury would know from the outset that they were dealing with a professional criminal, but even the most eminent legal authorities have overlooked this blatantly tactical revelation. J. P. Eddy KC followed Morrison's trial in the dual role of law student and journalist. 'I remember some time after the trial having a talk with Mr Abinger,' he recalled in 1961, '. . . he told me that his impression was that the jury knew or suspected that his client had a criminal record. I cannot think how he could have got such an impression and I feel sure it was unfounded.'[5]

14

6 March 1911 dawned grey and overcast, high winds and
squally rainshowers buffeting the little convoy from Brixton
bearing Stinie to his trial at the Central Criminal Court.
During the period of his remand, Stinie had got to know
several members of the Gardstein gang, among whom was
Yourka Duboff, who had been one of the three escorts to the
stricken leader in his last, terrible journey across Whitechapel
after the Houndsditch killings. 'Wish you success!' Duboff
had said to Stinie before a January remand hearing,[1] the
cheerful greeting assiduously noted down by a sharp-eared
warder, though it no way implicated Stinie in the Houndsditch
affair. Unfortunately, reports of the legal proceedings against
the Gardstein conspirators and those against Stinie were often
alongside each other in the papers, reinforcing the persistent
belief that a connection existed between the Houndsditch and
Clapham Common crimes.

At the Old Bailey, the grimly historic Newgate buildings
had recently been swept away and the new No. 1 Court was discreetly illuminated by electric lamps, a spacious room el-
egantly panelled in light cedarwood, expressing the last word
in modern forensic design. That morning the court contained a
vast concourse of counsel, solicitors, clerks, policemen, reporters, court officials and, inevitably, a crowd of curious spectators, filling the public gallery, many of whose number had
queued for three hours in the hope of being allowed into the
building. One notable and regular observer at the trial was
Seymour Hicks, familiar to thousands as the popular star of
musical comedy and West End revue, who took a decidedly
morbid interest in murder cases, which he would later describe
in lurid prose.[2]

Promptly at half-past ten, four sharp knocks heralded the arrival of the trial judge, accompanied by a motley but picturesque entourage of City officials. At the same moment, with military precision, Stinie was led up from the cell staircase into the dock flanked by four warders and, at the sides and the back, by a high screen of toughened glass. Any thoughts of escape were banished by the presence of a low, crowded well below the open front of the dock, into which a leap would be a risky business, exit being possible only along narrow gangways further complicated by oddly-placed steps.

Stinie faced his judge who, bowing to the court and the Bar, settled himself in a substantial chair, virtually a throne, behind which was displayed, perhaps a shade ostentatiously, the great sword of Justice. The little, shrunken figure of Charles Darling, thirteen years a High Court judge, contrasted uneasily with the grandiose scheme of the judicial dais. The judge's head, too large for his narrow, sloping shoulders, presented a gargoyle-like appearance which, when he affected to smile, gave the irresistible impression of a grinning skull.

Darling did not spring from the lawyer's classic mould, thus making a trio with Muir and Abinger. Born in 1849, his was Scottish farming stock, 'bonnet lairds' from the Lowlands, and his formal education, such as it was, took place at Colchester Grammar School. A literary dilettante, Darling fancied his abilities as a writer, contributing, in his early days at the Bar, to a host of long-forgotten periodicals and penning what must be some of the worst verse to come out of the nineteenth century.

He was on friendly terms, far too friendly, with Halsbury, the Tory Lord Chancellor, and Darling's elevation to the Bench in 1897 was widely criticized for being the political appointment it was. *The Times* commented sourly that 'to speak of him as an eminent lawyer or even a distinguished advocate would be absurd'[3] and Herbert Asquith, a future Prime Minister, declared the whole affair to be 'the most startling exercise of the right of public patronage ever recorded.'[4] In the event, Darling did little to improve his low standing with the press when, a year later, he jailed the editor of a Birmingham newspaper for contempt, though perhaps no judge could have ignored a leading article which likened him to 'Little Tich', the music-hall clown.[5]

This unattractive personality was very much a toady to the great and his ambition blithely crossed political boundaries. An unctuously-worded letter of congratulation, written to Winston Churchill on his appointment as Home Secretary in 1910, tells much about the writer's character.[6]

Darling's high opinion of himself as a wit encouraged his most notorious characteristic: the habit of making feeble jokes throughout court proceedings. A little humour, even in a serious case, may serve to break tension and humanize the inevitably remote atmosphere of the courtroom, but Darling always carried his jokes too far. Mostly they were excruciatingly bad as, for example, when a witness told of going into the Elephant Public House to make a telephone call. 'A trunk call?' inquired the witty judge, and next day the press dutifully awarded the accolade '(Laughter)' to the law report.[7] He made some effort to control himself in murder trials, where a man's life lay at stake, but such was his conceit that he could not for long resist the temptation to play the fool. With unerring aim, Max Beerbohm lambasted Darling in a cartoon which shows the judge's marshal, at his master's request, sewing bells on to the black cap.

Stinie's smart suit of green tweed, his fancy waistcoat and pale pink tie caught the attention of the watching pressmen as he took his customary stance in the dock, hand on hip, while the Indictment was read out to him. 'My Lord, if I was standing before the Almighty, I could give but one answer,' responded Stinie, rather melodramatically, 'I am not guilty.'

The jury was then sworn.[8] The twelve men who would try this extraordinary case came from an assortment of addresses in the London area but all were ratepayers and so, predominantly, middle-class. Four City businessmen were among their number, of whom two were perhaps Jewish though, like Abinger, they may have been from families long established in England, unsympathetic towards more recent arrivals from Russia such as the prisoner whom they had pledged their oath to try according to the evidence.

Stinie politely declined Darling's offer to be seated and

stood throughout the length of all nine court days of his trial which, as usual, began with an opening speech from the Crown, setting out in general terms the nature of the prosecution case and providing the jury with an outline of the probable evidence of the Crown's witnesses. Muir rose from his place, confident in his team of three counsel, each well versed in the technique of prosecution. Alongside Muir sat his brother-in-law, William Leycester, and behind him could be seen the most junior of the three, Ingleby Oddie, who already had ten years' experience in Old Bailey work. By contrast, the defence could muster Abinger and one very junior counsel, Alasdair MacGregor, who had been called to the Bar only two years before. When he fell ill after a few days, Abinger had to make do with young Roland Oliver, later to be an abrasive High Court judge, but in 1911 a mere fledgling barrister, just over a year's Call, employed mostly as a note-taker of evidence.

Speaking with quiet deliberation, Muir opened the Crown's case against Stinie Morrison in a concise speech which took just over an hour to deliver. Its comparative brevity and unemotional style belied the tremendous amount of work put in,[9] for Muir had visited Clapham Common twice, minutely studying the area in close liaison with Wensley, formulating his own estimates of the relevant timings and even dispatching one of his clerks to walk from Lavender Gardens to the scene of the crime, and from there to the rank at Clapham Cross, duly recording the time taken. Muir persuaded himself that this reading fitted closely into the evidence deposed to by prosecution witnesses.

Muir suggested that Beron had been induced 'on some pretext or another' to go to Clapham Common, a phrase which left matters deliberately vague, partly because the prosecution has no duty to prove motive, but also, for the more immediate reasons noted by his biographer, Muir omitted 'any mention of the motive that might have prompted [Morrison] to kill Beron because, in sober truth, he knew quite well that such a reason might easily be disproved by the defence.'[10] It was enough to demonstrate a close and unexplained connection between Stinie and the dead man in the three weeks before the murder. Muir gave the jury no inkling of Beron's true character. For the purposes of the trial he was a harmless eccentric, an 'old man' (at forty-seven), lured to his brutal death by the Warsaw's 'mysterious stranger'.

Stinie had been watching Muir's delivery with the closest attention except when aware that he was himself the object of careful scrutiny from the bench via the medium of the judge's gold-rimmed pince-nez. The prisoner looked up, returning a fixed gaze at Darling's face, and for a moment or two a fierce battle of wills raged until the judicial eye glanced elsewhere.[11] Stinie, proudly, foolishly defiant, had no intention of being taken for some cowardly lag cringing for mercy.

15

Various street plans were produced by the first witness, a police draughtsman, whose map of the East End caused Darling to demonstrate an ignorance of London which a modern judge would be at pains to conceal. Muir's reply blandly defined the boundaries of civilization within the Empire's capital.

DARLING: I do not exactly know where Whitechapel is.
MUIR: Beyond Aldgate, my lord.[1]

The court would soon have a number of startling insights into the ways of Whitechapel but the evidence in the case began, appropriately, on Clapham Common, with the discovery of Leon's corpse. Abinger established from PC Mumford that footprints were observable in the soil around the body (a flat contradiction of Ward's later evidence), quickly moving on to the tempting theme of the S-shaped cuts. Muir's sensitivity to the issue was apparent when Abinger tried to put in one of the police photographs of Leon, lying naked on the mortuary slab, showing the facial mutilations a little too clearly for Muir's liking.

MUIR: This is a photograph for which the prosecution are in no way responsible and it is put in by the defence.

ABINGER: It is supplied to us by the Director of Public Prosecutions . . .

MUIR: They were only supplied by the prosecution in this sense, that it was called for by my learned friend after it had been shown to me privately and it was produced and put in by him.

The judge, not yet fully understanding what Abinger was driving at, at first took his side against Muir.

DARLING: What is the point? They are photographs of the dead man, are they not?

MUIR: I am by no means clear as to what they are photographs of—as to how far they are direct photographs or touched up photographs or what they are.

Muir's strategic blustering, less than truthfully based, conflicted with his own instructions on the matter, for the next witness was the very police officer responsible for taking the photograph, who firmly denied re-touching the print in any way. In the event, it was not until well into the defence case that the coroner's assistant came forward to admit highlighting another print so as to give a clearer outline of the mysterious cuts to an eager press corps. Meanwhile, Darling became curious about this line of defence.

DARLING: I want to understand this. I do not want to ask anything embarrassing, of course, but I do not appreciate the point of this.

ABINGER: If I may say so, in a sense, the point is this: a part of the defence will be that the motive of the awful injuries was not robbery but vengeance.

This awkwardly phrased reply did Abinger's client no good at all. It was not 'a part of the defence' to show one motive or another in a killing for which Stinie Morrison denied having any responsibility: the true murderer might have been motiv-

72

ated by any one of a number of factors and the jury would have to decide whether Muir had proved that the murderer was Stinie. Seeking to combat Muir's case, which wisely eschewed motive, Abinger introduced, very clumsily, the possibility of revenge, using wild, unprovable suggestions and, by so doing, he played into the prosecution's hands. By trying, in effect, to prove that Beron had been murdered for informing on the Gardstein gang, Abinger left Stinie's position dangerously exposed if the jury came to reject this ramshackle theory—which may have originated in Abinger's own mind—a theory which was irrelevant to the central issue: had the prosecution proved that Beron was killed by Morrison, whatever the motive? Once revenge had been rejected, the jury would be left with the feeling that the defence had put up a smoke-screen. They might even come to think that Stinie knew a good deal more about the murder, and about Houndsditch, than they were being told.

Dr Freyberger, the pathologist, gave the detail of Leon's post-mortem. Abinger asked about the horseshoe-shaped wound on Leon's forehead, presumably in an attempt to show that an ordinary iron bar could have caused the wound, rather than a flanged blunt instrument, such as a jemmy. If so, the questioning produced exactly the opposite result when Darling intervened, ostensibly to help, providing the Crown with a most useful answer.

FREYBERGER: ... the injury may have been inflicted with an angled or a non-angled metallic instrument.
DARLING: Did you ever see a burglar's jemmy?
FREYBERGER: Yes.
DARLING: Could that do it?
FREYBERGER: Yes.

Abinger fared a little better with Dr Needham, the divisional surgeon.

NEEDHAM: I thought it was extraordinary that anyone should have stopped to inflict such wounds ...
ABINGER: Did you say that you thought they were some sign?
NEEDHAM: Yes, I said that at the coroner's court.

An attempt to follow this up with a series of questions about such dark expressions as 'spic', 'spickan' and 'sorreggio' (the latter a Camorra usage from Naples, which seems a little improbable) was baulked, quite properly, by the judge. Needham was not in any position to answer and, in the end, no expert witness was called by the defence on the issue, which remained a mere suggestion, unsupported by evidence.

Abinger's fumbling attempts to probe the mysterious under-world of secret societies was a mere curtain-raiser to the arrival of the first true Whitechapel witness, Solomon Beron, whose slight figure, 'dark, drooping features, with a suggestion of emotionalness and melancholy'[2] and oriental-type looks must have made the middle-class jurymen uncomfortably aware of worlds beyond their experience. From the outset, Solomon evidenced an oblique attitude to his responsibilities as a witness, as when Leycester, for the Crown, asked him to give Leon's age. Solomon's reaction was to pull a crumpled piece of paper from his pocket and gaze at it until Leycester testily prodded him to answer.

Solomon, unemployed in 1910, claimed to have been living on what he had earned in Paris. Replies came in a marked French accent.

ABINGER: What were you in Paris?
SOLOMAN: A placier—a traveller for my sister ... I brought over in London about £100, money what I have saved from what I have made in Paris ...
ABINGER: Where is it?
SOLOMON: In the Bank of England.
ABINGER: You mean you have spent it?
SOLOMON: Spent it, yes.

Solomon several times rebuked Abinger and the court for laughing at his answers but an attempt by Abinger to score over his strange adversary backfired badly.

ABINGER: Do you describe yourself as an independent gentle-man?
SOLOMON: Yes.

ABINGER: Living in a Rowton House at sixpence, I beg your pardon, sevenpence a night?

SOLOMON: What is that to do with the case? It has nothing to do with the crime. If you ask me independent [? impudent] questions, nothing relating with the crime, I will not answer you.

Unabashed, Abinger went on to ask a number of questions about the Beron brothers and their financial circumstances, which produced an interesting commentary on the ways of the East End, with never a mention of the unfortunate Adele Beron.

SOLOMON: If you want to know, from 1894 to 1905 he used to live along with us and . . . he has bought a watch and chain, because, you know, Jewish people like jewellery. They are fond of jewellery . . . They buy jewellery to save money, as you always get it back again.

Solomon knew nothing about the Anarchist Club, recently defunct, in Jubilee Street and none of the Houndsditch gang, though Abinger repetitiously put the notorious names to the witness. Evasive answers about the relationship between Solomon and young Jack Taw, a Warsaw regular, betray a close mutual involvement in marshalling evidence against Stinie.

ABINGER: Have you seen Jack Taw in the Warsaw restaurant . . . ?

SOLOMON: I do not take any interest in it. It has nothing to do with me in this case. I took no interest in it . . . Do not put me so many questions or I will go out from here.

ABINGER: Have you seen Jack Taw?

SOLOMON: I saw him, but I did not speak about this affair.

ABINGER: Where did you see him?

SOLOMON: In the restaurant. I saw him in court—all along. I do not care about it.

Fuelled by a bitter sense of loss for his dead brother, Solomon came perilously near to losing control altogether.

ABINGER: What is Jack Taw?

SOLOMON: He is a waiter, a kitchen boy... If you try to deceive me it is no good. I say to you he is a waiter.

Abinger missed a potentially vital line of cross-examination when Solomon appeared to be denying any acquaintance with Sam and Nellie Deitch, at least until after the proceedings against Stinie had begun.

ABINGER: Do you know Mrs Deitch?
SOLOMON: Only since she came here.
ABINGER: Do you know Mr Deitch?
SOLOMON: Never.

This must have been a lie, for Leon and Adele had lodged with Sam Deitch's father in the late nineties to Solomon's obvious knowledge. Abinger may not have been aware of that but he knew that Nellie had already deposed to an acquaintance with Leon which stretched back some twelve years before his death.

ABINGER: Have you seen Mrs Deitch at Snelwar's restaurant?
SOLOMON: I have.

The sight of a woman, other than the proprietor's wife, was a rare event at the Warsaw. Precisely what Mrs Deitch had been doing at the little cafe, the meeting-place of so many prosecution witnesses, might have been of value to the defence but the point remained unexplored, its potential unrealized.

Alex Snelwar took Solomon's place in the witness-box, his natural amiability masked by the effort of giving evidence in English, which was not his first language. He recalled Leon's habit of keeping gold sovereigns in a wash-leather purse, secured by safety-pin in an overcoat pocket. After some bumbling over the unimportant issue of whether Leon smoked or not, Abinger established that the dead man, whom Alex had known as 'the landlord', could not speak Russian and would converse in either Yiddish or French. Darling interjected with a pertinent inquiry.

DARLING: Do these people who come do business in your restaurant?
SNELWAR: No, they only come in to eat, that is all.

DARLING: Do they do business with one another while they are there?

SNELWAR: Nothing at all.

Alex was not going to put his reputation as a discreet restaurateur in jeopardy but at the same time it was necessary to distance himself from the dead man, whose business was probably well-enough known in the Warsaw.

ABINGER: Do you remember the murder of three constables in Houndsditch on 16th December?

SNELWAR: I remember that . . .

ABINGER: Do you swear you have never heard any of your customers discuss that in the restaurant?

SNELWAR: I swear I have never heard Beron talking about it. The customers have all been talking about it, but not Beron.

Snelwar was equally as anxious to put ground between himself and Stinie. When Abinger put to Snelwar that Stinie had also tried to sell his revolver, the reply was indignantly in the negative.

SNELWAR: I haven't got no customers for revolvers.

It was nearly five o'clock and time for the court to rise. The jury were told by Darling that they would be taken after dark, escorted by the City Under-Sheriff, to view the scene of the crime, after which they climbed aboard a horse-drawn brake, to be driven back to the Manchester Hotel where, firmly locked in, they would be forced to spend their remaining hours of leisure for the next nine days.

16

The Guildhall Justice Room, one of two City of London magistrates' courts, stood a ten-minute walk east of the Old Bailey.

As Stinie took up his position on the second day of the Clapham murder trial, the 'Houndsditch Seven' (as they would surely be called today) faced two former Lord Mayors of London, each resplendent in a cloak trimmed with Baltic fur, in the little courtroom. Poor, bewildered Rose Trassjonsky joined Nina Vassileva and five men—Peters, Federof, Rosen, Duboff and Hoffman—to hear a further day's evidence in their committal proceedings,* faithfully reported by *The Times* in a column alongside the account of Stinie's trial.

At the Old Bailey a score was being settled. Joe Mintz had been a waiter at the Osborne Street restaurant, lodging upstairs. Last summer he had tried to hang himself there, not his first attempt at suicide, and spent three months in Colney Hatch asylum before returning to his job, secured by the good nature of Alex Snelwar. On the morning of 31 December, Stinie was kept waiting for breakfast and, with brutal insensitivity, shouted down into the kitchen, 'Hello! Are you trying to hang yourself again?' Mintz was only too eager to tell the court about the brown-paper parcel handed in by Stinie for safekeeping on New Year's Eve. It felt like an iron bar, he insisted, and was heavier than a flute would have been: heavier, certainly, than Stinie's flute, which was handed to him as an exhibit. Strangely, no iron bar answering to Mintz's description was found on Clapham Common, although there were a number of ponds, thoroughly dredged, in which the murder weapon could have been thrown. If the prosecution theory were right, Stinie had handed over a highly incriminating object to the waiter, with whom there had been ill-feeling that morning, had transported it to Clapham Common for a deadly purpose and, presumably, had carried it away with him on two cab journeys, though none of the drivers mentioned seeing any suspicious bulges in the pockets of Stinie's overcoat. Young Becky Snelwar had a similar opportunity of assessing the weight of the mysterious parcel but she formed a very different view from Mintz. Probably because she was so

---

* In fact, Hoffman and Trassjonsky were discharged that day, Federof the following week. The three others were acquitted at this Old Bailey trial when Vassileva alone was convicted, of conspiracy to break and enter the Houndsditch jeweller's shop, but her conviction was later quashed.

young, she did not give evidence at the trial, though she did play a part in the appeal proceedings.

Like Solomon, Joe Mintz became distinctly evasive when pressed about the relationship between the Warsaw witnesses. Yet, as Abinger pointed out, Joe's memory was quite clear about seeing Stinie and Leon regularly in conversation together.

Towards the end of Mintz's evidence, there occurred the first of a series of interjections from the foreman of the jury, said to have been a surveyor.[1] The Clerk of Arraigns (or court clerk) considered this to have been the most extraordinary of several hundred juries that he had come across, a view borne out by the frequent direct questioning, which took place without Darling's veto, even though a jury is supposed to sit back while evidence is unfolded before them by the professionals. The first inquiry was boldly directed to the judge himself.

FOREMAN: Two or three of my colleagues wish to know if you would care to test the witness's sense of length. For instance, how long he considers this flute is . . .

And again, a few moments later.

FOREMAN: Did they send out from his restaurant for any alcoholic drinks to bring to their customers?

But Jews are not, as a rule, heavy drinkers and Joe could not remember ever having fetched liquor for a customer in the unlicensed restaurant, although it was already a proven fact that Leon had taken drink on New Year's Eve somewhere in London.

Another of the Warsaw's numerous lodgers was Henry Hermilin (also known as 'Deitch'), a Jew of German extraction who occupied a mean garret on the third floor. He was a furrier, employed in a Philpot Street workshop making cheap capes and feather boas, as well as dyeing rabbit skins in imitation of more expensive lines. It was an unhealthy occupation, poorly paid even by Whitechapel standards. But Henry had as sharp an eye for gold as was his ear for gossip. Loquacious as always, he described intimately the particulars of Leon's watch, chain and pendant. He recalled how Stinie (surely not the only one to do so) had held the watch in his hand, remarking how heavy it was.

Abinger, in lengthy, ineffectual cross-examination, tried to diminish the strength of the association between Stinie and Leon, contrary to the facts, and presumably on Stinie's express instructions. He pointed out that Hermilin, according to the deposition taken at the police court, had sworn, 'I have seen them a couple of times talking together.' There was obviously the possibility of confusion here, for Hermilin's grasp of English was not strong, but Abinger ignored the warning signs.

Eventually, Darling insisted that Abinger should read out the whole of the deposition, a course which did not help Stinie, since it showed that Hermilin had been broadly consistent in his evidence, both at the police court and at the Old Bailey. The jury cannot have been impressed by Abinger's petulant reply. 'Unfortunately, we have to deal with a foreigner,' remarked counsel charged with the defence of a man raised in the far-off Ukraine.

The last word lay with Muir, who crushed the rambling cross-examination by posing two simple but effective questions.

MUIR: You say you saw the prisoner and Leon Beron talking together a couple of times?

HERMILIN: Yes.

MUIR: How many times do you understand a couple of times to be?

HERMILIN: It can be ten times. It can be more.

The trial proceeded as young Jack Taw, said by the *Daily Graphic* to have presented 'an appealing picture',[2] recounted his adventuresome journey across Europe to England, made alone when he was all of thirteen. He now lived at Whitechapel's Rowton House and had no regular work, helping out occasionally at Snelwar's restaurant. Not only had he seen Stinie and Leon leave the Warsaw together at 11.45 on New Year's Eve but, he claimed, they were together again at

1.45 a.m., when he noticed them walking in Whitechapel Road, not far from the junction with Osborne Street, heading in an easterly direction towards Mile End.

Jack regularly hung about the Whitechapel streets in company with dozens of other unemployed youths until the early hours. The coffee stall near Gardiner's Corner was a popular rendezvous, where the lads would listen and sometimes sing to a piano played in a nearby tenement. It was from this vantage-point that Jack had seen Leon for the last time, walking with Stinie. But had this been on New Year's morning or on some earlier date? There must have been several occasions late in 1910 when the pair, so ill-assorted in height and build, had roamed about those streets, but Abinger did not raise the possibility of confusion in the date of the sighting, perhaps because it would only serve to emphasize the association between the two men, a fact which Stinie desperately wanted to play down. Indeed, Abinger's early cross-examination of the boy could only have attracted sympathy for the witness.

ABINGER: Then did you start earning your own living when you were thirteen?
TAW: Yes.
ABINGER: With your father and mother?
TAW: No Sir, I have got no father.
ABINGER: Got a mother?
TAW: Yes.
ABINGER: Where?
TAW: I do not know where.

Abinger was able to establish that Snelwar paid Taw seven shillings a week for his work but not on a regular basis and that he had been paid two shillings so far that month.

ABINGER: What month is this?
TAW: February.

As it was now 7 March, Abinger was emboldened to explore further.

ABINGER: What is the date today?

TAW: I cannot read. I cannot tell you the date.

But he was able to tell the correct time from the court clock and gave evidence about a church clocktower visible from Gardiner's Corner in Whitechapel.

Taw's was a sad little story, typical of many hundreds of other youths in the East End at that time, but there must be a possibility—though it was never openly suggested at the trial—that Jack had been forced to supplement his meagre income by taking to petty crime. The rent at Rowton House alone would have set him back half his weekly earnings from Alex Snelwar, an irregular source at the best of times. Furthermore, there is no doubt that he had a close association with a youth called Rosen who had a criminal background. There are reasons, therefore, for doubting the truth of Taw's evidence about the 1.45 a.m. observation and it is significant that he did not approach the police until the 3rd—accompanied by Rosen—after what appears to have been an attempt to sell their story to a Fleet Street newspaper, though this emerges from Taw's original statement to the police, which did not go before the jury.[3] Solomon Beron's evidence had betrayed considerable sensitivity on the topic of his association with Taw, but Abinger failed to raise this, choosing instead to cross-examine Taw mainly about his dealings with Rosen and scarcely touched on Solomon's position as ringmaster to the circus of Warsaw witnesses. A promising answer was missed.

ABINGER: Do you know Mrs Deitch?
TAW: Yes.
ABINGER: How long have you known her?
TAW: A few weeks ago I know her properly.

But Taw was not asked how well he knew her or in what circumstances they had met or what they had spoken about. He knew Sam Deitch as well, but everything was lost in a muddle when it emerged that Hermilin was sometimes known as 'Deitch'. Careful reading of the transcript shows that Jack was well acquainted with all three.

The next two witnesses for the Crown formed what was, in effect, a double act. The first was Jacob Weissberg, a kosher butcher, and the other was Isaac Zaltzman, a furrier. Muir's aim was to demonstrate that Stinie and Leon had been together at 12.45 a.m. on New Year's morning, said to have been walking westwards towards Aldgate in Whitechapel Road, opposite the entrance to Fieldgate Street. But, at best, their story is oddly muddled, and, at worst, two Warsaw regulars were giving false testimony at the behest of Solomon Beron.

Abinger, for once, made some headway with this strange brace.

ABINGER: ... You had been walking about since six o'clock?
WEISSBERG: I also met a girlfriend and had a conversation with her.
ABINGER: The three of you walked about—you, the girl and Zaltzman?
WEISSBERG: Yes ... The girl left us about eleven.
ABINGER: Then did you go on walking, backwards and forwards, from Aldgate to Mile End?
WEISSBERG: Yes.
ABINGER: How many times?
WEISSBERG: I cannot tell you exactly—five or six, or more.

Abinger established that Weissberg had not contacted police until 10 February, though the explanation was that, because Zaltzman had made a statement on 2 January, that had been somehow good enough for the two of them.

Zaltzman's evidence had to be interpreted. Abinger carefully sprung a trap for this witness, who had been outside No. 1 Court while his friend had been giving evidence and had not heard the story about the girl friend.

ABINGER: Did you meet anybody ... besides Morrison and Leon Beron?
ZALTZMAN: I have not seen any others.
ABINGER: Think carefully whether you did or did not meet somebody else and walk with somebody else.
ZALTZMAN: From the Mile End into Osborne Street somebody else walked with us, but I do not know him by his name.
ABINGER: Anybody else besides that man?

ZALTZMAN: Except this man nobody else spoke to us. I do not remember anybody else.

It was a skilful exercise in cross-examination and Muir's attempt to remedy the damage by a blatant leading question ('Did you have any conversation with any woman that night?') was disallowed by the judge in a rare forensic victory for the defence.

The scene was now set for a further sparring-match between Abinger and Nellie Deitch, still furious at allegations Abinger had made in the committal proceedings and just bristling for the fray. Nellie, amply bosomed and well-dressed, had known Leon since the nineties, when he and his wife Adele had lodged with Nellie's father-in-law in Brick Lane. By 1910 Mr Deitch senior had moved to Commercial Street, where a New Year's Eve party was held. Nellie had approached the police as early as the 2nd and her original statement referred to seeing Leon walking westwards in Commercial Road* with a young man, 'age twenty-six—he might be older', who carried 'a walking-stick and had patent boots and a smart cap'. Her statement carries a hint of that animosity prevailing amongst Jews from differing homelands. 'Look, there's Mr Beron,' she whispered to her husband Sam, 'and the fellow he is with looks like a Russian.' In this first account she spoke of leaving the party at two o'clock and, allowing for the distance involved and for stopping off on the way at a 'Ham and Beef shop', her sighting would have been at the better part of 3.00 a.m., hopelessly late for the prosecution's chronology, but she had been one of the gaggle of witnesses left to gossip among themselves before the identification parade on the 9th. By the time she gave evidence at the inquest, she blandly testified to seeing the two men at 1.15, a time fully in accord with the Crown's theory. She may have been prompted by Solomon Beron or by Sergeant Brogden, an over-enthusiastic member of Wensley's team, and she would also have had access to the very full press reports of what other witnesses had been saying in the preliminary pro-

---

* Between the junctions of Philpot Street and Bedford (now Cavell) Street, on the north side of Commercial Road.

ceedings. She had declared that 'knowing the deceased usually walked with his brother and seeing him at such a late hour drew my attention', but we know that Leon's nocturnal excursions were frequent and that he was not usually accompanied by Solomon.

Here were a number of useful lines for the defence to explore: she had identified Stinie as the 'Russian', whom she can only have had a few seconds to see. Gaslight is not the best illuminant and she was admittedly tired after the party. There was room for cross-examination which did not directly attack her integrity. Unfortunately Abinger had blundered in at the magistrates' court by suggesting that Nellie had been running a brothel above her husband's shop at 401 Commercial Road, not so very far from 2 Hardinge Street.

Ostensibly Sam and Nellie Deitch ran a combined gasfitting and bicycle-repair business, not too successfully it would seem, for half the premises had been rented out to a watchmaker not long since. Nellie had particularly resented the implication that her fur wrap, which bore a distinct resemblance to sable, had been paid for by the horizontal labours of women lodgers in her six-room house. It was a present from her mother-in-law, she had said, but Abinger had not pursued the intriguing point of how that lady, herself the wife of a humble gasfitter, could have afforded such a costly gift. At the trial, under a smart black hat trimmed in violet, she boldly wore the controversial fur. Nobody seems to have picked her up when she now said that it was a present from her husband, a strange extravagance if true, for the couple had left Jubilee Street only a year before after failing in business there. Whether Stinie was convinced that Nellie had some oblique motive for implicating him or whether the conduct of the defence was a crude, very nasty attempt to blacken a deadly witness will now never be known. Anyway, Nellie had been given the advantage of a practice run in the police court.

ABINGER: What are you?
NELLIE: What am I? I am a woman, of course!
ABINGER: I can see that, but what is your occupation?
NELLIE: My occupation? That is a fine question to ask me. I

am at home in the house, looking after my children, looking after my business.

No, she did not know Lizzie Holmes, Dolly Nevy or Lena Hall, and she categorically denied allowing them free rein in her house.

ABINGER: Is it true that Lizzie Holmes had a room at 5 Jubilee Street for which she paid 3s. a week?

NELLIE: No. I had a tenant for two rooms, but never a tenant for one room.

ABINGER: Used she to take men in to your knowledge?

NELLIE: No, no such thing.

ABINGER: And did they sleep with her or stay a short time?

NELLIE: Never such a thing happened.

ABINGER: Did she pay you 3s. for every man that stopped that night?

NELLIE: No. That is an untruth . . .

Abinger now seemed on the edge of a breakthrough, which in the end never came.

ABINGER: Whom were these rooms let to? . . . Give me their names.

NELLIE: I cannot remember their names.

ABINGER: Try.

NELLIE: No, I cannot. I can bring you the woman if you like . . .

ABINGER: What is her name?

NELLIE: Mrs Simmons, that is her name, a woman with her husband and two children . . .

Abinger pressed on with his intimations of immorality, which, far from being vague slurs, were surprisingly detailed. Nellie admitted that she did have a 'servant girl' called Lizzie, who had left about a month before. Darling then intervened to say that he expected to see Lizzie Holmes at court, so that Mrs Deitch could see her too, though there was no question of Lizzie, or any of the other prostitutes, giving evidence in this trial to contradict Nellie's denials. The rule is that evidence cannot be called to substantiate allegations which go merely to the credit of a witness. Anyway, Wensley, for his part, was confident that 'these ladies might have had some difficulties had it been allowable to cross-examine them'.[4]

Amid the few lulls in this questioning, Nellie was asked a little about Leon's background, but proved rather reticent. She made scant reference to his late wife, Adele, and none at all to the terrible circumstances of her death, from syphilis, of which the Deitch family must have been painfully aware. Her remark 'I never saw him with a lady after his wife died' stretches credulity to the limit, but at the time such statements as these were accepted at face value and so acute an observer as J.P. Eddy was not alone in regarding Mrs Deitch as an honest and deeply-wronged witness.[5]

The immorality allegations had backfired very badly indeed. The jury was now firmly prejudiced in Nellie's favour and regarded Abinger's cross-examination as a crude defence smoke-screen. Abinger afterwards declared, rather lamely, 'I must confess to a feeling of great hesitation before I subjected Mrs Deitch to questions concerning her character and possible credibility.'[6] He had discussed the matter fully with his junior and with Lumley before approaching Stinie, who gave direct instructions to attack her character saying that, if Abinger did not, he would try to do so. Abinger's view seems to have been that the allegations were purely gratuitous. If so, his proper course was to refuse to cross-examine on these lines and leave it to Morrison, the lay client, either to accept the position or to dismiss Abinger as his barrister.

The court was to be treated to a second, particularly noisy, instalment of the Deitch saga on the following morning but before then Muir had three important cards, possibly his leading trumps, to lay before the court.

17

'The evidence on which the case really turned was that of the three cabmen.' So wrote Fletcher Moulton, an early commentator on the Morrison trial, in a style irresistibly reminiscent of Beachcomber. But it was an accurate assessment of the position, and the jury, now particularly well-disposed towards the prosecution case after the Deitch fiasco, would hear first from Hayman, then from Stephens and Castling, of Stinie's alleged journeyings in and around South London during the first hours of 1911.

Perhaps Hayman did, as he maintained, ferry two men from Mile End to Lavender Hill. Perhaps, too, the smaller man was Leon Beron. The identification of Stinie Morrison as the other man is a different matter for, quite apart from the difficult circumstances of viewing his passenger on that occasion, Hayman had taken such a very long time to contact the police. Abinger was determined to plug away at this weakness but spoilt the effect, almost from the start, by declaring with a too-obvious relief, 'I am glad to meet an Englishman at last.' Preliminary questioning provoked an obtuse intervention from the judge.

ABINGER: When did you first go to the police station?
HAYMAN: About a week afterwards. I think it was the 9th, if I am not mistaken. It was on the Monday or Tuesday.
ABINGER: Which was it?
DARLING: What does it matter?
ABINGER: It is vital to my case.
DARLING: Whether he went to the police on the 9th or the 10th . . .?

Hayman admitted that he had read the account of Morrison's arrest before going to the police on the evening of 9 January,

the day of Stinie's first court appearance. The evening newspapers had brought out late editions giving detailed descriptions of Stinie and his clothing. The five o'clock edition of the
Evening News, for example, described him as 'tall, well-
dressed, clean-shaven', wearing 'a heavy overcoat of rough,
greenish cloth' and 'well-polished, fairly new boots. He looked
like a person in fairly good circumstances.' A still later edition
published a photograph of Morrison and the *Star* even
managed to produce the first sketch of Stinie in the dock,
wearing the notorious overcoat. In the event, Hayman had
plenty of time to collect his thoughts, for he was not required
to make a written statement until the next night, by which time
a welter of photographs, artist's impressions, descriptions of
and comments about the accused man had appeared in the
papers.

Hayman denied having seen any picture of Morrison before
approaching the police but his explanation for the inordinate
delay in doing so makes thin reading.

HAYMAN: . . . I went to the station as soon as I could.
ABINGER: Why not on the 2nd, 3rd, 4th, 5th, 6th, 7th or 8th?
    (No reply)
DARLING: Do you understand that question?
HAYMAN: Yes . . .
DARLING: What the learned Counsel wants to know is why
    you did not go before.
HAYMAN: I cannot give any reason for it . . .

But Hayman had seen the reward notice posted up in all the
yards and cab shelters. That was why he had come forward.

ABINGER: Then if you saw that police notice, offering a
    reward to cabmen, dated 6th January, why did you not go to
    the police station until the 9th . . .?
HAYMAN: I was driving night work at the time and I went
    home tired each day after doing my work.
ABINGER: . . . Why did you not go?
HAYMAN: I went when I thought proper . . . when I had the
    time.
ABINGER: . . . Why did you not go on the day you saw it?

HAYMAN: Because I was not sure whether I was—to tell you the truth, I did not want to have anything to do with the job at all.

Hayman would not be drawn about the mysterious first part of that answer, and there is always reason to doubt a statement prefaced by such expressions as 'to tell you the truth'. Abinger pressed him about the numerous likenesses of Morrison which had appeared in the papers on the 10th, receiving an odd response.

ABINGER: I have in my hand the *Daily Chronicle* of the 10th with a full-sized portrait of Morrison in it.
HAYMAN: I might go a week without looking at a paper.

The fact remained that Hayman was not asked to make a written statement until the evening of the 10th, after all that day's publicity, which must render his identification, made as late as the 17th, particularly suspect.

Muir's re-examination of the witness nearly came unstuck.

MUIR: When did you first form the opinion that the men you had driven to Lavender Gardens had something to do with the Clapham murder?
HAYMAN: I suppose when I saw this notice put up in the yard where I was driving.
MUIR: Not before?
HAYMAN: No.

But, in response to a solemn question from the judge, Hayman said he had 'no doubt whatever' that his identification was accurate: a claim that the jury was disposed to accept.

The second day of Stinie's trial ended with the reluctant presence of Sam Deitch, who definitely did not wear the trousers at 401 Commercial Road. He needed some judicial prodding to come out with his story, which did not really corroborate his wife's adamantly stated evidence.

On the following morning, there was an air of amused expectancy as Nellie Deitch stalked towards the witness-box for yet another battle with defence counsel who, overnight, had been provided, through the assiduity of his solicitor, with a couple of 'rather bedraggled ladies', in Abinger's words.[1] Confronted by Lizzie Holmes, Nellie firmly denied that she knew her, or that this Lizzie was her one-time maid. The advent of a second girl, Sarah Lask, caused a slanging match in No. 1 Court which threatened to eclipse the reputation of Billingsgate. Nor would Nellie admit to knowing Boyd Street or Batty Street, two little unsavoury rows off Commercial Road, or to approaching Lask, inviting her to come to her house, meet 'a nice man' and earn some money.

Muir then displayed the apparently respectable Mrs Simmons, wife and mother, but the Morrison camp had not exhausted their ammunition yet. After lunch, Dolly Nevy and Lena Hall made their appearance, the final exhibit being a young lady who went by the name of Becky Blue, but, as before, Nellie simply denied any connection with them and Abinger made no progress.

These undignified scenes prevented a proper exposure of weaknesses in the evidence of Alfred Stephens, testimony which, of all the three drivers, is most likely to have been perjured. There was a perceptible stir in court as he stepped forward, for it had been well-publicized that Stephens had been the victim of intimidation—or so Muir would have it—and a measure of sympathy was immediately forwarded to a man so obviously out of breath even with the modest effort of getting up into the witness-box. In a husky voice, he described the journey from Clapham Cross to Kennington and, though his opportunity of studying his fare must have been poor indeed, Stephens stoutly declared that it was the accused. 'I am quite sure,' he told Darling, but he, like Hayman, had waited a long time before approaching the police, well after the reward notice had appeared, and he frankly admitted that he had seen a picture of Morrison before doing so.

Under cross-examination, he revealed that he had been driving his cab continuously since two or three o'clock on the afternoon of the 31st, a matter of some twelve hours before the fateful journey to Kennington. Curiously, his passenger had come round the corner from Clapham Old Town, along The Pavement, which is not the most direct route from the scene of

the murder. After a great deal of peripheral inquiry, Abinger at
length came to the point.

ABINGER: When did you first hear of the murder committed
on Clapham Common?

STEPHENS: In the Sunday night, 1st January.

ABINGER: ...Why did you not go to the police on the
Monday?

STEPHENS: Because I did not connect it up then with that
man; I never thought of it at the time ...

ARBINGER: Then why did you not go?

STEPHENS: Because the general appearance of this man when
he came to me was like an actor or a professional man and I
thought he lived in the neighbourhood of Kennington Park.

This was a dangerous answer and Abinger would have been
wiser not to have pressed the witness, although there had been
a large number of references in the press noting Stinie's resemblance
to an actor (he had sometimes pretended to be one) and
of his being seen in some sort of make-up, probably deriving
from his fondness for the Yiddish theatricals. Stephens denied
having seen the *Evening News* on the 9th, but there is no doubt
that this edition was purposely left lying around in the room at
Brixton Police Station, where he was seen by Detective-Sergeant
Cooper at about noon on 10 January and made the
first of two written statements that day. Cooper's own account
makes damning reading:

> There is a desk where the typewriting machine is affixed ...
> Stephens sat opposite and to the best of my recollection
> there was an *Evening News* lying on the slope there with a
> photograph of the prisoner right in front of Stephens, but it
> was never shown to him and it was quite accidental that he
> saw it ... someone would have purchased it the night before
> for the purpose of reading it and would have left it on his
> desk.

By curious mischance, the paper was open at page three, on
which was the photograph. How careless of the police.

The two statements made that day are endorsed respectively
as being an 'original' and a 'corrected' version, although only
the first seems to have been made available to the defence.

Stephens had originally claimed to have picked up his fare at just before 2.30 a.m. on New Year's morning at the rank by what is now Clapham Common underground station. The man, whose description broadly tallied with Morrison, was driven to the Hanover Arms in Kennington Park Road, from where he walked hurriedly away in the direction of the Horns, the public house that persistently crops up in this story. Stephens' 2.30 a.m. was inconsistent with Hayman's story of picking up two fares in Mile End Road at about 2.00 a.m., allowing for the time needed to get to Lavender Hill, walk to Clapham Common, commit the murder and walk the half-mile to Stephens' rank. The corrected statement, perhaps 'corrected' in the light of what Hayman had said, gives the time of the pick-up as 'between 2.30 and 3.00 . . . some time after the last tram car left for Tooting.' Mention is also made in this second version of the man paying with his left hand, an amazingly accurate recollection after ten days, a feature which adds to suspicion that Stephens had been prompted by Cooper, just as Nellie Deitch may have been by Sergeant Brogden.

For whatever reason, Stephens' mind was set to work, even to the extent of visiting the tramway company's offices and examining the timetable. Apart from Cooper's intervention, there is a real possibility that Stephens and Hayman put their heads together about the evidence they were to give. Hayman very likely *did* journey from Mile End to Lavender Hill, though his identification is highly suspect, but it is doubtful if Stephens made the trip from Clapham Common to Kennington, at any rate in the circumstances he described. The facts certainly point to Stephens altering his times to fit in with Hayman's version, rather than vice versa, and there is evidence which suggests communication between the two. Towards the end of Abinger's cross-examination of Stephens, the foreman of the jury handed a note to Darling asking whether Stephens had seen Hayman before altering his timing. This question, which should have been the subject of pressing inquiry by Abinger, elicited an interesting reply, which was not explored, nor was Hayman recalled to deal with it.

STEPHENS: No. I have seen him. I have known him four or

five years, but I have not seen him during this case. I never spoke to him about this matter and I never knew he was a cabman at all until 17th January.

The latter date was the occasion of an identification parade held for the driver witnesses but it is remarkable that Stephens, a cabdriver for fifteen years, could have been unaware that his acquaintance of four or five years' standing had been employed in the same job. They lived within a mile of each other in the Kennington–Camberwell area and it would have been surprising if Hayman had not dropped into the Horns occasionally, as so many cabdrivers were in the habit of doing. Out of over seven thousand drivers in London, these two men—known to one another—would provide crucial evidence in the prosecution of Stinie Morrison. And neither man had chosen to come forward until after the offer of a reward.

The *Daily Telegraph*'s reporter considered Stephens 'cool and collected—an admirable witness' never at a loss for words.[2] Plainly, he impressed the jury, but his dealings with such known crooks as Rappolt, his desperate poverty (due to ill-health, gambling or a mixture of the two) and the possibility that he had been a regular 'copper's nark' were never canvassed in open court. His deadliest answer was reserved for another question from the jury wondering if the accused had opened his overcoat to pay his fare. The man did not unbutton his coat, said Stephens, but had the money in his hand. Then, looking towards Stinie's tall figure in the dock, head cocked in intense concentration, Stephens forged a link between the crowded courtroom and the misty, almost deserted cab-rank outside Kennington church. 'He looked the same look as he's got now—' he wheezed, '—on one side.'

The triumvirate of cabdrivers was completed by Alfred Castling's evidence of a mysterious journey from Kennington to Finsbury Gate, north of Finsbury Park underground station in Seven Sisters Road. Castling spoke of two passengers picked up at about 3.30 a.m. on New Year's morning outside Kennington church, one noticeably shorter than the other (though his original statement made to police on 6 January put them at about the same height). The taller, who spoke English with a foreign accent, had been wearing 'a long overcoat, a motor-shape fashion coat'. It was this man, identified as Morrison on 9 January, whom Castling had described in that first statement as '5′ 8″, fair', hopelessly removed from Stinie's appearance and height of over six feet, yet Abinger utterly failed to challenge Castling about this major discrepancy in his evidence. In retrospect, too, Castling's account of the second man ('bowler hat ... dark ... with a dark moustache ... 5′ 6″') might be thought to have fitted the recently-dead Beron himself and it is noteworthy that Castling admitted having read newspaper reports that the police, in the first days after the murder, were looking for 'two Frenchmen', and he ended his original statement with the words, 'They appeared to me to be Frenchmen.' There must be a possibility that Castling was trying to provide the police with what he thought they would want from him. At all events, it was not until after much newspaper publicity that he saw fit to call at a police station.

Before making the long journey to Finsbury Park, Castling had been on duty some fifteen and a half hours, even longer than Stephens' stint, but he claimed that he was not tired at Kennington. He could not afford to be.

ABINGER: When do you get tired, if you do not get tired after fifteen and a half hours?
CASTLING: When I have earned enough money to take home.

The most charitable explanation for Castling's evidence lies in a genuinely mistaken identification.* No material was ever forthcoming to explain how Stinie might have got back from Finsbury Park (reached at 4.00 a.m.) to Whitechapel, where he was seen up and about shortly before nine. It was mooted privately in official circles that the second man must have been a receiver (surely not Max Frank, based in Lambeth, or Rotto from Charlotte Street, nowhere near Finsbury Park) or even Hugo Pool, though Castling's description of a dark man does not accord with Pool's noticeably ginger colouring. For Stinie,

---

* Although he did live south of the river, a mile or so from Hayman and Stephens.

unhappily, the most important fact was his counsel's total failure to subject this witness to an effective cross-examination. There was no shortage of ammunition for it.

Muir called a contingent of police officers to prove that no one at Leman Street, other than the top brass, had possessed the slightest inkling that Morris Stein was the Clapham Common murder suspect and also that the first person to use the word 'murder' was none other than the accused himself. Wensley led the field in giving this improbable evidence and was duly questioned by Abinger about the personalities of the Houndsditch affair (in so far as they were already publicly known). The character of the dead man, so important a factor in the case, was barely touched on.

ABINGER: Had you known the deceased man?
WENSLEY: I did.
ABINGER: How long had you known him?
WENSLEY: Four or five years—probably longer.

Darling seems to have suspected that there might have been more to Beron than mere eccentricity and took the matter further at the end of Wensley's evidence. The replies were guarded.

DARLING: . . . What was he?
WENSLEY: He was reputed to be a man of some means. He apparently did nothing by way of occupation. He was chiefly in this Jewish restaurant in the East End and he was reputed to be a fairly wealthy man.
DARLING: Was he known to the police at all?
WENSLEY: Only by sight. He had some house property in the East End of London.

Wensley was not telling the whole truth but he was never asked in clear terms whether Beron was suspected or known to have been an habitual receiver of stolen goods or whether he had acted as a police informant in relation to matters other than the Houndsditch affair. Abinger had posed a melodramatic scenario, with Leon's death attributed to the vengeance of unnamed members of the Gardstein gang, a theory which Muir was able to destroy without revealing any of the unsavoury facts about Leon's true background.

MUIR: Was any information given to you with regard to these Houndsditch murders by Leon Beron?

WENSLEY: None whatever.

Nor was Mrs Deitch's house anything other than a respectable home, at least, as far as the Inspector knew.

Divisional Detective-Inspector Ward, filling almost the entire witness-box with his ample frame, ended the court day by recalling his first view of the body amid the scrub and bushes of Clapham Common. Questioned about footprints clearly visible in the soft soil and leaf-mould, Ward seems to have been protecting his less competent subordinates at Cavendish Road Police Station who had failed to make any record of the indentations before their destruction by the feet of sightseers or even, perhaps, by policemen's boots before Ward arrived on the scene.[3]

ABINGER: We have been told by a constable that there were upon the soft ground impressions of feet—footprints.

WARD: Yes ... but there were no distinct footmarks ... the ground is very hard.

ABINGER: It was not a frosty night, was it?

WARD: No.

Darling invited Ward to mark the position of the copse on an exhibited plan, whereupon the foreman, self-possessed as ever, blandly announced on behalf of his colleagues, 'We know the way exactly, to a man.'

The fourth day of Stinie's long trial began with Abinger's discovery that he was bereft of a junior counsel, as MacGregor had fallen seriously ill, but Ward was unsympathetic, in no mood to offer any help to the defence and stonewalled quite beautifully.

ABINGER: Is there a watchman's hut on Clapham Common?

WARD: Not now...

ABINGER: I am talking about December 31st.

WARD: Tell me where, sir, please. Clapham Common is a very large place.

ABINGER: I have never yet been to Clapham Common. Will

you kindly tell me if there is a watchman's hut on Clapham Common?

WARD: There was a watchman's hut near the road that runs parallel with the long path . . .

ABINGER: What is the name of the watchman?

WARD: I do not know.

ABINGER: Have you inquired?

WARD: He was seen by some police officer.

ABINGER: Have you inquired? . . .

WARD: Personally, no . . . Someone saw the man on the morning.

ABINGER: Did you give instructions?

WARD: Yes.

A blood-stained handkerchief had been found by a local woman on the morning of the 2nd near the Windmill public house, some two hundred yards from the scene of the crime and, although officers had checked every laundry in London, the laundry mark 'LT 109' could not be identified. Abinger made great play of this inconsequential discovery, taxing Ward with a sinister suggestion. 'Just look at the laundry mark,' he asked, 'I put it to you that it is a foreign laundry mark. What do you say?' But Ward candidly admitted that he was no judge of foreign laundry marks and there the matter rested. At any rate, there was no connection between the stained handkerchief and Stinie's clean washing, taken to the Japanese laundry by Annie Zimmerman and later collected by police, who were obliged to debit the Police Fund 8d. for the privilege.

Several watch mechanisms had been seized from Frank's shop, but none was found to be from Leon's watch. Ward went on to describe and time the reconstruction of Hayman's route from Mile End Road to Lavender Hill, a journey made by Stephens, who had driven Ward and Cooper—a tight fit—in a hansom. Stephens may have been the chosen driver because Hayman had started motor-cabbing, a sign of the changing times, early in the New Year.

Abinger rounded off his cross-examination of Ward by paying him an unnecessary compliment which would not have been endorsed by Stinie. 'You have been very fair in all the answers that you have made me. I do not quarrel with any one word you have said.'

In an odd manoeuvre, Wensley was recalled at Abinger's insistence to read the depositions of two youngsters, Eva Flitterman and Sam Rosen, neither of whom was to give evidence at the trial. This was an unnecessary exercise, establishing merely that the defence solicitors had unsuccessfully asked the Director of Public Prosecutions to have the pair prosecuted for perjury.

Eva, a sixteen-year-old tailoress,* had been billed as a major prosecution witness in the January committal proceedings when she said—or appeared to be saying—that Stinie had sported Leon's watch and chain on New Year's Day, deadly evidence if true. Stinie had certainly visited the Flitterman household that afternoon, changing a £4 cheque for gold half-sovereigns and astonishing the family by giving Eva £2 to buy the dress she had been outworking for her rascally employer (the aptly-named Abraham Stitcher). But Eva's testimony was hopelessly muddled and an incriminating '£5 piece' attached to the gold chain turned out to have been one of Stinie's own, bought late in 1910. An interesting example of police prompting a witness can be seen in this short passage of committal evidence. The sergeant in question was Brogden, who may also have influenced Nellie Deitch's answers.

EVA: The sergeant asked me if I had seen a £5 piece.
ABINGER: Did he ask you before or after you said you had seen a £5 piece?
EVA: Before.

The other recanting witness was the youth, Sam Rosen, regarded by police as a 'degenerate' (perhaps meaning homosexual) but none the less called to give evidence at the police court about seeing Stinie and Leon together at about 1.30 on the morning of the 1st, at the corner of Brick Lane and White-

___

* Stinie met Eva at the Hardinge Street brothel on Christmas Eve. She said she was the 'guest' of a man she knew only as Issy, who lived there with a woman known as 'Fat Nancy', sharing the premises with Hugo and Ethel Pool amongst others. Despite Eva's denials, it looks as if she and Stinie had a brief affair before the year ended, but she was hardly the embittered ex-mistress portrayed by Abinger.

chapel Road. Rosen later said that this was untrue and he had been asleep in bed by 11.30 on New Year's Eve. His proven association with Jack Taw suggests that either Taw or Solomon Beron put him up to giving false evidence on the first occasion but Stinie had friends too and Rosen, a weak character with known criminal associations, found himself under heavy pressure from both camps.

Further medical evidence, principally directed to the equivocal bloodstaining on Stinie's clothing, brought the Crown's case to an end. The few spots of blood (and mud) on a collar, cuff and shirt were plainly inconclusive—blood-grouping analysis was, in any case, unknown in 1911—and Abinger was able to pose a question of great value to the defence: how was it that no bloodstains had been found on the overcoat which Morrison had been wearing that fatal night?

Before Abinger began his opening speech to the jury, Darling ensured that a capital trial should not spoil the judicial levity when opportunity presented itself.

ABINGER: Would your lordship intimate that you will not sit on Saturday?

DARLING: I will think about it, but judges are not expected now to get fresh air on Saturdays. (Laughter)

FOREMAN: Nor juries, my lord? (Laughter)

DARLING: No, sir. Only the House of Commons. (Loud laughter)

After the court had quietened down, the foreman spoke for his jurymen colleagues in words which, with hindsight, bore an ominous import.

FOREMAN: That is hardly our wish... If you close the court on Saturday, it is practically two days for us to be shut up. It is two days absolutely wasted. We want to get this case over as quickly as possible.

18

Mr Justice Darling sat well back in his chair, resting his head on one side, apparently taking great interest in the ceiling lights of No. 1 Court. It was half-past three in the afternoon of a long court day, tea was but a faint prospect and Edward Abinger was making his opening speech for the defence. True to form, it would be a prosy affair, laden with peripheral detail; a faint smile was seen to cross the judge's face as counsel assured the jury that he would not put a single unnecessary question to any witness. There were some decidedly hackish moments.

ABINGER: Gentlemen, I am going to call the prisoner and he will have to go through an ordeal more terrible, I suggest to you, than the ordeal heretics had to undergo in the days of the Inquisition, because he, a man of imperfect education, as you will soon discover, fighting for his life, will have opposed to him a brilliant counsel, than whom there is no more skilful cross-examiner at the Bar. It will be a very unequal contest, as unequal as a fight between a professional prize-fighter and a curate.

This odd vision, the *Daily Graphic* recorded, 'raised a broad smile to the countenance of Gunner Moir, the best-known of British pugilists, who has been one of the most interested spectators at the trial'.[1]

Eventually Abinger stopped talking and called his first witness, John Greaves, a qualified surveyor, who had visited the vicinity of the cab-rank at Clapham Cross. His evidence, delivered in a calm, matter-of-fact way, ought to have destroyed the effect of Stephens' testimony had other things been equal in this remarkable trial. In the event, it seems to have made little impact on the jury, even though it confirmed that

Stephens would have had just a few seconds in which to get anything like a reasonable view of the man he was to identify as Stinie Morrison at a parade held some two and a half weeks afterwards, desperately important in a case which depended so heavily on identification evidence.

With the appearance of Annie Zimmerman, her husband Morrie and a woman neighbour, the court was once more plunged into the maelstrom of Whitechapel life.

Annie was charmingly naive, even to the extent of trying to supplement the interpreter's efforts with her own strange patois of Yiddish and English. Stinie, muttering that her evidence was not being translated properly, upset the interpreter, but Darling brusquely ordered him to get on as best he could. Annie made a great deal of the shrieking door-bolt, which Greaves had also described, together with the noisy, ill-fitting sash-window in Stinie's ground-floor room. She was positive, as was her husband, that she would have heard Stinie go out in the small hours and Mrs Grose, at No. 93, remembered seeing Stinie let himself in to the Zimmermans' house shortly after midnight and, she said, heard the bolt drawn behind him.

Muir handled these witnesses with care. They appeared honest, they could have been mistaken, and it would not profit the Crown to attempt an aggressive cross-examination. Abinger's next two witnesses, the Brodsky sisters, were not so fortunate but there can be no doubt that they both willingly gave perjured evidence on Stinie's behalf in a crude attempt to establish that Stinie had been to the music-hall on New Year's Eve: not a true alibi at all, because the performance was over well before midnight and, on Stinie's own account, he was back in the Warsaw at 11.45, when he saw Beron. The music-hall story was a stupid invention, born of Stinie's desperate desire to play down his association with the dead man—and, once disproved, strongly contributed to the ultimate verdict.

Esther Brodsky, the elder of the two, was first to enter the witness-box, trying, a shade too obviously, to hide behind the language barrier though, as Darling pointed out, she had lived in England for seventeen of her twenty-one years. Both she and her sister Jane were caught out by the simplest error: the price of a ticket for the orchestra stalls, normally a shilling, had been raised to one-and-six for the New Year's Eve crowds, who had, in any case, booked all but two rows in advance. Esther could not remember 'any particular performance that evening'—a telling admission. Muir, cross-examining, probed away at Stinie's flirtation with Jane and her continued association with him after his arrest, preparing the ground for the more important questions he would be putting to the younger sister.

Esther's looks and her smart appearance had been noticed in court but there was a distinct buzz when the sixteen-year-old Jane stepped forward. Underneath an elegant, black broad-rimmed hat, she presented an attractive figure, looking older than her years, with a pretty shawl about her shoulders, a lace-trimmed blouse and blue dress, armed with that essential item for a woman of fashion, a large fur muff. Asked to identify Stinie, she gave a broad smile as their eyes met and, presently, they both laughed as she described the sight of Harry Champion on the stage with his silly ginger wig and even sillier song, 'Ginger, You're Barmy!'

Stinie should have kept his usually impassive pose: the significance of those smiling faces was not lost on the unamused jurymen, mindful of Muir's thinly-veiled suggestions to Esther about her sister's relationship with Stinie. Indeed, Jane would shortly be telling the court about some four or five visits to Stinie in Brixton Prison. 'I went there at Morrison's request,' she declared simply, 'he wrote and asked me to come.' Jane had been the subject of extensive and repeated interrogation by the police about the association between herself and Stinie, which enabled Muir to pose some awkward questions.

On 7 January she had been taken by Stinie to Rotto's house in Fitzroy Square. Muir forbore to allege directly that sexual intercourse had occurred, but an outburst by Jane against the evidently strong police pressure upon her shows Wensley in a distinctly unfavourable light, with few scruples about alleging immoral conduct in the very young.

MUIR: What officer bullied you?
JANE: Inspector Wensley ... said ... that I have been going

about with Morrison from five years ago. I told Inspector Wensley if he knew how old I was at the time . . . I told him I was the age of ten or eleven and did not know Morrison then.

Nevertheless, she was unable to explain why she had not mentioned seeing Morrison in the music-hall on New Year's Eve in any of the numerous interviews with the police and, though Muir addressed her as 'madam', she made herself sound, on occasion, more like a cheeky schoolgirl than a woman of the world.

JANE: The next time I told them not to send for me, but to kindly drop a postcard if they should want me. They took no notice of what I said, but sent a police officer in private uniform.

After Abinger's re-examination, Darling hammered home the prosecution's case in a series of questions about the liaison at Rotto's house, showing that Jane and Stinie had been there for well over two hours and little credit was given to her assertion that Mrs Rotto had acted as chaperon. When, a little later, the two girls were recalled to face further cross-examination by Muir, now fully briefed about the Shoreditch Empire's ticket policy, they were utterly discredited. Abinger, in desperation, tried to persuade Jane into upping the price of the seats, but she obstinately repeated what Stinie had told her to say and would not be budged.

ABINGER: What did you pay?
JANE: Two single shillings, I think it was.
ABINGER: May you not have given three?
DARLING: Now, Mr Abinger, this is your own witness.
ABINGER: Yes, I know, but I have cross-examined so many days that I thought for a moment I was cross-examining this witness.

Irreparable damage had been done to Stinie's cause. He was shown up as a relentless seducer of young women: a man who did not shrink from persuading two young and impressionable girls to lie on his behalf. And the shame of it was that they had been such unnecessary, such unhelpful lies.

A senior bank official was called to prove, by comparing signatures, that Stinie had changed £35 cash—part proceeds, in fact, of the Holloway fraud—for seven £5 notes at a Commercial Road branch early in December. In court, at Abinger's request, Stinie had signed his name for the comparison, with suspiciously laboured effort, in an attempt to show that he was not short of money at the beginning of his association with Beron. Cross-examining, Muir skilfully turned the tables and, by putting two seemingly innocent questions, pointed the finger at Stinie, raising the grisly spectre of the dead man's mutilated face.

MUIR: The 'S' in the handwriting in the dock today is made differently to what it is on the exchange slip?
BANK OFFICIAL: Yes.
MUIR: The 'S' on the exchange slip is very open, like the open thing on a fiddle?
BANK OFFICIAL: Yes.

Florrie Dellow was determined not to disappoint her spectators—had she not once thought of going on the stage?—and, as Jane Brodsky had done, she entered the courtroom an object of eager scrutiny. The bright green of her high-shouldered jacket, with skirt to match, must have raised a few eyebrows, but the true sensation was reserved for her hat, trimmed with fur and sporting, on either side, a pair of exceedingly large wings, reminiscent of swallowtails, which bobbed alarmingly as she walked towards the witness-box. She told of her brief liaison with Stinie after their meeting at Max Frank's house on New Year's Day. Muir mercilessly questioned her about her true occupation in an episode which demonstrates his cross-examining skill at its very best, with a devastating repartee at the end.

MUIR: You have lived six months in this house?
FLORRIE: Six months, yes.
MUIR: Do you take ... different men home there?
FLORRIE: My friends. I do not take different men. I have my friends there.
MUIR: You are a common prostitute, are you not?

FLORRIE: I beg pardon, no.
MUIR: You have been convicted?
FLORRIE: I might have been. This is nothing to do with this case, is it?
MUIR: For prostitution in the street?
FLORRIE: Yes.
MUIR: More than once?
FLORRIE: Twice. The same detective that took me has been home with me twice.
MUIR: Then he made no mistake about you?

Further proof, if any were needed, of Morrison's powerful sexual appeal for so many women lay in Florrie's admission that she had visited the prisoner in Brixton Prison 'every day, except Saturday'.

Abinger called his last witness of the day at five o'clock sharp, when for once it was not necessary for the usher to summon anyone from the marbled vastness of the hall outside the courtroom. This witness came from the dock and, attended closely by a uniformed warder, Stinie passed directly in front of the jurymen to take his place in the witness-box. His evidence, over seven hours of it, would occupy the better part of three court days.

19

Stinie's approach to religious matters can only be described as eclectic: a convict listed as of no religion in his Dartmoor days, he asked to be sworn on the New Testament, though people thought he would take the oath as a Jew.

ABINGER: How old are you?
STINIE: Twenty-nine, between twenty-nine and thirty.
ABINGER: Where were you born?
STINIE: Australia.

If that first answer in evidence was odd, the second was a downright lie, as the court would soon discover. Throughout his long testimony, Stinie, a compulsive liar, intermingled fact and fancy, frequently telling lies when the truth would have helped him. Also, like many dishonest people, he had developed a habit of giving rambling, evasive responses to the simplest of questions. He spoke volubly in English, remarkably good for someone of his background, but which, unmistakeably, represented the voice of an alien immigrant, one of the thousands who had poured into the East End and who were now the object of so much suspicion and hatred, the 'foreign scum' of Seymour Hicks' florid pen.[1] Stinie would cough from time to time, a dry, nervous cough, while delivering his evidence in an accent which mingled eastern Europe with Cockney London, exemplified in his Dickensian habit of rendering 'v' as 'w' ('wery difficult to remember') and by pronouncing such words as 'opposite' with a long 'i'.

This shady circumlocution, plus Abinger's obsession with detail, made tedious listening for the jury impatient to return to business and family. Before the court rose for the day, an hour and a half of evidence had taken Stinie's narrative only to 31 December, with some unsavoury accusations against poor Eva Flitterman en route. True or false, they served only to underline, in an age very conscious of the middle-class proprieties, a disturbingly promiscuous pattern of behaviour by the man on trial. This answer is sadly typical of Stinie's mode of reply.

ABINGER: Did you know Eva Flitterman about that time?
STINIE: No, I do not believe I did—no, I did not—I believe I came to know her—Oh! yes, of course I did. I came to know her first about the 25th December, I believe. Somewhere about that time.

For an obscure reason, Abinger asked Stinie to reveal the make of the collar he was wearing that day. After a deal of confusion, Stinie was directed to remove the item for inspection, whereupon the foreman, wholly unprompted, stood up, leant over towards the witness-box and calmly helped undo the collar fastened about Stinie's neck: surely a most extraordinary episode in a murder trial, when hanging by the neck was the likely penalty upon conviction.

In spite of Abinger's desperate plea for a week-end's respite from the strain of defending 'a terribly difficult case like this', the trial resumed on Saturday morning, when the jurymen were subjected to the minutiae of Stinie's wanderings in the week after Leon's death. The judge vainly tried to stem the flow but Abinger was resolute in his view that everything had to be told and the morning was already well advanced by the time Muir got up to cross-examine. He had burned much midnight oil preparing for this moment once Abinger's opening speech had made it clear that Stinie would give evidence. An accused person cannot be compelled to go into the witness-box and be cross-examined and a more competent and confident advocate than Abinger would have hesitated before subjecting his client to cross-examination in this case, with so many gaps and contradictions in the Crown's evidence. Indeed, it might have been better not to have called any defence witnesses at all other than merely professional testimony on medical or allied matters; certainly the Brodsky girls had done far more harm than good. Whether Abinger considered this point with sufficient care is not known for Stinie, a powerful personality, may have insisted upon giving evidence, but there is no record of any attempt by Abinger to warn him of the danger ahead.

Assisted by many hours' consultation with the two senior police officers, reams of immaculately ordered papers in front of him, Muir launched his 'forensic barrage', the words of a contemporary advocate,[2] who felt that Muir 'at times ... pressed his prosecutions too far ... He regarded a Treasury prosecution as something sacrosanct and was apt to be led away by an enthusiasm almost evangelical.' The love of money is the root of all evil: greed for gold, in the form of watch, chain and coin, had been the object of the assault and the cause of Beron's death. There was no other credible reason for the killing and that was how Muir saw the matter.

MUIR: When you went to Flittermans on the 1st January, how much money had you in your possession?

STINIE: I should think I had about £28, not more than that. I cannot tell you exactly. I had four banknotes and I had £8 or £9 in gold.

Two of those banknotes, £5 each, had been changed from gold by Max Frank on New Year's morning, the others at Cook's in Aldgate, before Christmas. Muir repeatedly asked Stinie for the origin of the gold changed at Cook's, but answers were evasive until, to cover up the Holloway fraud, Stinie falsely claimed to have won £38 playing faro (a long-forgotten card game, popular with Edwardian gamblers) at a Whitechapel spieler early in December. Memory failed to recall the name of the croupier or any other witnesses to the lucky break, hardly surprising in view of the truth: Stinie had lost most of his ill-gotten gold at the gaming-tables within a few days of the Holloway coup. Another palpably false story lay in Stinie's claim that his mother, a shadowy figure from the steppes, had obligingly sent him £20 in English banknotes, but he was unable to provide any corroboration of the fact.

MUIR: Have you got any letter that came with the money?
STINIE: No.
MUIR: Does that, again, depend entirely upon your word?
STINIE: I destroyed that letter, for the simple reason that I did not wish to keep it with me.

That disingenuous 'for the simple reason' abounded in Stinie's evidence, particularly when awkward issues presented themselves. Once Muir had forced him to admit pawning the watch and chain on Christmas Eve (actually the only indication, and an ambiguous one at that, of financial problems at that time), cross-examination suddenly reverted to 30 November, the day of the Holloway coup, in a close scrutiny of Stinie's spree in a variety of clothing shops that day. Muir seems to have been primed by Wensley that Morrison was suspected of partici-pation in the fraud but, in the event, never accused Stinie directly of the Holloway crime, contenting himself with the defendant's failure to provide any credible account of his financial affairs between the end of November and the begin-ning of January. Stinie was in an impossible position and could not reveal even the semblance of truth without incriminating himself in the fraud, worth a good five years' penal servitude. Of course, a stretch like this was preferable to the neck-stretching consequent upon conviction for murder but Stinie seems to have been buoyed up by Abinger's initial optimism and much impressed by his counsel's wordy interjections, which often resulted in sparks flying between Abinger, Muir and the judge. Throughout the trial, even when the tide was plainly flowing against him, Stinie believed that he would be acquitted. He knew that he was not guilty of Beron's murder and he knew his barrister believed that, too. What he did not realize was that his counsel's incompetence was fatally under-mining such defence as there was, given the prejudices of the time and Muir's dirty tricks. Stinie, a gambling man, hoped that fate had dealt him a hand that would enable him to walk out of the Old Bailey free from the risk of further prosecution for a serious fraud. And there was a still darker secret of which his inner voices forbade any mention: the true reason for his in-volvement with Leon Beron.

Evasive answers allowed Muir to re-state an important part of his case under the guise of a question.

MUIR: What I point out to you is this. That on 23rd December you are pawning a gold albert; you have no document to show any money spent by you at all; and on 1st January, the day after this man's murder, you are in possession of £24.

The spotlight shifted to Stinie's friendship with the dead man, an association that had blossomed so quickly in the last three weeks of 1910. Stinie played it down, far too far down: all that would pass between them at the Warsaw, he said, was an oc-casional 'Comment vous portez-vous?' from Leon, prompting a reply of 'Très bien' (pronounced, noted an unkind reporter, as 'been'). In the face of the obvious, this kind of evidence failed to impress.

STINIE: That man has never in any way been friends with me. I never on any occasion walked with the man in the street as any two friends might have done ... I will admit that on several occasions we might have been sitting at the same table. There is no special table for anybody. Anybody can come in and sit where he likes.

Stinie compounded falsehood by denying that he had ever held Leon's watch remarking on its size and weight. Leon liked to show off this proud possession to fellow-customers in the restaurant and there cannot have been anything out of the ordinary in Stinie's interest, a curiosity shared by the majority of the money-conscious clientele; yet he would deny holding the watch, just as he had not realized that the early newspaper accounts of the murder referred to Beron. He was known to Stinie as 'the landlord', not the 'mad landlord' of the copywriters' script. A 'mad landlord' meant nothing to him. Most foolish of all, Stinie put himself among that army of New Year's Eve sightseers in Whitechapel, in the ranks of Taw, Weissberg and Zaltzman. He, too, had seen Leon with another man. It was about seven or eight minutes after midnight, at the corner of Sidney Street and Whitechapel Road. Muir asked for a description of the other party. 'I could only see his back,' said Stinie, 'he was very well-dressed indeed,' and, with a studied forgetfulness of Beron's name, he added that the man was tall, 'certainly taller than Mr What's-'is–name'.

Stinie was trapped and he knew it. He could no more reveal the truth about his association with the dead man than tell of the real source of his income in early December or, for that matter, why he had been on such friendly terms with Frank and Rotto. Neither of these two crooks was to be a witness in the case but Muir was determined that the jury should know as much as possible about them, putting some very prejudicial questions to Stinie, cross-examination to which Abinger should have objected, for the fact that both Frank and Rotto were men of bad character was quite irrelevant to the issue which the jury were trying.

MUIR: Do you know that Frank is a convicted receiver of stolen jewellery?
STINIE: I did not know anything of the kind till it was put in the papers after his being cross-examined by you at the coroner's inquest.

111

Stinie suddenly realized that he was playing into Muir's hands and, in a desperate diversionary tactic, alleged that Max had been offered £100 by the police to give evidence against him in court. This was a preposterous lie and, in the process, Stinie was forced to admit that Max had been to see him in Brixton, serving merely to reinforce the close association between the two men, which was just what Muir had wanted to do. For the judge, it was not enough that Max Frank was a convicted receiver: as in so many English trials, a fundamentally criminal matter became confused, to the detriment of the prisoner, with questions of sexual morality.

DARLING: Did you think that, if he had been a respectable man, he would have let a room to you to live with a prostitute?
STINIE: There are dozens of respectable men here in London, grocers and all sorts of people, who keep women in their houses.

Muir followed the judge's lead when he came to explore Stinie's long-standing friendship with Rotto, who was supposed to be a grocer but by no stretch of the imagination a respectable man.

MUIR: Do you know that he has been in custody for receiving?
STINIE: I did not.
MUIR: Do you know that he has been connected with the White Slave traffic? . . .
STINIE: Not that man. He is as respectable a man as I ever came across.

By now, the jury knew that Stinie's contact with the respectable world must have been slight but, so far, his own character had escaped searching cross-examination. Darling, mindful of Abinger's attack on Mrs Deitch, had given the prosecution that very morning carte blanche to explore and expose the defendant's character. Possibly Muir was not quite prepared for this and had designed his cross-examination of Stinie without reference to previous convictions, for he declared at the midday adjournment that he had not much more to ask.

Skipping lunch, Muir had a careful discussion with Charles

Mathews, Director of Public Prosecutions, who had been sitting in his traditional place to the left of the Clerk of Arraigns. Ward and Wensley were soon called in and the outcome was a decision to re-cast the prosecution's strategy. Cross-examination obviously could not go on that afternoon so, when the court resumed at two o'clock, Mathews climbed on to his seat, an ungainly manoeuvre, and held a lengthy, whispered conversation with the judge who, without asking the defence its view, promptly announced that it would be convenient to adjourn the trial until Monday morning, a nice example of judicial deference to the Crown, which contrasted sharply with Darling's summary rejection of Abinger's earlier plea that the court should not sit on Saturday.

A second visit to the Common was arranged for the jury, at the much later hour of 1.30 a.m., when twelve good men and true solemnly paced out the journey from the spot where Beron had died to Clapham Cross, probably taking the most direct route, forgetful of Stephens' evidence that his passenger had come from the direction of Clapham Old Town. They were, said the foreman, particularly anxious to check on the visibility at Clapham Cross 'after the surrounding lights of the business houses and so on had been put out', but the moon was almost full on 12 March, quite unlike conditions on the moonless, overcast morning of New Year's Day.

In the Temple, a light burned far into that night. Muir had been provided with a mass of material, all that the police knew about Stinie Morrison and his criminal associates such as Hugo Pool. If, during his waking hours in Brixton Prison, Stinie thought that he would soon be off the hook, he was much mistaken. There were some very unpleasant surprises in store.

20

Asking Stinie to speak 'very slowly and clearly', an optimistic request, Muir prepared his first forensic ambush. Unknown to Stinie, the police had rounded up Hugo Pool and Ethel Clayton and brought them to the Old Bailey, carefully concealing their presence from the representatives of the defence.

MUIR: Who keeps the house at 2 Hardinge Street that you said was a prostitutes' house?

STINIE: I cannot tell you ...

MUIR: Do you know a man named Hugo Pool who lives in that house?

STINIE: No. Never heard of it.

Stinie was not telling the truth, though, to be fair, he was in the habit of calling Pool by his underworld name, 'Shonkey', a sobriquet which never emerged at the trial. The pair were summoned into court by Muir; Pool's villainous appearance registering forcibly with the jury, who could have been in no doubt about Ethel's usual occupation. Muir may have been trying simply to blacken Stinie's character still further by producing these disreputable objects associated with the defendant, or there may have been a more devious motive behind their production to the court.

Morrison's known association with Pool by itself proved nothing. It may be that Muir hoped by staging this confrontation to provoke Stinie into some sensational admission. If so, he was to be disappointed.

MUIR: Look at these people.

STINIE: I know these people, but they are not the people who kept the house.

MUIR: How long have you known Pool?
STINIE: For several weeks before Christmas.

This was a lie but Muir was in no position to disprove it for there could be no question of calling Pool or Ethel Clayton as Crown witnesses even if Muir had got the judge's leave to re-open his case. Neither of them had at this time made any statement which took Stinie's association with Leon beyond 29 December and, besides, Pool was a man with a bad record for dishonesty. Ethel, too, seems to have been looked upon by the Crown as an unreliable witness. Utilizing their written statements, Muir contented himself by putting to Stinie that he had been accompanied by Leon when visiting the brothel on the night of the 29th. Beron was undoubtedly Stinie's companion but, as before, Stinie tried, unsuccessfully, to distance himself from the dead man. The replies were unconvincing:

MUIR: Do you say you have never been out in the streets at night with Leon Beron?
STINIE: No. Never at all. Never walked with him in the street. Never after the restaurant, on any occasion.

Muir pressed Stinie about the acquisition of the flute (provoking a silly lie, a denial that Eva Flitterman had seen the flute when she visited him on Boxing Night) and the mysterious revolver, but it was not until Muir dredged up that hoary chestnut, the mention of 'murder' at Leman Street, that Stinie's self-control began to crack. It was, of course, a thoroughly bad point for the prosecution to make and Stinie had good reason to feel bitterly frustrated. Muir's probing eventually proved too much.

STINIE: If Detective-Inspector Wensley did not charge me or say that I am wanted for murder in that restaurant, and if the detective whom I know now is Detective-Inspector [sic] Brogden, didn't, while walking along, say to me that I am wanted for murder, and if Detective-Inspector Wensley did not say in the police station that I will be charged with murder, may my innocence never be proved. Do you believe me now?

The words tumbled out in a spate of emotion, tears welling up, and a moment was allowed for recovery, but there was to be no relief from the pressure of Muir's cross-examination. Carefully dropping his voice, a favourite technique, Muir began his most telling inquiry, the exposure of Stinie's past. He worked back from the date of arrest.

MUIR: Were you, in fact, at that time a convict on licence?
STINIE: I was, but allow me to tell you that that has nothing to do with this case. That is just the reason why they are down on me. That is the only reason why they are building up this story. But for that they would not have dared to arrest me.

A brave speech, but there was no countering the catalogue of Stinie's actions which Muir was poised to reveal. Furthermore, given the public hositility to foreign immigrants, it went badly for Stinie that he would give no credible account of his origins. In the witness-box, he maintained that he had been born in Sydney, Australia, and taken to Russia at the age of two, but Muir had in his hand Stinie's petition to the Home Office, written from Dartmoor in 1909, unsuccessfully appealing for an early release so that he might return to the land of his birth—Russia. Indubitably his own words, Stinie had given what may have been his real name, Alex Petropavloff, providing some detail of his birth and upbringing in the Ukraine. For the jury, it did not matter where Stinie had first seen the light of day: he had given two contradictory accounts of the matter and, yet again, had been shown up as a thoroughly mendacious, untrustworthy character. He could not, or would not, even tell the court anything about his own mother.

MUIR: You decline to give the address ... to which you wrote to your mother?
STINIE: Certainly. I have no intention that my mother should be bothered by you or the police either, nor have I any intention to let her know that I am in such grievous trouble.

The jury watched impassively as Stinie broke down weeping for a second time, but scarcely had composure been restored than Muir, in that deceptively soft voice, was inquiring the date of Stinie's first conviction for felony. His criminal career was minutely dissected before the court, providing excellent copy for the pressmen who appreciated Muir's dramatic sum-moning into court of the policemen who had arrested him before the 'two five-year stretches' of 1901 and 1906. Only a modicum of mental arithmetic was needed to discover that, of twelve years' residence in England, Stinie had spent almost eleven in prison. Muir cleverly utilized the burglaries to strengthen his case that Stinie was the murderer of Leon Beron. Darling's intervention during the defence cross-examination of Dr Freyberger had established that a burglar's jemmy could have caused the fatal injury to Leon's skull, though this remained simply a possibility, for Freyberger's stated opinion had referred, more generally, to 'a blunt metallic instrument, which need not be heavy'. In other words, a simple iron bar was just as likely the murder weapon as a flanged jemmy, but burglars are in the unfortunate habit of carrying jemmies around with them on their criminal ex-peditions. It was very much in the prosecution's interest to present the deadly weapon, which had not been recovered, as a jemmy, and Muir built up neatly to this point.

MUIR: On 14th January 1906 ... the charge against you ... was ... having housebreaking implements in your possession?

STINIE: Yes.

MUIR: Were a brace and bit the things you had in your pos-session when you were arrested ...?

STINIE: Yes.

MUIR: And a jemmy?

STINIE: I do not remember having a jemmy. I never had one in my life. I had a chisel with a blade about four inches long.

No one was going to believe that answer and Stinie soon gave away the truth, reducing the distinction between chisel and jemmy to a mere question of semantics.

STINIE: I say, so far as I can remember, I never had a jemmy in my life, but if it was, it could not have been more than that length (indicating) ...

FOREMAN: He indicates nine or ten inches with the handle; he puts the blade at about four inches and the handle at about six inches.

117

The jury could not have realized from this analysis of Stinie's criminal career that, in law, the fact that he had been convicted of burglary might show a 'general disposition to commit crime' but could not prove Stinie to be the murderer of Leon Beron, though they did go to show that the accused was a dishonest man, unlikely to be telling the truth. Muir's detailed treatment of Stinie's record inevitably encouraged an erroneous reasoning among the jury: Stinie, a professional burglar and, generally, a Bad Thing, had on this occasion gone just too far and killed for gain, an attractively simple proposition, which drew attention away from major defects in the Crown's case.

To round off his cross-examination, Muir asked Stinie about the spots of blood found on the shirt and collar he was wearing on the day of his arrest. Predictably, Stinie's response was a long, rambling and none-too-convincing explanation, but heavy censure lies against Muir for exploring the point at all. His very last question exemplifies Churchill's privately and cryptically expressed view of Muir's conduct: 'Hard riding by the Crown in disclosing character and generally in the prosecution'.[1]

MUIR: Did you say a word to the Inspector Ward about your nose bleeding?
STINIE: No, of course not, because I did not think of it at the time, but that is a fact just the same.

The implication of this was that Stinie's nosebleeding episodes had been brought on deliberately to explain away the presence of blood from the dead man on his clothing. As has been shown, bloodstaining was always a weak point in the Crown's armoury and, well before the trial started, warders' reports were in existence, one of which, dated 15 February 1911, details an attack of bleeding which came on just before Stinie was due to leave Brixton for a remand appearance at Lavender Hill Police Court. 'The bleeding appears to come on quite natural,' wrote the jailer who gave evidence to that effect, called by Abinger as part of the defence case. Dr Dyer, Medical Officer at Brixton, confirmed this privately to the Home Office. 'The prisoner has been closely watched and examined,' he reported, 'but I have been unable to discover any reasons for making the inference that the nosebleeding was self-induced.' In this situation, particularly since this was a capital case, Muir should have exercised restraint, but in this regard, as in so many others, he fully lived up to his reputation of being 'a completely remorseless Crown prosecutor', the words of his usually sympathetic biographer.[2]

Not until after the trial was over was the press free to comment on Muir's handling of the case.[3] *The Times* congratulated him, but several papers referred unfavourably to the severity of his cross-examination of Morrison, with the *Evening News* and *Yorkshire Post* openly critical of Muir's approach. The *Penny Illustrated Paper* trenchantly condemned the 'unusual and extreme bitterness of Mr Muir'.

Abinger tried to resuscitate Stinie's case in re-examination but the task was hopeless. Muir was then allowed to call strong, cogent testimony from the manager of the Shoreditch Empire to rebut the bogus alibi put forward on Stinie's behalf, and at his behest, by the Brodsky girls. Abinger could do little with this, though the manager, Mr Munro, was on quite friendly terms with Sergeant Brogden and both men apparently were fond of a jar or two.

Seven days of evidence from sixty-five witnesses had come to an end. In the normal course of events a speech for the defence would be followed by a speech by Muir on behalf of the Crown, after which the judge would sum up and the jury retire to consider its verdict. In the normal course of events the judicial process runs fairly smoothly: not so in this strange case, where the even tenor of the judicial way had already been subject to considerable interruption. More dislocation lay ahead in the two remaining days of the trial.

21

Edward Abinger, tapping his snuff-box, took a large pinch of its contents, wiped his nose with a silk handkerchief, and embarked upon his closing address to the jury. It was to last six hours and cannot be regarded, even by the most charitably minded, as a triumph of forensic advocacy. Indeed, much of the time was taken up by futile arguments with the judge. Some good points were scored: Muir had carefully avoided the awkward issue of the S-shaped mutilations and had ignored motive, but the studied arrangement of the corpse, face upwards, one leg crossed over the other, the rifled overcoat re-buttoned and a large black silk handkerchief about the head forming a kind of shroud (a handkerchief which had not belonged to Leon and which could not be traced to Stinie) suggested that the dead man might have been killed as a punishment for informing on some individual criminal or gang. Abinger's mistake was to latch on to the Houndsditch crime when there was no evidence of any connection between the Gardstein conspirators and Leon Beron. Had the police revealed what they knew about Leon's character, Abinger might have been on stronger ground for, once proved to be a receiver, Leon the police informant was a more credible character. As things were, Abinger could only attempt to make bricks without straw.

He set about Muir in a manner which was altogether too personal, even allowing for Muir's unfair and aggressive presentation of the Crown's case. 'You cannot convict a man in a murder case by rhetoric,' he boomed, 'it must be facts, gentlemen, not eloquence.' Yet, within seconds, the jury was to be subjected to the purplest of passages, ruining the argument vital to the defence that Beron's murderer must have become heavily blood-stained as a result of the brutal assault. 'Why, there must have been blood all over his clothes!' he shouted across the court, 'Blood! Blood! Blood!' an emotional outburst which left the jury, business and professional men as they were, wholly unmoved. When Abinger dragged in Eva Flitterman's erratic performance, Darling intervened.

DARLING: Mr Abinger, what do you want? Do you want the prosecution to call her or not?
ABINGER: No, my lord, I do not want them to call her. It would be a terrible spectacle.

But no more terrible than the ham performance which Abinger was putting on for his client, destroying the last scintillae of credibility which the defence case might otherwise have possessed.

While Abinger had been tediously analysing the events on Clapham Common, a slight figure, unnoticed at first, crept from the back of the court, past the dock and then made straight towards the astonished Abinger, shouting, 'When are you going to stop?' This was not a protest at the boredom engendered by Abinger's speech. The frail form was that of Solomon Beron, for whom the strain and excitement of the trial had finally proved too much. He swung a punch at the hated advocate, which probably would not have done much harm if it had connected, which it did not, since Abinger had sufficient common sense to duck down in his seat. For a moment all was uproar in court while Solomon was dragged away; the efforts of three policemen being needed to overcome him. People in the aisles and galleries stood up to see the performance, though the judge, who had been making a note while Solomon had been stalking his intended victim, remained still, as did Stinie, who observed the episode calmly, with a faint smile. Far off, in the great hall of the Old Bailey, Solomon's reedy voice could still be heard, shrieking, 'He's going to get him off! He's going to get him off!'*

---

* Two days later, after the end of Stinie's trial, Solomon tried to get into Darling's room at the Law Courts. He seized a large bundle of papers from a startled solicitor's clerk, shouting, 'They're mine! They're mine!' as he made for the judge's door, but his attempt 'to make an application' was frustrated and, after a medical examination at Bow Street Police Station, he was committed to Colney Hatch asylum, where his sister-in-law, Adele, had died so terribly nine years before.

Once calm had been restored, Abinger continued his speech; it would have taken more than Solomon's interruption to stem the relentless flow of verbiage. Towards the end, Darling gave way to exasperation and made an observation which showed, all too clearly, his opinion of the defence case. Abinger had been complaining that cross-examination based on Morrison's 1909 petition to the Home Secretary had been a breach of confidence.

DARLING: I ... absolutely disagree ... If you wanted a topic of lament, I think you might lament that the Home Secretary did not allow him to go to Russia when he asked.

This was going much too far for any judge but the judicial patience had been sorely provoked and not for the last time, for Abinger's final words to the jury would amount to an implied accusation that Solomon had committed fratricide. 'Take, for instance, Solomon Beron,' he mused, 'who would benefit from the death of Leon Beron?' This was a silly approach to the facts of the case, even sillier than the Houndsditch informer theory, which was weak enough. Abinger had never cross-examined Solomon on the footing that he was the killer and Darling was moved to intervene, at length. The effect of a well-deserved rebuke from a judge at the end of a defence speech is often disastrous to the fortunes of the accused. Vainly, Abinger tried to explain that the facts did not point to Morrison alone, but the advocate was unmasked; there had been too many tricks of the Newgate trade. The jurymen were undeceived. At the end of the marathon address, the foreman stood up and, as if dismissing all that Abinger had said, blandly asked the judge if there was any hope of finishing the case that night. In its collective mind, the jury had decided upon conviction.

Abinger's speech, damp squib though it may have appeared to the jury, had infuriated Muir, whose orderly mind could not cope with so untidy, emotional a presentation, with all that sloppy criticism of the Crown's case. Ward and Wensley, for example, had been praised in one breath, snidely attacked in the next, but the real provocation to Muir lay in an attack upon his integrity. There is a convention at the Bar that counsel should avoid making personal remarks about each other. In

Stinie's case, both Muir and Abinger had already been guilty of breaching that basic, and sensible, rule. 'It has been suggested by Mr Abinger,' said Muir, his face crimson with rage, 'that it is consistent with the duty of counsel for the Crown to suppress facts, to pick witnesses and to argue on untenable bases.' Almost shouting now, Muir reminded the jury of a typical Abinger paradox, which had deeply wounded Muir's very considerable amour propre. 'At the same time, he has been showering compliments upon me as the soul of honour. Heaven save me from the compliments of my learned friend if that is his sense of honour or duty!'

Yet there was more than a grain of truth in Abinger's maladroit comments on the conduct of the Crown case. A more skilled advocate, counsel of greater standing than the unfortunate Abinger, might have been able to demonstrate the hollowness of Muir's claim that no fact had been suppressed which told in favour of innocence and no witness kept back who would be favourable to the accused. 'Everything which could be in favour of the prisoner has been admitted,' declared Muir, in a sweeping statement which, effectively, he made as a witness of facts untested in evidence, 'and everything doubtful, <u>and in some cases not doubtful,</u>* has been excluded in favour of the prisoner.'

Ignoring his own tactics in the Rappolt case, Muir condemned the defence argument that he had brought in Morrison's criminal past to persuade the jury to convict in a weak case. 'A more terrible accusation could not be brought against a responsible man conducting a case for the Crown,' Muir said solemnly. 'It was with the greatest reluctance that I put those questions as to previous convictions,' (an explanation which does not bear the stamp of truth) and Muir was anxious to explain why all this material was relevant. To be sure, he reminded the jury that such cross-examination goes to the credibility of a witness but Muir could not resist a second, dubious, submission. Morrison was a 'practised burglar' and, as such, it was of direct relevance that the implement which had caused Beron's death was 'in all probability a jemmy',

---

* Author's underlining.

employed to cause death for the purpose of plunder. The phrase 'in all probability a jemmy' was, of course, an unwarranted extension of Dr Freyberger's evidence but there was no intervention from the bench, no protest from defence counsel. The supposed jemmy, plus Morrison's record of burglary chronicled so thoroughly by Muir, pointed inescapably to a killing by Stinie for gain. Or so the responsible man conducting a case for the Crown would have the world believe.

Just before the court day ended, Muir had even tried to suggest, obliquely, that Stinie was one of Gardstein's gang, a thought which must have already crossed the minds of the jurymen and which Abinger's own tactics had done something to reinforce. Nevertheless, this sort of forensic speculation came ill from any 'responsible' counsel for the Crown.

MUIR: Supposing this was a murder for revenge directed by the Houndsditch murderers. Who were the Houndsditch murderers?—Russian burglars.

Darling managed, with difficulty, to suppress Abinger's wrath and tackled Muir for an explanation.

DARLING: (To Abinger) You are suggesting that there was no evidence . . . I was waiting for an opportunity to call on Mr Muir to tell me what there was.

Muir's response was pure bluster.

MUIR: My lord, any facts so notorious that the jury may be presumed to have knowledge of them may be evidence . . .
DARLING: Mr Muir . . . You must not say that they were Russians or that they were burglars.
MUIR: No, their names, gentlemen, were Fritz Svaars, and some other similar-sounding names.

This rude reply, directed at the jury over the judge's head, directly contradicted the spirit of his ruling but went unrebuked, enabling Muir to end his powerful speech on a confident note.

22

That evening, Abinger returned to his chambers in the Temple deeply depressed. 'A web of circumstantial evidence, which I found it impossible to destroy,' he recalled, was 'slowly but surely sending my client to the scaffold.'[1] Still nursing that obsessive, unshakable belief in Morrison's innocence, Abinger described himself as 'overwrought ... on the verge of collapse'.

All this gloom was temporarily lifted by the last delivery of post for the day, which brought a letter marked 'confidential' from PC George Greaves, already the author of numerous letters to Wensley about the Houndsditch affair, which Wensley had firmly dismissed as being utterly useless. Greaves had manned the switchboard at Leman Street the day Harry Jeffery's excited voice had told of seeing Stinie returning to his old lodgings on the day of his arrest. Abinger had never heard of George Greaves and was amazed to read his account of the goings-on in the charge-room at Leman Street shortly after Stinie had been brought in. According to Greaves, Stinie had asked what he had been brought in for, to which Brogden had replied, 'I told you before. You're brought here on ... suspicion of murder.' If true, this was a complete contradiction of the evidence given by Wensley, Brogden and no less than four other officers, and squared fully with Stinie's account of proceedings.

Greaves went on to ask, optimistically as it turned out, that his letter should remain confidential, 'for if the Commissioner of Police should discover I have sent this letter to you it would probably cause my instant dismissal from the police service ... I wrote solely with the object of giving fair play to Morrison.'[2]

125

A calmer, more reflective advocate than Abinger would have realized that this information, though of considerable importance, was not an answer to the prosecution case. But Abinger had convinced himself that he had 'Morrison's liberty in my pocket', as he rashly told his wife that night. In normal circumstances Abinger should have contacted Lumley, the solicitor, but the excitement of the news prompted Abinger to take a highly unusual course, and he approached the Attorney-General, who was, by a stroke of luck, his old school friend Rufus Isaacs. Perhaps it was too late to get in touch with Lumley that night, or possibly Abinger may have been concerned that the judge might have refused a postponement of the next day's sitting to allow inquiries to be completed. Abinger made straight for the House of Commons, where he persuaded Isaacs to see him. According to Abinger, the Attorney gave Abinger permission to deal with the matter himself and obligingly dispensed with the usual rule that only solicitors should take statements from contentious witnesses. Abinger left the House armed with a note of introduction to the Metropolitan Police Commissioner, Sir Edward Henry, and with Isaacs' final words of advice, 'trust no one', a caution which sprang from the Attorney's wily mind and which plainly embraced the police themselves.

Not surprisingly, the Commissioner had already left Scotland Yard for home, but the indefatigable Abinger took a cab to South Kensington where the astonished Sir Edward found this highly excitable barrister on his doorstep. Abinger told of receiving the letter, though, with rare prudence, Abinger refused to identify Greaves, revealing merely that his man was attached to Leman Street station. Henry was not at all offended, even when Abinger, in a wild outburst, threatened to go directly to Winston Churchill if the Commissioner obstructed him in any way. Henry's affable response was to offer his involuntary guest a drink and a sandwich. After telephoning around, Henry told Abinger to go over to Leman Street where Sir Melville MacNaghten would meet him.

When Abinger arrived at the police station, shortly before midnight, he found MacNaghten, immaculately clad in evening dress, waiting for him in his private motor car. Sir

Melville reflected tartly that he had been dragged from a West-End dinner-party to attend this peculiar rendezvous: 'The Commissioner's been telephoning for me all over London,' he said grumpily, unimpressed by Abinger's emotional declaration that this was a life and death matter. Keeping the air of mystery, Abinger refused to reveal the name of his quarry, blind to MacNaghten's logical statement that it would be difficult to find the man if Abinger would not provide his name. In the end, with some assurances that there would be no victimization, Abinger spoke to the Night Duty Officer, who provided details of Greaves' beat, and this unusual policeman was run to earth not far from St Mary's Church in Whitechapel High Street. Back at the station, Abinger questioned Greaves, while MacNaghten acted as scribe, writing out a statement which Greaves was eventually to sign.

Abinger returned to the Temple in ecstatic mood. It was well after two o'clock when he got back to his flat but he seemed to feel no need for the usual sleeping pills. Brimful of news, he was already awake and speaking to Rufus Isaacs on the telephone at seven o'clock the next morning.

23

Stinie of course knew nothing of these developments. His only concern in waking moments was that today, Wednesday 15 March 1911, was sure to be the last day of his trial, the day of judgement. Backed by a chill east wind, a heavy fall of snow greeted the prison van as it passed through the turreted gateway of Brixton Prison, a fine example of that sham medievalism much loved by Victorian penal architects. By the time Stinie and his entourage had reached the Old Bailey, the snow had given way to heavy rain, which fell in squally showers for the rest of the day. There was always a long wait before he went upstairs into the dock and today there was an hour's frustrating delay before he could stand in his usual position, the centre of interest in the packed court.

Outside, people had been queuing in the hostile weather, hoping to share the excitement of so sensational a capital trial. Eva Flitterman slipped into court, later to be snapped by an enterprising cameraman as she smilingly leapt on a tram to avoid a crowd of the curious. A fair sprinkling of fashionably dressed women was noticed in the public gallery and those who had been unable to get seats inside gathered around the main entrance to the building. They would have a long, cold wait for the verdict.

On Isaacs' advice, Abinger had seen the judge in private, with Muir, before the hearing resumed. He faced a cool reception as Darling bluntly asked, 'What right had you to take yourself the evidence of a witness?' But reference to the Attorney-General mollified the judge's concern and Abinger was simply asked to ensure that Muir had an opportunity of reading Greaves' statement. Darling need not have troubled himself about Muir: the probability is that MacNaghten had been on the telephone to the Director, perhaps to Muir himself, as soon as Abinger had left Leman Street with Greaves' statement in his pocket, and had given a thumbnail sketch of the night's events to the prosecution team and ordered an immediate investigation into the man's background. Muir was by mid-morning well briefed about Greaves' unorthodox police career. It is a measure of Abinger's naivety that he was genuinely surprised by Muir's devastating cross-examination of the star witness who would shine all too briefly.

The delayed start had the effect of heightening tension so that more people jumped than usual when the four staccato raps preceded Darling's entry into court. Abinger formally asked leave to call further evidence and, after Darling had firmly squashed the prospect of yet another defence speech, PC Greaves went into the witness-box to depose that murder had indeed been mentioned in Stinie's presence at Leman Street on the day of his arrest.

Greaves was an untypical policeman. A Roman Catholic, he was, at thirty-six, unmarried and in many ways a 'loner'. An insensitive refusal to admit him to a section-house had obliged

7 *Top* Baroness Hilda von Goetz in March 1914, during her successful legal action against a former protégé, con-man Hugh Dalrymple (inset).
8 *Above* On the left, Jane Brodsky, Stinie's 'sixteen-year-old sweetheart lass', seen with her elder sister Esther during the trial.

STINIE MORRISON'S ORDEAL IN THE WITNESS-BOX

9 *Above* A panoramic view of South-West London Police Court, 29 January
1911. Stinie stands in the dock, his tall presence looming over the
courtroom. The magistrate, de Grey, takes a note of Abinger's cross-
examination of Jack Taw (far left). Muir is sitting to Abinger's right at the far
end of counsel's row.

10 *Left* Number One court at the Old Bailey during Muir's relentless cross-
examination of Stinie. Abinger sits at the end of the front row of barristers;
Wensley and Ward face him on the far side of a table laden with exhibits.

PRICE ONE PENNY.

THE PRISON LIFE OF
STINIE MORRISON

REPRIEVED BUT TORTURED

11 A romanticised view of Stinie as depicted on the cover
of James Timewell's 1914 pamphlet.

STINIE MORRISON GOES FROM PRISON TO GRAVE.

12 Stinie Morrison's funeral on 28 January 1921.

him to take lodgings in Whitechapel with a garrulous Jewish family with whom he can have had little in common. After eight years in the army, seeing action in the Boer War when he was decorated, he had been discharged with an excellent character. In fact, it was some time after joining the police force in 1903 that things began to go wrong: in 1909 he was disciplined for 'making unfounded statements of generally tyrannical conduct on the part of a Sergeant', though, with the harsh code prevailing at that time in the police force, he may have been guilty only of speaking his mind. Also, there was no question of a Catholic joining the protective folds of the Masonic brotherhood, so widespread among police personnel, then as now. Unfortunately, he made a further mistake in writing about his problems to John Syme, an unbalanced ex-Inspector of police,* who had been using the populist columns of the *Penny Illustrated Paper* (P.I.P.) to air his views about the shortcomings of the force. This slight, but demonstrable connection between Greaves and a patent agitator was enough for Muir, who had earlier softened up his target after Greaves had given an evasive-sounding answer.

Not for the first time, the jurymen were unimpressed with a defence witness. Muir quickly capitalized on this mood by pressing Greaves on a most important point: why had he not approached a senior police officer earlier on this matter, rather than writing, so late in the day, directly to the defendant's barrister? The answer was, of course, that after his experiences in 1909, Greaves was wary of doing anything of the sort. He had, he said, mentioned the matter a couple of days before to another constable, who was immediately sent for by Darling and broadly confirmed what Greaves had said, though not before there had been a further acrimonious exchange between Abinger and the judge about how this second officer should be escorted to the court.

DARLING: It is not to be expected that I shall go and fetch these witnesses [sic] myself. If it were, I suppose even I

---

* On 4 July 1911 Syme was convicted at the Old Bailey of threatening to kill a police inspector and was sentenced to six months' imprisonment.

would have to take the Defendant along with me to see that I did not do what was wrong.

It was all rather feeble. If Greaves had genuinely been ruminating over this injustice to Morrison, he had taken a very long time before doing anything about it. But it was what had been written to Syme which provided Muir with his deadliest ammunition.

MUIR: Are you in the habit of seeing ex-Inspector Syme from time to time?
GREAVES: Not since about eight months ago.
MUIR: Have you corresponded with him?
GREAVES: I have sent him about two letters . . .
MUIR: Is ex-Inspector Syme a man who was dismissed from the police?
GREAVES: He was.
MUIR: Is he the same man who was prosecuted at Bow Street for threatening the late King?
GREAVES: He was.

The connection with Syme thus demonstrated and magnified, Muir introduced the disciplinary proceedings of 1909. Reference to all those useless letters to Wensley served to complete the rout. Greaves was destroyed and Abinger's short, confused speech showed that all was lost. Darling intervened, blandly dismissing the whole point, despite the major attention given to the issue by the prosecution until well into the trial.

DARLING: It did not appear to me to be at all unnatural that a man arrested without explanation should assume, with nothing said, that he had been arrested for one or other of those murders.

Muir, taking this cue, promptly jettisoned the whole episode, and was able to hammer home the prosecution case all the more effectively as a result. He spoke for three hours, twice interrupted by Stinie, on whom signs of strain were already showing all too clearly.

The judge's summing-up lasted little more than an hour, a short time for a trial that had lasted nine days. While he personally felt no doubt that Stinie was guilty, Darling considered that the evidence before the jury was 'in the nature of things not sufficiently cast-iron to act as the basis of proof in a criminal charge'. He recalled this dilemma many years later in a letter written to the Home Office.

> I gave him a very good chance in my summing-up, for I felt that, with my eyesight, I couldn't have identified the person who took a cab in the early morning as certainly as the cab-drivers did. I therefore had the jury taken to the place . . . in the same circumstances as the cabdrivers deposed to and the jury were perfectly satisfied.

This is a revealing passage, not least because the lighting was quite different at the time of the jury's inspections and because no reconstruction can ever prove what has passed through a witness's mind.

Darling, however, did not rely solely upon the reconstructions, and he gave some guidance on the identification evidence, reminding the jury of the newspaper photographs of Morrison which had been published before many of the identifications had taken place. To a modern eye, the direction does not seem nearly robust enough and does not spell out with sufficient clarity the dangers inherent in all identification evidence.

Another criticism arises from his dismissal of the facial mutilations ('I can only say that anyone who sees the figure 'S' in either of those scratches has either better eyes or a more vivid imagination than I can possibly claim to possess'), in which the judge chose to ignore the evidence of Freyberger and Needham about the matter; Abinger, however, had called no expert evidence—which at the time apparently was available—to back up the 'spic' or 'schlosser' theories.

Overall, Darling's summing-up leant towards the defence. Even the exploded alibi was gently treated, the judge giving a little evidence of his own in terms that may be read as faintly patronizing to the world beyond England.

DARLING: Ask yourselves, do you or do you not know that it is very common among people of certain classes and of certain

131

nationalities if they have a good case not to rest upon that case? If you have ever talked to anybody who has administered justice in India...

Muir, conscious perhaps that he had gone too far with Morrison's past, reminded the judge that he had promised to direct the jury on the proper approach to previous convictions. 'Bear in mind,' said Darling, 'that the only use to be made of these convictions is to show that when you rely upon his word as contradicting something stated by somebody else ... you have not the word of a person who has done nothing wrong, who has never told any lie and who has never broken the laws of England.' Darling added a little sting to the tail of his otherwise defence-minded directions:

DARLING: It has a bearing ... on the capacity or not of the prisoner getting in and out of a house without making as much noice as a person would make who had never done it before.

This was a clear reference to that awkward sash-window in Stinie's ground-floor room in Newark Street, the room in which, he and his witnesses said, he had been sleeping at the time of Leon's murder six or so miles away.

Darling must be criticized for sending his jury out to consider their verdict in a murder case so late as eight o'clock in the evening. Juries are not supposed to be put under any pressure to arrive at their conclusions and there had already been over seven hours' worth of evidence, speeches and summing-up to absorb that day. In reality, of course, concern on this score would have been academic. The jurymen were well aware before the trial started that Stinie had two five-year stretches to his name. There can be little doubt that they had made their minds up long before to convict, influenced by a prevailing public opinion that was desperately in fear of all that the alien immigrant might do, or be about to do, to the fabric of life in England. In these circumstances, it is surprising that they remained in their retiring-room for as long as the thirty-five minutes it took them to return with their verdict.

CLERK: Do you find Stinie Morrison guilty or not guilty of the murder of Leon Beron?

FOREMAN: We find the prisoner guilty.

CLERK: You say that he is guilty and that is the verdict of you all?

FOREMAN: That is the verdict of us all.

Stinie, who had been proudly standing with folded arms to hear the verdict, turned deadly pale at the foreman's words, and his eyes filled with tears. Abinger, sitting in counsel's row, buried his head in his hands, utterly crushed, while Muir was dispassionately tying up his papers with the traditional white ribbon. There was a moment's stillness, in which only the reporters' scribbled shorthand could be heard, 'the very rustle of the wings of Death' noted the *Daily Graphic*.[1] Then the clerk put a formal question:

CLERK: Stinie Morrison, you stand convicted of wilful murder. Have you anything to say for yourself why the Court should not give you judgement of death according to law?

Stinie made as if to step forward, catching his breath in a way which sounded like a sob. Four warders moved with him in unison as he leant over the front of the dock to make a confused declaration, which ended as a desperate plaint.

STINIE: I have a great deal to say. For one matter, the evidence against me as to the funds which has been seen on me on the 1st January being the proceeds of the murder. I can prove that in November I had a sum of £300 and out of this £300 I have still got £220. If I can prove that, will that in any way alter the jury's verdict?

The rights and wrongs of the Holloway fraud were of no moment, for alongside Darling stood a tall, gaunt, grey-haired figure in white cassock and bands—the judge's chaplain, who even now was placing the notorious 'Black Cap'—a square of black cloth—upon the judge's wig, a terrible but faintly ludicrous ritual. In a brief address to Stinie, Darling seemed to imply that he did not associate himself with the jury's verdict,

133

'... the only conclusion, as it appears to them, consistent with the whole of the evidence against you'. Moments later, sentence was pronounced.

DARLING: It is that you be taken hence to the prison from whence you came; that you be taken thence to a lawful place of execution; that you there be hanged by the neck until your body is dead. And may the Lord have mercy on your soul.

Defiant to the last, forgetful of his reference to the Almighty at the start of the trial and of his oath in the witness-box, Stinie unrepentently challenged destiny.

STINIE: I decline such mercy. I do not believe there is a God in Heaven either.

He turned and walked slowly from the dock, pausing for a moment to survey the court in which he stood condemned. Some thought he was looking out for a friend, maybe Pool, but, if Stinie's private life is any guide, he was searching for the face of a Jane, an Esther or a Florrie. Whatever was in his mind, he gave no indication of it as he passed from public view down the steep flight of steps leading to the Old Bailey cells.

The crowd outside, marshalled across the road from the entrance to the building, quickly melted away, thinned by the chilly weather, and there were few who remained to see the prison van leave, bound for another destination. Stinie was not being taken back to the prison whence he came, but to Wandsworth, the home of convicted prisoners, site of the condemned cell.

24

The press, now that matters were no longer sub judice, felt free to comment boldly on the trial, as well as upon the wider issue of immigration control which had been raised by the exposure, as many saw it, of this dangerous Russian murderer.

'At last,' proclaimed *The Times*, in its leading article,

> this country will be rid of a cold-blooded assassin and a most undesirable alien. This long trial will confirm very strongly the impression prevalent of late—that the East End ... counts among its population a large number of very dangerous, very reckless and very noxious people, chiefly immigrants from the Eastern and South-eastern countries of Europe.

The writer noted their 'extreme untrustworthiness, since lying, especially in the witness-box, appears to be their natural language.' Repeating Muir's unwarranted extension of the medical evidence, it was noted that Stinie, a burglar, was 'therefore accustomed to the use of the "jemmy", which is just the weapon with which the murder was probably committed.' The article ended by applauding Muir. 'Mr Muir conducted the case with his customary ability and with that due regard for everything that could tell in the prisoner's favour which is one of the best traditions of the English bar.'[1] An especially charitable endorsement in view of Muir's ungracious reference to 'those bloodhounds of the press' in his closing speech for the Crown.

On the page opposite the leader lay another blast against the newcomers, under the banner headline, 'ALIEN LONDON TODAY. A NEW GHETTO.' 'The Judaism of the people,' observed an anonymous author, 'adds to the problem ... The mutual helpfulness of the sons of Israel tends to make the East-End immigrants an exclusive cast. They gradually oust the Englishman, be he shopkeeper, fellow-workman or business competitor.' Many were law-abiding but 'there has entered an appreciable element of criminals,' which included, 'the Russian burglar, the Polish thief, the Italian stabber and the German swindler,' an impressive array of national stereotypes.

In the popular press, the *Evening News*, too, was stridently hostile,[2] condemning, 'the few shrieking sentimentalists who believe in making these islands the rubbish heap of Europe' and lamenting that 'Israel remains a people, practising its own

135

virtues, sinning its own sins... In how many generations shall we make Englishmen out of these stubborn folk?' The *Pall Mall Gazette* struck a more practical note, with a hint of a doubt about the correctness of the verdict:

> Whether he murdered Leon Beron or not, the prisoner in the dock was a man whom it was very undesirable to let loose again upon society if the law could possibly hold him back ... an alien morally as well as racially among honest men, a danger and a pest.[3]

None of the mass-circulation papers, however, approached the hostility expressed in the *East London Observer*'s editorial, whose tone was distinctly anti-Semitic. Under the heading 'THE STEPNEY ALSATIA', the editor took the *Jewish Chronicle* firmly to task.

> The organ of the aristocracy of Anglo-Jews is dejected by the revelations in the Beron murder trial concerning the Jews born in alien lands and herding in the East End of London. There is no real Judenhetze in Stepney,

continues the leader, as if regretting its absence,

> but there is a most earnest and insistent demand that the great municipal Borough of Stepney shall not be regarded as the modern Alsatia, the haven of unrepentant vampires of society.[4]

Only a small number of periodicals could be found sympathetic to Stinie's predicament or to pose awkward questions about the case generally, and of these, the best-known (or most notorious) were the *Penny Illustrated Paper* and *John Bull*, neither of which could have been described as the home of responsible investigative journalism in 1911. But other voices were being raised, in weightier tones, concerned, if not about Morrison's fate, at any rate to probe the stark conflict of evidence between the Leman Street officers on the one hand and PC Greaves on the other.

The establishment, already anxious about the whole alien question, was deeply troubled by the Greaves episode, despite Muir's excellent demolition job. Public confidence in the police was shaken and the authorities were most concerned to re-establish faith in the word of the man on the beat. Promotions were issued to Ward and Wensley immediately after the Morrison case and, even before 16 March, when the *Daily News* became the first newspaper to call for an inquiry, the Home Office had, it seems, decided to hold a private investigation, though it was soon clear that matters were too important to be debated behind closed doors. On 20 March, an MP asked the Home Secretary, disingenuously, 'if he knew that the evidence given by a police witness in the Clapham Murder trial was in direct contradiction to five other police witnesses and if there was to be an inquiry'.

CHURCHILL: The argument founded upon the incident in which the evidence was contradictory was expressly withdrawn from the jury by the prosecution and the judge directed the jury to disregard it. I feel however that the occurrence requires to be investigated.

By a strange coincidence, that very day, the Home Office saw fit to release the text of the Metropolitan Police Commissioner's judgement of 1909 upon Syme's disciplinary charge. This document, issued as a White Paper, must have had the effect of discrediting Greaves ahead of the inquiry, as a proven associate of the unstable ex-Inspector.

Although the Lord Chief Justice, Lord Alverstone, had privately expressed his strong opposition to an inquiry in a letter to the Home Secretary, Churchill eventually decided, after some prodding by George Lansbury and others, to have a public hearing and the inquiry opened on 30 March 1911. George Cave KC (later to become a Tory Lord Chancellor) presided and it proved a curious affair, almost a re-run of the trial, with Muir appearing on behalf of Wensley and the other Leman Street personnel and Abinger representing Greaves (Roland Oliver mysteriously switched sides to become Muir's junior). The evidence, which was not taken on oath, was largely predictable and there were moments of light relief, as when Sir Melville MacNaghten was questioned about the detention of an unnamed man, possibly Hugo Pool, in the early days of the investigation.

ABINGER: Was that man detained?

MACNAGHTEN: Yes, but not on a charge of murder. He was asked what he knew.

ABINGER: Was he taken to the police station?

MACNAGHTEN: No. He was asked to go. He was morally persuaded.

Whether there was laughter at this urbane euphemism is not recorded but considerable merriment did occur when, at a crucial moment in Wensley's evidence, the ample frame of Richard Muir proved too much for his chair which suddenly collapsed under his weight. Learned counsel, however, managed to retain both his balance and his dignity.

In the end, the Cave Report,[5] was very much an 'all shall have prizes' affair. The police evidence, it concluded, was given in a straightforward manner but Cave was at pains to add that he was not satisfied that Greaves 'deliberately swore what he knew to be false . . . he may have assumed that the charge of murder had been mentioned to the prisoner . . . Greaves is regarded by his comrades in the Force as "eccentric" and I am disposed to think that this epithet is not undeserved.'* As for Stinie, his version of events was totally rejected, but it was quite possible that he might have gathered that he was wanted for murder from reading newspapers or 'from the observations of the crowd which followed him to the police station'.†

Cave had decided not to see Stinie, who remained undisturbed in the condemned cell at Wandsworth. When Abinger visited his client there, he was surprised to find that the 'cell', far from being the expected dungeon, was 'a large, airy and pleasant room, with terra-cotta wallpaper, a large gasolier, a bright fire burning, and in the corner a bed with a pretty

---

* Greaves is noted as 'formerly PC 86' by September 1911 and is stated to have emigrated to the USA: Home Office papers.

† Detective-Sergeant Brogden, upon whose evidence much reliance was placed both at the trial and during the Cave inquiry, is said to have been dismissed from the police at some time in the First World War, possibly for drunkenness (an inkling of his drinking habits may be gleaned from the evidence of Munro, the manager of the Shoreditch Empire, quoted at page 119) and, by the early 1920s, had been reduced to the status of doorman at Bella Burge's boxing ring in Blackfriars Road: see Arthur Harding to Raphael Samuel 'East End Underworld'.

coverlet, and a large table strewn with newspapers'. Stinie, for once on the best of terms with his gaolers, was sitting nonchalantly in a comfortable armchair, with his feet up on the mantelpiece, and smoked a cigarette as he perused the day's press. He looked 'the very picture of a healthy and well-groomed man' and Abinger was particularly impressed by Stinie's neat pair of camel-hair slippers.[6]

This apparent calm in the face of approaching death may have been a tactical device, but the brief correspondence he was allowed to make with Florrie Dellow and Jane Brodsky indicates a certain resignation to what then seemed inevitable. A few of these letters found their way to the Sunday press and it is tempting to think that Stinie encouraged their publication as an aid to release, although his appeal against conviction had not then been heard and when the time came to prepare a petition for reprieve, Stinie would have none of it and refused to sign. He may have wanted these former lovers to profit a little from their association with a condemned man.

When the letters first made their appearance in the *People*, *Reynolds* and *Lloyds Weekly News*,[7] the Home Office, in the personality of Ernley Blackwell, Assistant Under-Secretary, took a distinctly suspicious view of the writer's motives. Blackwell, then aged forty-two, was a Scot of middle-class background, of the dourest aspect, whose thin features were perfectly complemented by the delicate gold frames of his spectacles, behind which lay the cold gleam of his eyes. Promoted to Legal Assistant Under-Secretary in 1913, the most notorious episode in his twenty-year tenure of that post would be his involvement in the decision to execute Roger Casement for treason in 1916. One writer[8] has shown that Blackwell was primarily responsible for circulating copies of the 'Black Diaries' (which showed that their author, Casement, was a passive homosexual, with a penchant for recording his sexual experiences in the greatest detail), a stratagem which successfully countered the international campaign for Casement's reprieve. Inglis noted that a memorandum, prepared for the Cabinet by Blackwell and his senior colleague, Edward Troup (another Scot, the author of *Place-Names of West Aberdeenshire*), 'might have been written by Counsel for the Prosecution', a comment which could equally apply to the many entries in Blackwell's hand to be found throughout the Home Office papers on Stinie Morrison.

Before the question of the published letters came to vex his mind, Blackwell was already preparing a lengthy memorandum on the case for the Home Secretary, in which Blackwell concluded that the evidence of the three cabmen 'can be relied upon and for that reason I have no doubt in my own mind that the prisoner is guilty'. An example of Blackwell's approach to this evidence can be seen in his commentary on Castling's account of the man, whom he later identified as Stinie, being five feet eight inches tall and fair-haired. Blackwell omits any reference to height, postulating,

> the fact that he describes prisoner as 'fair' goes a long way to disprove any suggestion that the statements made to police were prompted. The man has thick dull black hair with a fresh complexion. Castling may well have recognized his features although in the lamplight he got the impression that he was 'fair'.

Troup added a gloss, declaring that the case 'was an extraordinarily strong one,' yet his note goes on to reveal some highly signifiant private doubts, resolved only by the linchpin of the cabmen's evidence:

> As we have read it from day to day it has appeared to be weakened by the failure of one point after another on which stress had been laid by the prosecution. The evidence from the blood on the prisoner's tie and the inference drawn from his statement on arrest have quite disappeared from the case and not much now can be made of the parcel he left with the waiter—of his supposed disappearance from Whitechapel— or even of his alleged want of money ... The critical point in the whole case is the identification by the three cabmen. I have read all their evidence and the statements they made to the police—and they strike me as very good identifications by trustworthy witnesses.

The plain truth was that neither Blackwell nor Troup was prepared to make a disinterested investigation into the contradictory, suspect or often inherently improbable aspects of that crucial evidence.

Blackwell considered it important not to let official judgement be swayed by any strongly aroused opinion in favour of Stinie. As usual in any capital case, letters soon began to flood into the Home Office (some via King George at Buckingham Palace) from people who thought that the conviction was wrong: the letters to Florrie and Jane might well provoke an elaborate and, to Blackwell's ordered mind, tiresome campaign on Morrison's behalf.

Stinie's letters, written in a clear hand with a few spelling mistakes, show that his English was remarkably good, though one to Florrie, kept back by the authorities, must have been composed with an eye to the press, with its references to being 'very hard to die for a Crime one has had nothing to do with' and to 'my Darling mother hopping [sic] and longing to hear from her boy'. As for Jane, 'no Angel in Heaven (if there is such a thing as a Heaven and Angels) could be purer, better or more beautiful than my 16 year old Sweetheart Lass,' an extravagant compliment which endorses a journalist's view that during his trial Stinie used every artifice to gain sympathy, but overdid it. In a letter to Jane he had written gloomily of his prospects. 'My first trial lasted for 9 days and no justice has been given me; do you think they are going to give it me now? Dear girl, all that Appeal business is only a matter of form, nothing else.' But it was another letter which particularly angered Blackwell.

My Own Loving Little Janie,
... I know that you believe my Innocens, but I am writing a statement about the £300 I told You about, which I will ask permition to sent to you, so that You may be able to see for Yourself how ridiculous it is to supose that I have commited the Murder.

But the real reason why I write it, is, I want you to sell it to a newspaper agent. Such a statement will be worth to them hundreds of pounds ... whatever You do get, You are to pay a half of it to my Solicitors who have done such a lot for me ...

141

> All my Love and Heaps of kisses to You, from your unfor-
> tunate Boy—Stinie

Not unnaturally, Blackwell was firm in his view that this
traffic should be stopped, reminding the Home Secretary that

> the permission to write and receive letters is given to pris-
> oners for the purpose of enabling them to keep up a connec-
> tion with their respectable friends and not that they may be
> kept informed of public events... Any which are of an
> objectionable tendency, either to or from prisoners, or con-
> taining slang or improper expressions, will be suppressed.*

Churchill agreed that no more letters of this kind would be
allowed out. Stinie's response was to repeat his request to
'write a statement on his life for the newspapers,' a plea that
was brusquely refused.

25

Stinie's appeal against conviction opened at the Royal Courts
of Justice, in the Strand, on Monday 27 March, before the
Lord Chief Justice, sitting with two other High Court judges.
Abinger had vainly tried to persuade Lord Alverstone to
postpone hearing the appeal because, he wrote, 'the terrible
struggle at the Old Bailey had completely unnerved me,'[1] but
he was told, politely but firmly, that the date for execution had
already been fixed and that even the Lord Chief Justice could
not possibly interfere with the Sheriff's arrangements.

As during the trial, crowds gathered outside the building,
and the court, as well as the corridors leading to it, was packed
with curious people hoping to see something of the action.
When the three judges entered the tall, narrow courtroom and

---

* This is in fact the standard wording on the front of the letter form used by prisoners.

bowed to counsel, Stinie was escorted into a small dock at the left-hand side. Dressed smartly in a green suit, he remained standing, in his distinctive pose, throughout the proceedings.

The judges must have known what to expect from Edward Abinger, who rose to address them from a counsel's bench which, as the *Star* reported, resembled nothing less than a chemist's store in miniature,[2] for in front of the wordy advocate were laid out a glass of water, a green bottle of smelling salts, a screw-top bottle of throat and voice lozenges, and a box of snuff.

Abinger's principal themes, in an address that roamed over three days of court time, were that Muir had wrongly introduced the allegation of Morrison volunteering the word 'murder' immediately after his arrest; this was an issue which had somehow prevented the defence from cross-examining the police thoroughly for fear of revealing that Morrison was a convict on licence; a complaint that Darling had made it appear that the murder weapon was most probably a jemmy; that the questioning of Mrs Deitch ought not to put Morrison's character in issue; and that Muir's snide references to the bad character of Frank and Rotto should not have been made. In addition to his argument, Abinger called three witnesses: two women, who gave quite valueless testimony about seeing Stinie in Whitechapel in the week after the murder, and ten-year-old Becky Snelwar. Becky's pretty, dimpled face and attractive manner were disarming and she was photographed outside the court, after giving her evidence, in a smartly cut short overcoat, her long fair hair crowned by a little pillbox hat.[3] Inside court, it had quickly transpired that she could add very little to Stinie's case, except to confirm, in part, his evidence that the brown-paper parcel handed to Mintz was in fact a flute. But the judges were, in all probability, minded to agree with Troup's view that little could be made by the Crown from this evidence anyway, and Becky had never been shown the parcel's contents. The overwhelming problem was that Becky had been approached by the defence only eight days before the appeal hearing (her teacher, she recalls, was furious at the thought of her young charge giving evidence: 'They've no right to ask you,' she had said fiercely, 'you're far too young'),[4] though she had been seen by Ward and Wensley, but not very closely questioned, on the third day of Stinie's trial.

Not long before the end of Abinger's case, Alverstone raised a pertinent matter.

LORD CHIEF JUSTICE: You said you would let us have your theory why Beron went to Clapham Common.

ABINGER: . . . As to the inducement which Beron had to go to Clapham Common, I can only discuss hypotheses. One was that he went to see his father. It was said that he was fond of women, so a woman might have got him there. Assume he is a receiver, I do not say he was—no evidence. On the contrary, Wensley said 'I have known him for some time and he had some property.'

After this journey into the realms of speculation, Abinger asked for more air in court, as he felt faint. Despite the applause from the public gallery, it was all over. Muir would give no answer from the prosecution side to Abinger's theories for, as the court had already decided to dismiss the appeal, he was not called upon in reply and the last opportunity for the authorities to shed light on the mystery of Leon's character was lost.

Not that Muir was to be let off totally by the court. The first words of the Lord Chief Justice were an implied, but nevertheless powerful rebuke to Crown counsel in the controversy over the use of the word 'murder'.

LORD CHIEF JUSTICE: It is most important that those conducting prosecutions should not raise issues of comparative unimportance and thereby enormously lengthen the proceedings and, at times, increase the difficulties of coming to the right conclusion.

Likewise the trivial evidence of specks of blood on Stinie's clothing was rejected by the Appeal Court in no uncertain terms.

LORD CHIEF JUSTICE: Having regard to the prisoner's habits and the facts as to his linen, I think that ought not to have been brought against the prisoner.

But the court, nonetheless, upheld the exposure of Stinie's character by the prosecution on the simple ground that Abinger, in cross-examining Nellie Deitch, had plainly put his client's character in issue. That the jury must, in all probability, have known a good deal about Stinie's background before the trial started, as a consequence of the Rappolt proceedings, was never raised in the Appeal Court, which decided that there was 'no ground for thinking that the verdict was unreasonable or that the trial was not painstaking'. The court was, to be sure, appalled by the publication of Stinie's photograph in so many newspapers, but declined to impeach the identification evidence, a fundamental issue never properly dealt with by Abinger in his lengthy submissions to the court. There was, said Alverstone, no miscarriage of justice.

LORD CHIEF JUSTICE: I can only say it is impossible for us, without usurping the functions which are given to us, to say that there has been any misdirection or mistrial. If there had been, we should not hesitate to say so. Bearing in mind that we are not entitled to put ourselves in the position of the jury, we can only come to the conclusion that the appeal must be dismissed.

Stinie, confident to the end that his conviction would be quashed, took a step back at the judge's words and, his face noticeably flushed, left the silent courtroom. Some saw a personal expression of dissent in those words of judgement but Lord Alverstone, at least, had no doubts about the matter. Sir Hall Caine, the novelist, met Alverstone in a publisher's office barely an hour after the appeal had been dismissed. Sir Hall had been one of the mighty crowd of spectators that afternoon and remembered Stinie's air of self-possession, as if the man was standing there for justice to his cause. 'I can't get the sight of that man's face out of my mind,' confessed Caine, but the judge was less easily impressed.

'No wonder,' he said, 'he's a splendid fellow, isn't he? But he is a bad one, I'm afraid, a real bad one.'[5]

26

Stinie's execution was fixed for 9.00 a.m. on 20 April 1911. Abinger tried a last legal move on behalf of his imperilled client by seeking leave to appeal to the House of Lords. At that time, such an appeal could only be brought if the Attorney-General were prepared to certify that a point of law of exceptional public importance was involved in the case and Abinger, accordingly, went to see his old school friend. Rufus Isaacs was affability itself, not a whit concerned when Abinger reminded him, uncomfortably, that all three parties to the argument (Morrison, Isaacs and himself) were Jews.

'I'm anxious,' pleaded the ever-neurotic barrister, 'that your judgement should not be warped by any racial sympathy.' Proffering Abinger his cigarette-case, Isaacs assured his agitated listener that he need have no fear on that score and, after an hour's fruitless argument by Abinger, refused leave.[1] A few days later, Horatio Bottomley MP, proprietor of *John Bull* and an accomplished fraudsman, invited the Attorney-General to bend the law in Stinie's favour.[2]

BOTTOMLEY: Does not the Honourable and Learned Gentle-man think that, having regard to the somewhat remarkable character of the evidence, he might strain the technical point ... in favour of giving the man the right of appeal?

But Isaacs would not be budged and the last hope of overturning the verdict in the courts was gone. The only course open to Stinie's supporters lay in persuading the Home Secretary to advise the King that the royal prerogative of mercy should be used to commute the death sentence into one of penal servitude for life. Spearheaded by Lumley and Abinger, a campaign for

Morrison's reprieve quickly got under way, with Lumley's Fleet Street office open twelve hours every day to accommodate the signatories. In the space of a fortnight, the names of over 75,000 people ('three-quarters of a mile of signatures', according to one press estimate[3]) appeared below a lengthy petition, which Abinger had drafted on the basis of his arguments in the Court of Appeal. Those who signed, noted the *Morning Post*, included 'barristers, solicitors, doctors, Army officers, clergymen and a stipendiary magistrate. Forms bearing signatures were received from all parts of the Kingdom, as well as from Italy, Belgium, Alsace Lorraine and the Channel Islands.'[4]

One important signature was missing. Stinie flatly refused to endorse the petition, even when Abinger, on his visit to the condemned cell, had begged him to do so in an emotional interview which ended with Abinger in tears. All that Stinie would talk about was the Holloway fraud, which he claimed to have brought off by himself—less than the truth, but he may have been reluctant to peach on his friends. As for the petition, Stinie politely thanked Abinger and his friends for their efforts, but he would not sign. 'I'm innocent. I am not going to cry mercy to any man. If they are going to hang me, they must: after all, a man must die sometime. I'm not afraid.'

When a day or so later Jane Brodsky visited Stinie, it may have been to thank him for his watch and 'some cheap jewelry' (Blackwell's words) which Stinie had asked should be given her as a memento. Jane proudly told him that she had persuaded eight hundred people to sign, but Stinie was unmoved: he did not want anything to do with the petition, but then added some words which a sharp-eared warder swiftly relayed to the Home Office. 'If I liked,' said Stinie, 'I could say who did the murder and it would bring three more into it, one a woman.' But, by doing so, he would have to confess to another, unspecified crime, 'which would send me back to Dartmoor for seven years and I'd sooner die,' an inkling of that deep secret never revealed at the time. The murderers of Leon Beron had, according to Stinie, done others . . .

Jane, a shrewd girl, passed this startling information to Claude Lumley, who immediately took steps to interview his

147

client. A warder was at hand to record the outcome:

> Very near the whole of the conversation was as to who the persons were whom he says committed the murder, namely three men and one woman. Mr Lumley wished him to give him the names of these persons or something for him to work on, but the prisoner would not and when Mr Lumley said he would come and see him privately tomorrow if he would write out a statement for him, he declined.

Perhaps Stinie had some underworld knowledge about the death of Beron; there would have been gossip not only while he was at liberty but also during the long remand period in Brixton. In any case, a condemned man was likely to come out with all sorts of desperate statements as the prospect of the gallows grew nearer, despite, in Stinie's case, those brave words spoken to Abinger.

Letters continued to pour in from all over the country asking for a reprieve. If one section of the British public had been baying for Stinie's blood, another had found its sense of fair play outraged by the Crown's conduct at his trial. 'Reprieve Stinie Morrison,' wrote an anonymous correspondent from Braintree. 'Hang Lloyd George and Churchill'; but a more reasoned approach could be seen in the letter of a London barrister, E.A. Harvey:

> Many members of the Bar hold a strong opinion that in this case there has been a miscarriage of justice... His past record, his being one of the aliens against whom not a little feeling exists, rendered it hard for a jury to impartially weigh the evidence of identification.

In the correspondence columns of the press, too, interest continued to be shown in the controversial case. G.K. Chesterton championed Stinie's cause in a colourful letter to the *Daily News*:

> Everyone knows that the case for the prosecution was from the first in a state of collapse. Its chief supporter [presumably Solomon Beron] behaved like one possessed of devils... The prosecuting counsel went on, with fatuous radiance, pointing out that there were still some parts of his

148

case that had not been knocked to pieces.[5]

Concern was voiced from all quarters. The *Evening Standard* reported that there was 'much sympathy ... for the prisoner from the miners of Wales, some of whom, being unable to write, had made their marks.'[6]

Behind the closed doors of the Home Office, a sense of unease had developed. Sir Edward Troup had, of course, no personal doubt about Morrison's guilt, but, as he minuted to Churchill early in April,

> it is impossible to exclude from consideration the fact that the circumstances attending the trial have left on the minds of many intelligent people the feeling that Morrison's guilt is not proved beyond all doubt. This results inevitably from the failure of several points that were relied on and strongly pressed by the prosecution and from the unexplained facts connected with the case.

Both Darling and Alverstone, the Lord Chief Justice, had been approached for their views: Darling also made the point that the evidence had failed to explain many features of the crime and that there was a 'strong possibility' that another man was involved, but, even privately, Darling knew nothing about the identity of any suspect.

Alverstone's observation that the mystery was 'still unfathomed' had a marked effect on the Home Secretary, who quoted the expression in his minute of the reprieve. Churchill's interview with the Lord Chief Justice also revealed the concern felt by the Court of Appeal about Abinger's handling of the defence. Alverstone believed that if Stinie had been well defended he would have been acquitted and, although that might afford no logical reason for a reprieve, it left an uneasy feeling in the mind. In fact, Churchill had already decided to advise commutation before he spoke to Alverstone, but it is obvious that the Lord Chief Justice agreed with the course, which, as Churchill's minute shows, was taken for two reasons: firstly, the mysterious background to the case and, secondly, because it was thought that 'another was accessory before or after the fact'. On the information available to the

Home Office, it was impossible to say with any degree of certainty what Stinie's role had been, although no one in authority seems to have had any doubt about his involvement, somehow or other, in the crime.

Sentence of death was duly commuted to one of penal servitude for life which, at that time, involved at least twenty years' imprisonment. The decision was made public on the morning of 13 April 1911, the same day that Cave's report on the Greaves episode, vindicating the police evidence, appeared in the press: an event which can hardly have happened as a coincidence. The London *Star*, whose earlier hopes that Stinie would 'meet the fate he so richly deserves'[7] were thus disappointed, was dismayed at what was seen as an illogical compromise and several papers took up the theme that 'if he was guilty, he should have been hanged; if he was not guilty he should be released' anticipated in Troup's minute to the Home Secretary. More soberly, the *Daily Mail* thought that, on the whole, Churchill had acted wisely. 'The public mind is not convinced,' read the editorial, 'that the crime has been brought home to him clearly. There were many gaps in the evidence.'[8]

The struggle for Stinie's life became, overnight, a campaign for his release, spearheaded by Lumley and Abinger, which would go on, intermittently and without success, for almost ten years, but within two days of the announcement of the reprieve, Stinie won a rare accolade, which may have provided some grim consolation to the prisoner. At Madame Tussaud's, his wax effigy was set up in the Chamber of Horrors.

27

On 12 April, the day before Stinie heard that he was not after all going to be hanged, a young French airman, pupil of the immortal Bleriot, took off from Hendon in a primitive monoplane and proceeded to fly non-stop to Paris, taking just under four hours to make the trip, at an average speed of 60 m.p.h. He was the first man ever to perform this feat. M. Prier landed at a village outside Paris at 5.33 p.m. That same morning, a well-dressed, attractive Englishwoman, probably then in her forties, boarded a Paris tram in the Avenue Kleber, near her home. Mrs Maude Rider, the wife of a publisher,[1] had lived in Paris for some time, understood French very well and, indeed, had armed herself with a French newspaper to read on her journey. Sitting behind her in the tram was, as she later discovered, a tall, dark man, with an attractive trim moustache and 'long, well-shaped hands, very well tended', with two prominent moles on one of the fingers of his right hand. He was soberly dressed in a grey overcoat and brown felt hat and carried a portfolio, in which Mrs Rider glimpsed an architect's plan, coloured in. He walked with a slight but perceptible limp.

Her attention was first drawn to this fellow-passenger when he called out, 'Hello Georges!' to an altogether less prepossessing character, a short, plump Frenchman ('a Jew' she thought) with dark hair and a lighter, rather straggly beard, which concealed the lower part of a distinctly pasty face, 'hardly any eyebrows at all,' his little fat hands clothed in brown gloves. He wore a green tweed suit and a bowler-hat with a low crown.

At first the two men spoke unexceptionally in French, but Mrs Rider, who had been following the Morrison case, was suddenly startled to hear Georges say the equivalent of 'What are you doing in the affair Stinie Morrison?' pronouncing Stinie as 'Steen'.

The first, taller man, told Georges to be quiet, looked round and said, 'Speak English,' which Georges attempted to do, badly and with a marked French accent. The first man spoke English well, with a Cockney twang, but it was obvious to the listener that he was neither English nor French.

Mrs Rider groped for the library book she had with her and, heedless of future readers, scribbled a few shorthand notes of the ensuing conversation. She had to strain her ears to hear it, for there was a good deal of background noise and the two men would, occasionally, speak too quietly to be heard.

GEORGES: All right, are you going to do anything?

FIRST MAN: No. Why? Gort's life is more valuable to us than his.

GEORGES: Yes, but we cannot let him hang. Cannot you write a letter?

FIRST MAN: That is no good. We did that before.

GEORGES: When?

FIRST MAN: In 1907.

GEORGES: That was not so serious. They did not hang him. They will this man.

FIRST MAN: Well, I am not going to interfere. I am not going to get the police on me. We cannot spare Gort.

Mrs Rider wondered if the name was Cort, but considered Gort more likely. The drift of the conversation suggested that neither man knew Morrison, though the first man had seen Stinie's photograph in a newspaper. She heard other fragments of speech.

FIRST MAN: Have you heard from ... (inaudible)

GEORGES: Yes. His eyes are still bad. He is fixed up at Marseilles still. Seely (or Seebay) had a baby, you know, there.

FIRST MAN: What, already?

It does not seem to have occurred to Mrs Rider that 'Seebay' might have represented a pair of initials in French 'C.B.' or, perhaps, 'J.B.' and that the word 'baby' might have been a slang term, not to be taken literally. As for Marseilles, apart from the great seaport there is a Rue Marseille in Paris not far from La Villette, then a quarter notorious for harbouring criminals of all kinds, including, at about that time, the anarchist bank-robber Jacques Bonnot. At all events, such non-French names as Keritoff and Conrad studded the conversation, as well as another Georges, and a Peter.*

Georges got up to leave at the Rue de Rome and the two men shook hands before the little man waddled away. His companion stayed on for the short distance to the Rue Tronchet, where he got down, followed at a discreet distance by Mrs

---

* Fletcher Moulton claimed in *The Trial of Steinie Morrison* that the French police had recognized some of the names as those of an international gang of criminals, but the source of his information is not given.

Rider, now revelling in the role of female Sherlock Holmes. Indeed, she hazarded that the first man had come from Auteuil, to the south-west of Paris near the Bois de Boulogne. That was the direction the tram had come from and she had heard him say, in French, 'I go by Seine boat,' possibly a reference to his return journey. Near the Opéra, that extravagant memorial to the follies of the Second Empire, he boarded another tram, leaving at the Boulevard de Magenta. He made his way into the Rue de Deux Gares, close to the Gare de l'Est, and was seen to enter No. 11, the Hôtel des Amiens. The Rue de Deux Gares stands less than a kilometre from the Rue Marseille.

At this point, Mrs Rider called off the chase and returned to her husband's office, no doubt bursting to tell all. At Mr Rider's suggestion, they went to see the editor of the *Daily Mail*'s Paris edition, an old friend. He referred them in turn to his manager, who decided to telegraph Mrs Rider's statement, or the gist of it, to the paper's London office by 'private wire', to avoid any leak of the story. According to Mrs Rider, she persuaded the manager not to publish anything in his paper before the French police had taken steps to have the first man watched. She was over-optimistic on two fronts: there was no guarantee that the man had stayed at the hotel for any appreciable length of time and, furthermore, there was precious little co-operation between the French and British authorities.

For three days she waited in vain for news of official steps in the matter. On the 15th, she asked Lane,* the manager, to telephone the *Daily Mail* office in London. He confirmed that her account had been relayed to Scotland Yard but revealed that the police had decided to do nothing about it. In the interim, a reporter from the *Daily Mail* had spoken to Superintendent Froest. On being told that no 'Cort' or 'Gort' was known to police, the reporter, rather feebly if Froest is to be believed, said that he would not use the story. Froest's view was robust: 'The information contained in the telegram emanated from a

* Ralph Norman Lane (1874–1967) is better remembered as Sir Norman Angell. He wrote the anti-war book *The Great Illusion*, first published in 1908, which sold more than a million copies.

person suffering from delusions or from some sensational journalist for the purpose of his [sic] business.'

There the matter would have rested, but for Mrs Rider's determination. She wrote to Abinger, enclosing her statement. He was, predictably, elated by the news but pointed out the problems caused by the delay, already nearly a week by the time Abinger had received her letter. The police, without doubt, sat on the information—the complacent attitude adopted by Froest appears to have been endemic—and Abinger must be given credit for ensuring that some attempt was made to investigate the story, though the lapse of time was to prove fatal. The trail had long gone cold by the time the Home Office was moved to ask Scotland Yard for a report at the end of April.

On May Day, the official view at the Home Office was that 'any communication to the Paris police on ... this story told by Mrs Rider would give it quite undue importance and could not lead to anything of consequence, except perhaps to prejudice some innocent party'. There was 'not the remotest chance that the Paris police could do anything,' wrote Troup two days later, but this sublimely aloof posture received a rude shock when, at last, Churchill saw the papers. The reaction of the Home Secretary, who relished a mystery, was tersely to the point: 'This should certainly be followed up as far as possible.'

The permanent officials, who had hoped to 'lay by' the episode and forget about it, were reluctantly compelled to act. The Yard sent the statement—perhaps not even translated into French—to Paris and asked if a French officer might interview the lady, but Mrs Rider was unimpressed when on the 11th, a month after the strange conversation, a detective called. He said, apologetically, that he had only just been instructed and knew nothing whatever about the Morrison case.

The proprietors of the Hôtel des Amiens, a Monsieur and Madame Noël, knew nothing of a man answering the description given by Mrs Rider, staying at their hotel or visiting it. The Paris police, however, seem to have given no details about the background of the Noëls and, anyway, the pair must have been approached at about the time of the detective's visit to

Mrs Rider. If the man was merely a casual visitor, they could hardly be expected to recall him after four weeks had passed.

'Lay by?' Troup wistfully queried at the end of May, but the Rider affair could not yet be relegated to the limbo of the Morrison file. Mrs Rider decided to approach the Home Secretary personally and wrote to him in June, expressing concern at what she saw as the 'perfunctory character' of inquiries into the truth of the story. She offered to attend the Home Office for examination, adding that 'the conversation made such an impression on me that I cannot rest, notwithstanding the fact that a certain amount of publicity would have necessarily to attend the re-opening of the case and that would be very disagreeable to me...' Churchill was impressed; he wrote to Troup:

> The letter is a very good one and shows the writer to be credible and competent. I am not at all satisfied that any inquiries worthy of the name have been made and no doubt the delay which occurred at the beginning reduced the chance of their being successful. Inform me now exactly what was done before replying with proper consideration to the representations of this lady. WSC 18.6.11.

This was tough talk from the Boss, and Troup should have been stung to action, but time was his ally. It was, of course, far too late for anything significant to emerge, and Blackwell's minute, prepared on Troup's instructions, had the desired effect of dampening Churchill's enthusiasm. The Paris police, wrote Blackwell, would have 'resented' the dispatch of a French-speaking Yard officer to make inquiries in Paris; anyway, Mrs Rider would have complained, he surmised, that such an English officer would have been 'unacquainted with the Parisian criminals or Anarchists amongst whom she would expect her two fellow travellers [sic] to be found'. The possibility of a joint Anglo–French investigation did not cross Blackwell's mind.

> Personally I do not attach the smallest importance to her story. I am inclined to think that Mrs Rider's story is a concoction. If it has any foundation at all, I think she heard two

men ... possibly of some Russian society in Paris who habitually interest themselves in capital cases and write deprecating executions ... and that she supplied certain details prompted by a vivid imagination.

The Home Secretary was persuaded and there things rested for over a year, during which Mrs Rider seems to have enlisted the support of Mrs T.P. O'Connor, wife of the famous 'Tay Pay', Irish Nationalist MP and journalist. In October 1912, Mrs Rider wrote asking to see the Home Secretary but Churchill had moved to the Admiralty and his successor, Reginald McKenna, evidently knew little about the case. 'The man is a blackguard,' conceded Mrs Rider, 'but what hurts me is that he is suffering for a crime he did not commit. If you had heard that conversation, you would have no doubts...' But official-dom was unmoved and the response was chilly, merely a formal acknowledgment of her letter.

Fletcher Moulton reprinted Mrs Rider's sworn statement under the initials 'MAR' in his 1922 account of the Morrison trial, considering that her testimony 'cannot be brushed aside as the result of imagination'. Blackwell must be censured for making no attempt to test Mrs Rider's credibility in an inter-view, a technique already adopted when Abinger came forward with Stinie's story about the Holloway coup. Abinger was questioned at some length by both Blackwell and Troup, even though the information was second-hand. Blackwell admitted, 'we know nothing of Mrs Rider's credibility,' but took no real steps to investigate it. 'The *Daily Mail* may know a great deal,' he wrote vaguely, 'as she is a journalist resident in Paris who may'—vague again—'have supplied copy to their office...' He then made a very unfair attack. 'The fact that they did not make use of her story is very significant. Her letters show her to be competent and are at any rate plausible; but were Farn-combe's (Mr Bottomley's agent) when from his lodgings at Croydon he was describing his pursuit of Piggott from the 'Abode of Love' all over England and across to Paris.'

The relevance of this peculiar anecdote to Mrs Rider must remain obscure, but the unproven suggestion that the paper had decided not to print her story because of doubts about its authenticity does not carry much weight; many more sensational, more flimsily based stories have appeared over the years and Blackwell had brushed aside Mrs Rider's own words, when she had specifically asked the paper not to print, at least until investigations had been made, as well as the distaste for publicity expressed in her letter to Winston Churchill. Whether she was a 'journalist' in the accepted sense is not known, but she was certainly, as 'Maude Annesley', a fairly prolific writer of romantic fiction, whose published work appeared between 1907 and 1923, under such breathless titles as *Nights and Days*, *Blind Understanding* and *The Sphinx in the Labyrinth*. Of her prose style, one reviewer noted that she 'has a distinct facility for seizing the vivid moment, both in incident and in character,' a comment which unkind people might apply to her account of the conversation in the Paris tram. Curiously, the Home Office team seem to have been unaware, in 1911 at least, that four Maude Annesley novels had already appeared (two published by John Lane and two by Methuen, both well-known houses), though Troup and Blackwell might be forgiven for not having such *oeuvres* in their bookshelves.

In her one, supposedly factual book (*My Parisian Year—A Woman's Point of View*), published in 1912, she makes no mention of that extraordinary conversation. Nevertheless, official handling of this episode must leave a sense of unease, as with so many other 'unfathomed' aspects. Perhaps the last word should come from Blackwell. In a minute prepared for McKenna in October 1912, Blackwell wrote, revealingly,

> I hope sincerely that if S of S *sees* anyone on this v. difficult case he will go into it first with me & let me be present at the interview. Otherwise we are likely to be landed with another ... Oscar Slater case!

28

The early spring of 1911 had been cold and stormy, with frequent falls of snow but, by the perversity of the English climate, April saw the start of a glorious summer, which would form so brilliant a backdrop to the Coronation.

A fortnight or so after the reprieve, Stinie, moody and deeply depressed, was bundled into a prison van and driven to Waterloo Station for dispatch, yet again, to Dartmoor. But he was not going to let the moment pass without a public demonstration of his feelings towards authority. The early morning sunshine filtered through the grubby glass of the station roof above the open doors of the van; for several minutes no one emerged, while muffled strugglings took place inside. Eventually, Stinie was removed by force, his hands manacled, and he was frogmarched towards the waiting train. He looked surprisingly fit, wearing the drab khaki suit of the convict, and had several days' growth of beard. Once out of the van, his considerable strength was proving very difficult for his escorts to control.

'This is the way they treat a prisoner,' he yelled to a gathering crowd of incoming commuters, declaring, questionably, 'I am a gentleman. You see how they treat me. Leave me alone!' Safely lodged in the compartment, he calmed a little and, before the blinds hid him from public gaze forever, Stinie was seen to take a long, resigned look in the direction of Waterloo Road, vainly hoping for a farewell glimpse of the good-hearted Florrie or the curvaceous Jane.

Stinie's air of weary resignation proved to be short-lived and he behaved truculently on the way to Tavistock, celebrating his arrival at Dartmoor by throwing his dinner ('12 oz of bread and 5 oz of corned beef') at the nearest available jailer. A little later, an offensive remark by a warder prompted Stinie to empty the almost boiling contents of a can of cocoa over the unfortunate man's head, a gesture which resulted in a lengthy stint of bread and water. For a while, Stinie morosely refused to speak at all and began a hunger strike, but he did not remain passive for long and was to compound his earlier unruly behaviour when he flatly refused a peremptory order to strip. Stinie punched a warder in the chest and shouted, 'You can murder me before I will take them off.' A general struggle ensued, in which Stinie's clothing was forcibly removed and he was left naked in his cell until the Medical Officer, Dr Murray, arrived to examine him. After transferring the prisoner to the hospital wing, Murray posted two warders on night duty in Stinie's cell, for a fear of a suicide bid.

In June, Stinie was petitioning the Home Secretary, with accuracy, 'My reason is already weakened. And it requires very little trouble more to send me into a lunatic asylum.' This was followed by a curious declaration: 'I am able to speak in 7 different languages and I can allways [sic] overhear a great deall [sic] in the hiding places of the London Criminals . . .'

But the world outside Dartmoor had not yet forgotten Stinie or the ramifications of Beron's death. In mid-June the English authorities were startled to receive a request from the Paris police asking for a detailed description of Beron's watch. They had, it seems, told Lumley that an English £5 piece had been pledged in Paris during March. In the event, nothing emerged from this line of inquiry. A month later, Lumley wrote to the Home Office, protesting that Scotland Yard had made no attempt to find out about Leon's life and associates in France before the family's abrupt departure to England. If Lumley's information were right, it conflicted with press copy appearing soon after Beron's murder, which spoke of liaison between London and Paris, but Home Office minutes do not confirm these reports and, indeed, Blackwell's note boldly defends the investigative failure. 'Beron came to London in 1894,' he wrote, 'and had lived here ever since. There was, therefore, no need to inquire as to his life or associates in Paris 16 years ago. His habits in London were well known . . .'

Perhaps Blackwell's complacency had been reinforced by

the sight of a Scotland Yard memorandum that purported to describe a conversation between a police officer and a 'very reliable informant', who, of course, remains anonymous. The officer was Sergeant David Goodwillie. According to Goodwillie, the informant stated

> very deliberately that Max Frank ... came to the informant on New Year's morning and said I have earned myself £10 this morning by a deal I had with a baker whom I knew many years ago, although I have not seen him for 7 years until a day or two ago. He used to bring me property which he had stolen when I had my shop at Walworth Road. The informant said to Frank, 'What was it you bought?' Frank replid 'A watch and chain.' About two days later, Frank again called on the informant and said 'For the love of God don't say a word to anyone what I told you about that watch ... I got rid of it at Weisens ...'

'Weisens' was the nickname of a 'jew watchmaker and jeweller' in Walworth Road.

At first reading, this gobbet of information looks bad for Stinie, but other factors may well have been at work, leading Goodwillie to embroider a conversation with one of his regular 'snouts' in order to advance his career. In the first place, Goodwillie's report is dated 5 July, over six months after Max Frank's supposed indiscreet disclosures and subsequent panic. Unless the informant had been very recently recruited by the police (which is unlikely, for such a reputation for reliability has to be earned) it is curious that he or she did not whisper anything about the matter into Goodwillie's ear rather nearer the time and, in any case, six months is a long while to carry the details of any conversation. A second doubt arises from the character of Goodwillie himself: he seems to have felt keenly that he had not achieved rightful recognition of what, he claimed, were unique investigative scoops of his own in the Morrison case and he had not been called as a witness at any stage in the trial or in the legal preliminaries to it. In 1925, he retired from the force with the modest rank of Detective-Inspector and promptly penned a series of sensational articles for a Sunday newspaper about his life and work ('During the

Great War, disguised in horn-rimmed glasses and with a pronounced American accent, Detective Goodwillie walked the streets of Berlin and picked up many secrets that greatly helped his native land'), including one about the Clapham crime, a copy of which was passed on by a worried C Division, at Scotland Yard, to the Home Office.

'I was able to prove,' he claimed in the article, 'that the watch which was known to have belonged to Leon Beron passed through the hands of a well-known receiver in South London. Of course, I am not suggesting for a moment that there is any proof existing that Morrison himself disposed of it . . .'[1] which suggests that the only lead given to Goodwillie in 1911 was a reference to Weisens, leaving Frank's supposed admissions as an embellishment, probably deriving as much from newspaper reports (for example, of the Rappolt case) as from any official sources.

In early August 1911, a gold watch was dredged up from a large pond on Clapham Common. Excited speculation was quickly dampened by confirmation that the watch had, in fact, been stolen and dumped by a loose and light-fingered lady, who had stolen it from a man unwise enough to fall asleep after making love on the Common one night. 'It was in consequence of my investigations,' declared Goodwillie, in his usual modest vein, 'that, when . . . a gold watch was found . . . in a pond on Clapham Common . . . we were able to say definitely that it was not the one worn by Leon Beron.' For weeks afterwards, though, until the storms and floods of autumn broke the remarkable Coronation Summer, shoals of eager swimmers paddled about in the muddy waters of Mount Pond, fruitlessly searching for similar treasure.

29

Stinie submitted five petitions to the Home Secretary in the remaining months of 1911. They illustrate an increasing tendency to mental instability, a process that reached its climax the following year. In the first, fairly rational petition, Stinie asked, quite simply, to be hanged. Blackwell minuted angrily, 'He should be stopped arguing that if he is guilty he ought to be hanged.'

But the Home Secretary was more sympathetic. 'A painful letter,' wrote Churchill. 'There is no reason why he should not petition freely.'

In September, Stinie again pleaded for execution, but the tone had become disturbed, ending with a bizarre Latin quotation. 'And whoever grants this petition, Deus Omnipotens adimpleat omnem benedictionem in vobis!' This, thought the Home Office officials, was 'theatrical and rather impudent,' but the next instalment from Dartmoor caused a much greater rumpus.

Stinie complained of being 'messed about by every dragged-up-in-the-gutter, chewing beer-drinker who wears a uniform and calls himself an "Hofficer"!' and once more invited authority to hang him. In a passage which cut officialdom to the quick, he wrote, 'I demand that this, my petition, may reach the hands of the Home Secretary himself. It is not to be kept back by a subordinate,' causing Troup to renew Blackwell's argument that Stinie should be stopped from petitioning altogether.

Churchill, who remembered his own time in a Boer prison camp, again mollified the harshness of authority. 'I share so keenly his feeling that death would be preferable,' he wrote in October 1911, 'that the petition does not seem inexcusable in its violence. It is not necessary therefore to take any steps this time. If he goes on—no doubt he will have to be warned.'

Stinie did go on. The next month he was writing 'Why point out the moth in my eye,' slightly re-wording the Sermon on the Mount, 'when you can't see the lamp-post in the eyes of your honourable detectives?' He concluded in verse of doubtful quality:

> Come, sweetheart Death and kiss me,
> I'll gladly be your slave
> Only hasten to release me
> From this filthy living grave!

This was wisely ignored by the new Home Secretary, McKenna, but Stinie's next contribution was altogether too much for the authorities consisting as it did entirely of doggerel (some forty-odd lines of it). Two stanzas and a 'chorus' must suffice as examples:

> I had enough of convict life,
> My heart is getting chilly
> Enough of bread-and-water strife
> And officers to knock me silly.

> Rt. Hon. Sir, I beg you hear my humble plea
> And send—'Granted'—in reply!
> If you will not give me my liberty
> I pray you let me die.

> Chorus!

> My Freedom or my Death
> Nothing else will satisfy me!

Blackwell and Troup were outraged and Stinie was forbidden to petition for twelve months.

Stinie's worsening mental condition may have been exacerbated by the long period of solitary confinement he underwent after reaching Dartmoor. No doubt his own violent and eccentric behaviour encouraged the authorities to take this course and it seems that prison officers were officially instructed to give Stinie a wide berth although, as in any institution, there were members of staff who could not resist verbal or, at times, physical abuse of the inmate. Some inkling of Stinie's mental decline can be gathered from his own accounts, smuggled out of Dartmoor and later printed in an underground pamphlet.[1] He wrote, 'I began to lose weight, slept badly at night, could not read, began to talk to myself, saw a heavy cloud of mist before my eyes and felt a heavy pain between my eyebrows... Felt a strong desire to smash the furniture in my cell. Fought hard against it...' A week or two later, 'I smashed up the furniture ... I tore up my clothing ... I could not sleep for more than two hours out of every 24.'

He had, it seems, been allowed some association, but after an ugly incident in the tailors' workshop late in October 1912, Stinie was forcibly returned to his cell, where he was found by the Medical Officer stark naked, behaving quite irrationally. He was transferred to a malodorous padded cell, where his condition rapidly deteriorated. No amount of bromide in the prison tea could subdue him.[2] The MO noted ruefully, 'His strength is considerable. He has burst himself out of two restraint jackets (one being a perfectly new one) and tore his bedding made of quilted No. 1 canvas.'

Other reports confirm chronic insomnia, with Stinie 'wandering or crawling about his cell' and 'talking rapidly to himself all day, apparently in Yiddish...' This was not, as Blackwell had been suggesting all through that year, some elaborate sham to gain sympathy. By early December, though, it was reported that there was 'some improvement but still highly delusional, still violent and destructive, but he no longer has the constant restlessness, the garrulity, the rapid utterance that characterised the first period of his illness'. There was 'still some incoherence with slipshod articulation and salivation. At one time there were fine tremors in the tongue when protruded...'

Stinie was transferred to Parkhurst Prison on the Isle of Wight on 13 December 1912. Blackwell's brutal comment, 'It seems to me that this convict is probably insane' was, in the event, not justified and Stinie slowly recovered in a period of exhausted tranquillity. At Parkhurst, Dr Treadwell, the prison MO, noted that Stinie was 'both physically and mentally reduced on reception,' but he was eating properly at last and quickly gained seven pounds in weight. After three weeks, Treadwell could report that Stinie had 'been quiet and orderly ... and has given no trouble'. Despite the considerable reputation for ferocity that has grown up around Stinie's memory, he took a further year before settling down and remained reasonably well behaved until shortly before his death.

Somehow or another, reports of these traumas had seeped out of prison and appeared in the press, but the Home Office refused to comment, maintaining total silence on the subject, and refused permission for Abinger to visit his old client to see how he was getting on. Lack of communication, both inside and outside prison, undoubtedly caused Stinie a bitter sense of isolation. He was never officially allowed to see any of his legal advisers and, he claimed, received only four outside visits during the first three years of his sentence. Lumley made numerous applications over the years, on a variety of pretexts, but access was invariably refused, even when, in mid-1912, a remarkable legal action was mounted on Stinie's behalf, but probably without his knowledge, against Alfred Stephens. Abinger applied for a summons against Stephens, alleging that he had committed perjury in the Morrison trial. The evidence included the declarations of three men (including, it must be said, Lawrence Rappolt), recounting what they could remember of Stephens' conversation at the Horns the day after the Clapham Common murder, the sad story so different from the evidence he gave to the jury at the Old Bailey.

Whatever the merits may have been, a legal technicality defeated the enterprise, for there was no affidavit from Morrison, the only person who could have been regarded as having the necessary 'real interest' in the proceedings. The court dismissed the application, a decision upheld in the High Court, who found it unnecessary to consider the wider question of whether a convicted man could be allowed to initiate a prosecution for perjury against a witness in his own trial.

When making his application at Guildhall, Abinger declared that he was acting on behalf of, but not on the instructions of, Morrison (access was denied to Lumley, even for the purpose of obtaining Morrison's sworn affidavit). Abinger added that the action had been initiated by an unnamed 'person of title', who was paying the legal costs. It is at this point that the Baroness Hilda von Goetz enters the Morrison story.[3] The lady, who was, in the Edwardian phrase, 'darkly handsome', claimed to be an Austrian Baroness, and was certainly quite rich. She had, it seems, taken a keen interest in Stinie's trial and wrote to the Home Office, in a royal third person, during May 1911, requesting a visit, as she was 'desirous of impressing on him to be patient and resigned and that she is interesting herself in the steps which are being taken to effect his release'. She referred to 'her place at Aldingbourne, Sussex' (actually, a forty-acre farm), where six discharged prisoners were, she said, already accommodated.

Her interest in ex-convicts may have been purely altruistic and it was later stated on her behalf that likely candidates were forwarded by the Church Army. Nevertheless, Stinie was a well set up, healthy-looking man, whose sexual adventures had been well publicized and, while it may be pure chance, Hilda was in the process of ridding herself of a tiresome protégé at the time of her letter to the Home Office (who, predictably, turned down her application). 'Hugh Dalrymple'—otherwise Dillon, Crawford, Dalton etc.—was a rogue with many previous convictions, including bigamy, a fact of which the good Baroness was well aware when she took him into her service. The Baroness was unmarried and 'Dalrymple' later referred to a mutual 'sporting turn of mind' between the pair, both interested in 'horses and country life', which led to their mutual presence in the bedrooms of sundry hotels from 1903 onwards. According to 'Dalrymple', the Baroness wrote him a large number of letters over the years, many of which were addressed to 'My Dear Pal Onions'. She claimed that the correspondence was mostly forged, the incriminating bits anyway, but Onions or no Onions, the man was employed at Aldingbourne for over a year until the early summer of 1911, when Hilda evidently decided to end the association.[4]

With the help of the Baroness's considerable financial clout, a renewed campaign for Morrison's release got under way in 1912. Lumley had been allowed to forward some written questions, in a form approved by Blackwell, asking Stinie if he knew anything of 'Gort' and allied matters overheard by Mrs Rider. But Stinie was unable to give any help.

In September 1912, Lumley's request to see Stinie with a view to settling a petition was brusquely refused, Blackwell minuting that 'It is clearly impossible to allow every convict who can afford it to be attended by solr. and counsel for the purpose of working up a petition to S of S' and, after Stinie had recovered from his illness, a similar plea was turned down.

'Let me find there is someone doing something for me,' Stinie wrote, rather pathetically, 'and perhaps the injustice I am suffering may not be so heavy to bear,' but the Home Office was unmoved. It would be difficult to see, wrote an official, what would be gained by allowing an interview.

The Baroness, however, a forceful lady, was not going to allow more officialdom to prevent *her* meeting Stinie, who seems to have been the object of much of her waking attention at that time. When in March 1913 the time came for one of the rare visits allowed to Stinie, a plot was hatched between Lumley, the Baroness and Jane Brodsky. Jane, as a personal friend, was allowed to bring two others, without specifying their identity. On the 8th, in defiance of Blackwell's policy, the three visitors were shown into Stinie's hospital cell, where they found Stinie sitting at the far end, a warder standing between them at the foot of a bed. Like an inspecting committee, the three sat, side by side, on chairs arranged along a wall. Lumley at once introduced the Baroness as 'the lady who takes so much interest in your case'.

Unknown to the participants, the conversation was reported in detail to the Home Office. There was general talk about the trial and Stinie, rather idly it seems, mentioned a man called Braddock, who looked like him and, once a Devil's Island convict, now lived in an unidentifiable address off Vauxhall Bridge Road. (Mention of 'Braddock' put the authorities in a quandry: if the name was later put to Stinie, he would realise that his visits were being carefully monitored.) Little emerged, however, from this doubtful source, and Stinie was concerned mainly to repeat his three goals: release, or hanging, or re-trial. He said he wanted no new evidence bespoken, had never asked for a reprieve and declared that the Home Secretary had had no right to reprieve him, adding, ungratefully, that Lumley had had no right to get up the petition against his wishes. The Baroness, it was reported, 'was very much alert and seemed to listen most attentively . . . Mr Lumley did most of the talking; Miss Brodsky said a good deal; Miss le Gortz [sic] said very little.' The visit lasted three-quarters of an hour and ended in Lumley's over-confident assertion that Abinger would soon be along to visit Stinie and had suggested 'pamphleting the country' to draw attention to the Morrison case.

Blackwell was furious. 'It will be time enough to take note of his [Lumley's] conduct when he next applies for a visit or makes an application on the convict's behalf grounded on the information he has obtained.' A directive was soon issued laying down that applicants for prison visits would all have to be named in future, with provision for a blacklist of those considered undesirable by the Home Office.

Undeterred by Stinie's vehemently expressed view, Lumley and Abinger organized a second petition. The first, in April 1911, had called for reprieve: the second boldly claimed that Stinie ought to be released. The hospital wing of a prison was often one of the easier places from which to conduct a 'clandestine correspondence', as officialese termed it. After the now-notorious visit, a secret channel of information was opened up between Stinie and the Baroness, aided, it seems, by a sympathetic warder and the position of Stinie's cell, on the ground floor, with the added advantage of sliding ventilation panels and a cell door open during working hours.

Stinie was searched, a routine and random procedure, early in May 1913 and a letter in the Baroness's hand was found, though Stinie, absurdly, claimed to have written it himself. She wrote, with brio, about the progress of a campaign for which Stinie had scant enthusiasm.

Cher Morrison,
J'ai en [eu?] bien du plaisir à recevoir votre lettre et de savoir que vous vous portez bien. Voilà les nouvelles. They are getting a good many signatures at the Office, the notice appeared in most of the papers—probably you have received

168

the cuttings by this [time?]—hundreds of forms have been sent to various parts of the country. Mr L has received a good many letters on the subject—he has been promised 5000—I hope to get some 3000 & am trying some of the big shops and several friends have promised their assistance . . . Mr L's son is now going round in a motor getting signatures. We hope for the best & even should it fail, Mr L expects great things of it and says he will not be at the end of his resources. The result probably will not be known for some time—perhaps you will have a visit before then—if so send it for Janie not Tillie [Jane's younger sister] and be careful not ti [to?] mention viafa froidfa.

Kind regards from everyone
H. G.

Unfortunately, there is no recorded translation of 'viafa froidfa'. The Baroness added, in a postscript, 'I shall shortly be in your neighbourhood to see what can be done there,' causing the prison's Deputy Governor to suggest that she 'might be looked for and, if found, watched'. Stinie was duly punished, probably by reduced diet, but this was by no means the last of this underground post, as will be seen.

The petition had no effect upon official attitudes, and was almost the last major public effort in Stinie's cause. Some 42,000 people signed, 'from all walks of life', in the well-worn phrase. Carefully preserved amid the substantial Home Office file devoted to Stinie Morrison and in a bold, flowing hand can be seen the signature 'Roger Casement, H.M. Consulate-General, Rio de Janeiro, Brazil.'

30

The petition, a handsomely printed document running to fourteen pages, laboriously rehearsed the familiar arguments in Stinie's favour. There was, however, a significant new claim, which would prove to be the means of keeping Stinie in prison, the precise opposite of the effect which had been intended. Ethel Clayton is about to make a baleful re-appearance in this story.

Abinger's autobiography, published in 1930, is a sloppy work, notoriously inaccurate, but his account of Ethel's visit to his chambers (he called her 'Mrs S.') 'some months after Morrison had been reprieved', her sensational version of the events around and about New Year's Eve 1910 and her no less sensational interrogation at the Home Office, have found their way into the mythology of the Clapham Common crime. Abinger appears to have invented the Home Office interview, said to have been conducted by Troup and Ward in Abinger's presence, at which Ethel, questioned by Ward, blurted out that Pool had left 2 Hardinge Street with Stinie late on the night of the 31st, a revelation which, according to Abinger, at once proved fatal to the campaign for Morrison's release.

The truth about Ethel Clayton's involvement in the matter is very different, although one of her many versions of what happened between Pool, Stinie and Beron in the last days of 1910 was seized on by Blackwell and Troup as an excuse for keeping Morrison behind bars.

In mid-February 1911, Ethel had given police the first of several written statements. It was an odd account, beginning with the story of her early life in Huntingdon, setting out a wholly untrue story of meeting Pool at a dance there, and of marrying him at a local Registry Office. The marriage was a concoction: at the time the statement was made, Pool and Ethel were living together in Whitechapel, he as pimp and she as prostitute and a miserable life it must have been for her.

Later on in the statement, more truthfully, she confirmed that Stinie was a frequent visitor to Hardinge Street:

The last time I saw Morrison was on the 30th December last.* At about 12 o'clock that night, he called with a man, whom my husband afterwards told me was Beron . . . I . . .

---

* There is reason to think that she meant the visit of 29 December.

asked my husband not to go out and he agreed not to do so. My husband and Morrison had a conversation in a foreign tongue, after which Morrison left and I have not seen him since.

Here, of course, was nothing that particularly incriminated Stinie or, for that matter, Pool, in the murder of Beron and there her part in the case ended (apart from her brief exhibition during Stinie's trial) until well into 1913, not just 'some months' after Morrison's reprieve, as Abinger wrote, but nearly two and a half years after Beron's death. In the interim it is clear on the available police evidence that Ethel had been hovering on the brink of utter destitution, at any rate since Pool had left her for America (she puts the date of that event variously at December 1911 and November 1912, a divergence which does little for her credibility) and, in one 1913 statement, she refers significantly to having 'mentioned the matter to some girls'—working colleagues, presumably—before contacting a middle man, Harry Freedman, who took her to Lumley's office in the Strand, where she gave an account which seems to have been noted down verbatim. She afterwards declared that she was paid half-a-crown by Lumley.

What happened next is not quite clear, but a copy affidavit, dated 5 June 1913, is in the Home Office file, a document which was presumably compiled from the declaration made a fortnight before. Lumley then decided to instruct Abinger, as counsel, to re-draft the affidavit, which was to be sent to the Home Office along with the petition. Unfortunately, by the time this second affidavit was ready to be sworn, Ethel had moved from Brick Lane and disappeared. On 24 June, Lumley was writing to the Prison Commissioners, asking to see 'Ethel Wood' in Holloway. Ethel, who was not in prison, was shortly afterwards tracked down to an address in Shoreditch. Lumley's letter to the Commissioners had referred to Ethel's affidavit, saying that it 'required revision', an unhappy expression. Lumley seems to have been referring to some minor alterations between the first affidavit of 5 June and the one drafted by counsel which Ethel swore to on the 25th. Nevertheless, it was foolish of Lumley to have destroyed his record of the original declaration made in May; Blackwell was convinced that there was skulduggery afoot, with both Abinger and Lumley involved in suppressing the facts.

'I think Ethel Pool should be seen,' Blackwell minuted on 11 July, 'she may be able & willing to give more information than Messrs Lumley & Abinger have thought fit to embody in this statement.' And the proper officer to follow this up was of course Ward, who, attended by Wensley, saw Ethel at Scotland Yard on 15 July, when she made yet another statement (her fifth), which contained some significant differences from her previous accounts.

Broadly speaking, the content of the two defence affidavits sworn by Ethel in June is to the same effect. She omits any reference to 30 December, but tells of an unidentified someone knocking at the door of Hardinge Street on the 31st. Then follows something that was completely new.

I did not know who it was as I was upstairs in my bedroom. I heard them talking in a foreign language which I do not understand and they both left the house together. Paul [sic] didn't return home until 3 days after and at night time. I found blood on his shirt sleeves and down his shirt front . . . I asked him where he had been. He refused to tell me and swore at me. I know he carried a knife like a dagger . . . in his hip pocket. I said to him, 'Where does this blood come from?'

He said, 'I've been fighting.'

I said, 'I'll take it to the laundry.'

He said, 'No, I'll tear it up.'

He tore it up there and then and put it on the fire and told me if I was asked about blood I was not to tell anyone. He took his knife out and said, 'I'll draw this through you if you do,' and this he said for a long time afterwards each time he went out. When I heard Stinie Morrison was arrested and mentioned it, he said again, 'Be quiet and not a word about the blood on the shirt,' and threatened me again with his knife.

She went on to say that Pool had no money on the 31st, but when he returned he had gold and silver. He would also say,

172

when drunk, 'There is nothing like a Jewboy to keep his mouth shut.'

Ethel's confusion over the exact date of Pool's departure for the USA is reflected in her inability even to remember the date she was eventually married: Christmas 1911 in the first affidavit, 'about June 1911' in the second and 'about April or May 1912' in her statement to Ward. The true date was 10 June 1911 at the Registry Office for St George's-in-the-East district. On the certificate, Hugo Pool described himself as a tailor, but the space for Ethel's occupation, perhaps wisely, was left blank.

Ethel's atrocious memory, her obvious intellectual limitations and her crying need for money to support herself, support the view that, like the proverbial pillow, she bore the imprint of the last backside to sit on her. In the case of Alfred Ward, the backside was literally, as well as metaphorically, substantial. Taken to Scotland Yard, she provided Ward with everything he wanted. Stinie, she said, had told her during a supper-party with Pool and Beron at the Warsaw Restaurant on Christmas Eve that Beron was 'a very wealthy man and had got a lot of property'. She put in some detail about 30 December, but contradicted her first statement by saying that Pool did go out with Stinie that night, adding the entirely new expression, 'I was convinced in my own mind that they intended to rob Beron,' adding that 'on Saturday 31 December . . . Stinie came to our address alone, as near as I can remember it was about 11.00 p.m. He stayed a few minutes and he and Hugo left together. Hugo did not say where they were going, and I did not ask them, but I thought they were going out to commit a robbery.' This was the crucial part, the first time she had ever suggested that Morrison had called at 2 Hardinge Street late on New Year's Eve. If true, of course, it was damning—a murder plot could be the only inference.

She went on to repeat the story of the blood-stained shirt and added that the news of Stinie's arrest was brought by a 'young German Jew', who was dispatched by Pool to visit Stinie in Brixton and according to police records did so.

After Pool had been pulled in for questioning he adjured Ethel, 'If you have got to go to Leman Street, don't you say a word about the blood on my shirt or that Stinie was at our house on the Saturday or that we left together,' which she promised to do. As to the first defence affidavit, she claimed that she had not read it carefully before she signed it.

Ward noted triumphantly, 'It is obvious that Mr Lumley has omitted facts which told against the prisoner Morrison and only embodied those which cast suspicion on Pool,' sentiments wholeheartedly endorsed by Blackwell, who used a quotation from Lumley's letter to the Prison Commissioners in support of this contention.

'The submission of this statement by Ethel Pool carefully "settled" or rather garbled by Messrs Lumley and Abinger,' Blackwell wrote early in August 1913, 'is in keeping with the lack of judgement displayed in the defence of Morrison.' The received Home Office theory on the case was now this, as minuted by Blackwell:

It appears now that Morrison about 11.00 p.m. went round to 2 Hardinge Street (under 1 mile [from the Warsaw]) and called out Hugo Pool ... Morrison could easily have slipped out, seen Pool & returned to Snelwar without the witnesses noticing ... I suggest that he sent him off to Clapham Common to wait for Beron and himself, who would turn up later. Pool could get there easily in an hour by train or bus. One need not speculate as to how Beron was induced to journey to Clapham Common. He was got there somehow and the bait may have been the purchase of stolen property or a woman. Hugo Pool did not return to 2 Hardinge Street till dusk* on 3rd January and the evidence of Ethel Pool as to his conduct, the blood on his shirt, his threats and allusions to the 'Jewboy who would hold his tongue' all point to him as having been Morrison's accomplice. After the murder, Morrison and Pool separated. Morrison went on across the Common to Clapham Cross where he took Stephens' cab. Pool probably reached the streets by a shorter cut, picked up a cab and got to the rendezvous at Kennington Church,

---

* In fact, Ethel said it was 'at night-time' in the two defence affidavits, but told Ward that it was 'in the afternoon'.

174

where he was awaiting Morrison and whistled to him as Stephens' cab drew up. They then took Castling's cab to the Holloway Road [sic].

In so far as Blackwell was not quoting the orthodox prosecution line, his theory inevitably involved acceptance of Ethel's latest statement. Blackwell does not seem to have addressed his mind as to why she had not come forward earlier with these startling revelations. In the defence affidavits, she claimed that 'it was only when I was satisfied that Pool was out of the country that I ventured to speak of the matter in the interests of justice'. But Pool had been on the other side of the Atlantic for either six or, more likely, eighteen months (depending on Ethel's chaotic chronology) before she got in touch with Lumley. To Ward, she tried to explain her very different statement of February 1911 by saying that she was in fear of Pool at the time adding, feebly, that 'the only reason that I have not made a statement before is because I have never been asked for one'.

Blackwell concluded his minute with these words: ' ... the full statement by Ethel Pool to the police ... enormously strengthens the case against Morrison. Had her evidence been available at the trial there is little doubt that Morrison and probably Hugo Pool would have been executed.' Troup agreed. So the three earlier versions, each signed and in two cases sworn to on oath by Ethel, were to be disregarded. But were the Home Office officials justified in taking the Ward/Wensley statement as gospel, which is, in effect, what they did? The efflux of time—two and a half years after the events deposed to—must weaken the force of her allegations, but there are other factors which cast substantial doubt upon her reliability. Ethel's background and personality do not encourage the belief that she would have made a reliable, a truthful witness. The statement itself contains a significant illogicality. Pool, she said, was always very careful to keep things from her. Furthermore, at all relevant times, Pool, Morrison and Beron would speak in Yiddish, which she did not understand. Yet, according to Ward, she was 'convinced' on the 30th that Stinie and Pool were going to rob Beron and similarly she was 'always

. . . convinced' that they had murdered him. Why she felt so
convinced, if in truth she did, was never explained. Ethel
seems to have been a pitiable creature, willing to say whatever
she thought her listeners wanted to hear. There is little doubt
that Lumley paid her in return for swearing the affidavits and
it would be surprising if Ward had not also oiled that very desperate palm.

Perhaps the clearest indication of Ethel's character arises
from her conduct eight months after declaring that her 1913
statement to police was a true account. In May 1914, *John Bull*
carried a 'startling story' from 'a certain young woman' who
was, of course, Ethel, making her sixth statement in exchange
for five shillings, paid to herself and a man she had recently
taken up with in Spitalfields. She now attributed the observation about Beron's wealth, made at the Warsaw supper-
party, to a man she called 'A' (plainly Hugo Pool). She
described, in terms similar to those of her very first statement,
the visit Stinie and Beron had made to the brothel a few days
(the report says 'weeks', which must be wrong) before the end
of the year, but she made no reference to that vital knock from
Stinie at the door of 2 Hardinge Street late on the night of the
31st. Later on, though, the blood-stained shirt was duly aired
to thrill the magazine's readership.

Blackwell was distinctly ruffled. 'I do not suppose it is
possible to prevent this woman making statements to newspapers.' Ward was called in again and ascertained from Ethel
that Sam Rosen ('possible [sic] in the pay of Morrison's
friends') had put the story to *John Bull*.

Ethel also told Ward that, when she had made her 1913
statement, 'I forgot to tell you that Povl [sic] and Morrison
were committing burglaries together for some six weeks before
the murder,' which may well have been true for once, but it
accords ill with the prosecution case at the trial, which maintained that Stinie was desperately short of money in the last
week of 1910.

Ward was able to confirm that Pool had gone to America and
was currently serving four years eight months for receiving
stolen property. He had been sentenced on 1 May 1914 and
was safely lodged in Auburn Prison, New York State under the

name 'Sam Mellor'. Wensley, in his memoirs, wrote cryptically, 'I heard that he had been executed for a murder and robbery in the United States, although I never troubled to verify the report,' rather out of character for Wensley who, a senior Yard officer until 1929, could have done so without difficulty.

As for Ethel's story about the blood-stained shirt, the authorities eagerly seized upon it, accepting the episode without reservation but, in retrospect, it seems decidedly improbable. Where had Pool been in the intervening days? Whitechapel was alive with policemen chasing the Houndsditch gang. Why had he gone on wearing the hopelessly incriminating garment for so long? He was a professional burglar and Ethel herself had referred to an occasion when Pool had come home with a suitcase full of clothes. It would have been easy for Pool to have broken into a home or shop and effected a complete change of clothing.

Pool was a thief, a bully and could be extremely violent, in and out of drink. He and Ethel were both experienced practitioners in the art of rolling tipsy sailors. He used Ethel abominably and, when he left her penniless, it is hardly surprising that her memory of him was bitter and when opportunity offered itself to make a little money (Ethel had, on her own admission, discussed the matter with 'some girls' early in 1913 and it does not need much imagination to work out what passed between her and her fellow prostitutes) she took it, whatever the source might be. To Lumley, she would say one thing, to Ward, a second, and to the *John Bull* reporter, a third. Her story of the visit by Stinie to 2 Hardinge Street late on New Year's Eve 1910 is simply not credible, since it was an assertion made for the first time over two and a half years later. The probability, too, is that the melodramatic scenario enacted around Pool's shirt was an invention with an eye to money-making and, perhaps, as a means of getting back at the man who had treated her so callously. Preoccupied with the sheer problem of staying alive, Ethel could not afford to let Stinie's interests stand in her way.

Blackwell mooted a possible course of action, making passing reference to another contemporary *cause célèbre*. 'The

recent inquiry in Oscar Slater's case,' he wrote, was 'likely to
direct attention to that of S. Morrison & if ... the case were
taken up by a more reputable paper than *John Bull*, public
opinion might render it necessary to re-open it.' Blackwell's
wording suggests a reluctance to encourage anything of the
sort, but he ended by noting that the case could be referred by
the Home Office to the Court of Criminal Appeal. 'Ethel Pool's
evidence certainly constitutes a new fact,' he conceded, adding
that 'it may at some time become advisable to do so, but her
full statement made to the Police would be included in the reference & it would be for the Court to decide whether they
should not have her examined before them.' An interesting
suggestion—but it remained no more than a suggestion and, in
the event, nothing was done. Ethel's credibility was never
tested, as it ought to have been, in a court of law.

31

Some people have been moved to confess to crimes they did not
commit, even when the consequence of such lying claims
might be death itself. The Morrison case was no exception and
a crop of would-be assassins emerged from obscurity. Some,
like the male inmate of Cane Hill asylum, are known only from
the pages of the Home Office file, which records an insane declaration prompted by 'drink and syphilis'.

At about the same time, September 1911, though not as a
confession, there were widespread reports of the arrest in
Boston Mass. of John and Jacob Goldberg and Harris Rothstein, three criminals suspected at one stage of involvement in
the Houndsditch affair. Home Office records showed that the
Goldbergs had left England in November 1910 and had been
out of harm's way in an Austrian jail on that fateful 1 January.
Oddly, the Home Office papers suggest that Lumley had been
visited by Rothstein later that month. The man had spoken of

Stinie's innocence of the Clapham crime and the probability is that he was one of Stinie's associates. In the event, the Goldberg–Rothstein episode provided anti-British newspapers along America's Eastern Seaboard with useful copy in the last months of that year.

Men with more rational minds than the Cane Hill inmate used bogus confessions as a means to an end. In July 1912, a naval stoker told Australian police that he had killed Beron, but it was soon clear that the matelot had been aboard HMS *Revenge* at the material time and, moreover, had jumped ship the following May. The Home Office thought that this was all a ruse to enable the man to get home, where he would no doubt pay the price for desertion and the confession was retracted just a month after it had been made. Perhaps the man had a closer ear to the ground than other would-be murderers, for he claimed to have committed the crime with the help of one 'Hugo Volgt', conceivably an echo of some underworld buzz around the name of Hugo Pool.

Gunner Veare, unlike the ex-stoker, made the august pages of *The Times*[1] when in June 1913 he admitted the murder and was duly confined to the garrison guardroom at Port Royal, Jamaica. Declared sane, he insisted that he had committed the crime for revenge, being of Jewish descent, brought up in the East End. Tormented by his terrible secret, he had decided to reveal all. In fact, Veare was at home, which was not Whitechapel but St Luke's Road, Clapham, at the time of the murder. Later, he admitted that he had used the story as a means of procuring his discharge from the army.

The Home Office was also deluged with useless information from correspondents, who ranged from the well-intentioned and intelligent to the malicious or simply dotty. One such unwanted helper, Jesse Charley, was noticeably persistent with coffee-stall gossip, 'a crazy individual with a mania for notoriety,' in Blackwell's opinion and Charley's attempts to persuade Ward of the truth merely resulted in a painful 'bang on the mouth' (Charley's words) at the hand of that robust Inspector.

Another eccentric was one 'G. Wells', who wrote in that name from the irreproachably suburban address of Orpington,

Kent, on the day before Stinie's reprieve. Poor Mr Wells had walked three miles in pouring rain to Farnboro' Police Station to give his information, only to be told that he must write to Ward, who, wisely, did not reply. Mr Wells informed the Home Office that Leon Beron was, in reality, Henri Jaques of the Ligue Fraternité Internationale, a shadowy organization, with which Mr Wells had had an unexplained connection, dedicated to the exposure of foreign influence, particularly by the Imperial Russian Government. Blackwell's minuted 'apparently mad' must be endorsed, but there was to be an extraordinary sequel in 1924.

That year, the year of the first Labour Government and a great scare about Reds, whether under beds, in the streets or elsewhere, saw the publication of *Famous Crimes and Criminals* by the aptly-named C. McCluer Stephens. Concealed in an otherwise routine compilation could be found a heavily elaborated version of Wells' 1911 letter to the Home Office. Stephens carefully acknowledged that his information had come from an anonymous source, but the public sensation was considerable. Beron had been murdered because the LFI suspected him of informing on a fellow-member, 'son of a Riga shipman', whose ferocious sister, 'a strong muscular young woman and absolutely devoid of fear,' had, alone, killed Beron, who was at that time 'carrying out an intrigue with a woman who lived on the outskirts of Clapham Common'. The S-marks did not stand for 'spy' or anything of the kind. No, said Wells, unconscious of any alternative meaning, the LFIs badge had consisted of 'three small ivory balls' and the sign 'was such as one man would make in trying to indicate to another the nature of the badge, namely an S-shaped circular movement of the right forefinger'.

Wells had posted the original letter on 10 April 1911, though the Home Office did not receive it until after Churchill's decision to reprieve Stinie. 'I placed my fateful missive in a wall letter-box at St Mary Cray station,' declared this Orpington Pooter, who had convinced himself that his agency alone had saved Morrison's neck. For good measure, he told the credulous McCluer Stephens how he had foiled a plot to murder Churchill himself after 'certain extremists' had tampered with an aeroplane in which the Home Secretary was due to fly.

The publication of the book was heralded by a number of sensationally-worded reviews in the weekday and Sunday press. Churchill, in Opposition and searching for a political identity, was astonished and wrote to Blackwell on 2 April, plaintively asking if the Home Office had any information on the subject. Blackwell had the very answer, which was crisply expressed: 'Mr McCluer Stephens has had his leg well pulled.'

32

In May 1913, King George and Queen Mary travelled to Berlin, guests at the wedding of Prince Ernst Augustus of Hanover and Princess Victoria Louise, daughter of the German Emperor. This last, resplendent gathering of Imperial Europe was also attended by Tsar Nicholas, in whose realm of All the Russias Stinie had first seen the light of day thirty-odd years before. Whatever the personal bonhomie between the Royals, bitter nationalistic rivalries pointed ineluctably in one direction: the path of war. But things were not exactly peaceful at home, either. The suffragettes were on the march and smashed plate-glass windows, poured acid into pillar-boxes and over golf greens, burned down several houses and two railway stations and, it was said, had even planted a bomb in St Paul's. Many women when imprisoned went on hunger strike, and were forcibly fed in brutal, degrading fashion. And at the Derby, Emily Davison threw herself under the King's horse and died.

The Baroness Hilda, if not a militant herself, seems to have had contacts among the women's movement, some of whom, living in the vicinity of Parkhurst, were eager to help operate the secret underground correspondence which undoubtedly ran throughout 1913 and into the following year, possibly until heightened wartime restrictions and surveillance put an end to it.

During the period of his mental breakdown late in 1912, and for many months afterwards, Stinie was accommodated in the prison hospital which, as has been seen, was ideal territory for the secret mailing system. By autumn 1913, Blackwell, irritated by a series of petitions from Stinie, 'more or less insolent', which repeated pleas for execution, retrial or release, decided to visit the Isle of Wight and see for himself this tiresome thorn in officialdom's flesh. Blackwell, whose scrupulous attention to detail rendered him almost the apotheosis of the Protestant Work Ethic, was dismayed to find Stinie 'lying full length on the floor . . . reading'. An appalled Blackwell wanted leave-to-petition withdrawn immediately and urgent consideration given to putting the prisoner to work. 'He has now settled down,' he wrote firmly '. . . should be kept for the full twenty years,' and should not be 'given the impression that he is being treated differently from other convicts.'

Stinie's discharge from the prison hospital was marked by an unfortunate disclosure. In the morning, the warders came to transfer the moody prisoner to the ordinary cells and he was summarily ordered to strip for the customary full body search. The impending transfer must have come as a surprise, for that very morning Stinie had written a letter, plainly destined for the Baroness, in pencil on the back of 'undefaced pictures from a library book, stamped with this prison's government mark,' (in the solemn reportage of Mr Tabuteau, Deputy Governor at Parkhurst). As Stinie reluctantly undressed, the folded paper, which he had stuffed down the back of his underpants, fell to the floor. Stinie grabbed at the incriminating document and tried to swallow it. A violent struggle took place, several officers intervening before the letter could be recovered from Stinie's tenacious grip. The text, enlivened by a little black humour, was not designed to appeal to the official mind.

S. Morrison at the Separate Cells 17 November 1913
Hearty thanks for your letter, bountiful——There are all sorts of people on the landing above mine, bankers, doctors

and solicitors, chaplains... We only want the H[ome] Sec[retary] to make up the set. I find myself quite well, thanks to you, noble——. But my life is a torture here, the more so because I am young and strong and my blood boiling hot. But however difficult my life here may be, I have no intention to give in. I'll fight for my rights tooth and nail ... I am going to make myself a thorn in their eye continually until justice is done me... Another chap broke his contract with the H. Sec. on Sunday morning. Did he die naturally, I wonder? Just think of it. 6 to the grave, close on 50 to the Lunatic Asylum and several dying now and all in one year. Not bad for a Christian country...

If I had my way, I'd kick all the male longheads out of the government service and open the doors to the dear little suffragettes. They are the plucky ones of the land... As regards the printing of my letters, why not rub out anything you do not wish printed and then send them on anonymously...

God bless you, Mr M. and Mr C. [unidentified] I sincerely hope that you are all in the best of health ... I kneel and kiss the hem of your robe, kindest—and remain, ever your humble servant.

Stinie Morrison

PS ... Love to G [? Jane Brodsky] and all her darling sisters.

SM

Jane Brodsky was, on the infrequent occasions when visiting was allowed, accommodated by the Baroness, whose 'place' at Aldingbourne in West Sussex was conveniently sited for journeyings to the island prison.

The discovery of this attempt at secret correspondence led to a reduced diet, and this, coupled with the transfer from the prison hospital and consequent restriction upon those unorthodox channels of communication, re-awakened deeply depressive feelings of isolation. Once more he gave way totally to despair and, on 12 December, tried to commit suicide. How he made the attempt is not stated in the Home Office papers, but it may have been a go at slashing a vein in his arm with a piece of broken glass. Wensley, in his memoirs, refers to a somewhat ludicrous leap into a pond found to be only inches deep, though this incident, if it occurred at all, was on an earlier occasion, perhaps while Stinie was in Dartmoor.

Stinie gradually recovered his spirits and embarked on a long period of good behaviour, though Blackwell was angered when, in February 1914, the prisoner indicated that he was going to petition the Home Secretary for his next visiting order to include the Baroness and Claude Lumley. Blackwell, mindful that the authorities had been outwitted by the pair less than a year before, was in no mood to agree.

By the next month, Jane, at any rate, had already been allowed in, for Stinie's petition is a loud complaint about Ethel Pool's activities. 'I fully believe,' he wrote, with possible justification, 'she has been put up to it by someone working on behalf of the police ... to upset the petition.' Less credibly, Stinie went on to suggest that the mysterious New Year's Eve visitor to Hardinge Street was Pool's 'pal Max (I think), who is so like me that if he were put alongside of me, you would not be able to tell the difference between us'.

In this petition Stinie had been rather indiscreet and Blackwell's suspicions were aroused: 'There has perhaps been more trafficking by the Baroness von Goetz, but Brodsky may have told him enough to write this petition. Nil EB 18.3.14.'*

Nevertheless, the trafficking went on and, in the spring of 1914, Stinie enlisted a pamphleteer to his cause. James Timewell, founder in 1902 and now honorary secretary of the 'Police and Public Vigilance Committee', a group that in modern times would be regarded as Civil Liberties campaigners, went into print in March with a tract entitled *Is Stinie Morrison Innocent?*, a re-working with Abinger's help of the 1913 petition for Morrison's release. The pamphlet received

---

* After 1914, the Baroness disappears from this story: perhaps, with the coming of war, she returned to her family in neutral Denmark. It is possible that she was the 'lady of benevolent disposition' swindled out of £35,000 by Harry Benson, whose fraudulent 'Prisoners' Aid Society' brought in considerable revenue from Stinie's more gullible sympathizers between, it is said, March 1914 and Benson's death on 22 October 1917. Stinie seems to have been unaware of the fraud: see Charles Kingston, *Gallery of Rogues*.

favourable notices in the *Daily Citizen* (later to become the *Daily Herald*), the *Star*, in *John Bull* (of course) as well as a surprising boost from the Belfast Protestant Daily, the *Northern Whig*.

Three months later, Timewell produced another broadside, *The Prison Life of Stinie Morrison—Reprieved But Tortured. Price One Penny*, prefaced by a flintily-drawn likeness of an anguished Morrison clad in arrowed tunic, breeches and prison cap. Timewell, described by Earl Russell,[1] Bertrand Russell's elder brother, as 'a fanatic', prepared to believe anything ill of the police, certainly spared the public no detail about Stinie's alleged mishandling in prison. Much of the text is in Stinie's own words, a recognizable style, supplemented by facsimiles of his handwriting, culled from eighteen months' worth of underground post.

Stinie's words spoke bitterly of prison conditions, the awful food, constant winter cold and damp, and of regular beatings administered to troublesome inmates. There was, of course, a powerful vein of exaggeration at work, but life in Dartmoor and Parkhurst, then as now, was unlikely to have been a bed of roses. A number of incidents, such as bursting open the straitjacket—a formidable feat of strength—can be traced in Home Office papers. Stinie's unquiet mind is well illustrated by this extract from the pamphlet: 'When asleep after a sleeping draught, I was always disturbed by dreams of the three officials in the punishment cell beating me with their sticks. I was oppressed by such dreams for a long time ...'

Two contributions from 'ex-prisoners' rounded off Timewell's squib. One anonymous informant revealed that Stinie was 'most emphatic that several of his ... friends know beyond a shadow of doubt who the murderers are and, further, where they could, with very little trouble, be found.' Another correspondent had spoken only once to Stinie, shortly after one or other of his abortive suicide attempts, for Stinie was found 'walking about on the path in the prison yard ... with no laces in his shoes'. When the curious prisoner asked Stinie what he had been doing, the response was both a declaration and a melancholy prophecy: 'I am an innocent man ... and I do not mean to do the time.'

33

Britain declared war on Germany at midnight on 3 August 1914. It would not be over by Christmas as optimists thought and, as foolhardy cavalry actions were succeeded by the amphibian immobility of trench warfare, people banished other contemporary issues 'for the duration'. The Irish question and women's suffrage were in cold storage. In Flanders, many finer men than Stinie Morrison were to be killed or maimed every day of those ghastly four years. The coming of the Great War effectively extinguished any hope of a successful public campaign for Stinie's release.

Stinie did, however, make a convert in the prison's resident rabbi, S.P. van Raale, with whom a distinct rapport was established as 1914 wore on. 'After a long conversation,' wrote van Raale, petitioning in the third person, 'he accepted him [Morrison] as a Jew on condition that his behaviour improved. He has, during the year, behaved exceedingly well... He seems like a different man.' Van Raale frequently visited Stinie's cell and 'noted that the prisoner is an educated man. He is fond of good literature and does not by any means appear to be the depraved creature that he was represented to be.' Stinie was 'most anxious to give up his life—if need be, to join the allies against the common foe (he is Russian)'.

The upshot of van Raale's petition was an expression of belief in Stinie's total innocence of the Clapham crime, an unusual declaration from a 'prison Minister', as the rabbi was officially termed. Stinie's partiality for 'good literature' would not have impressed Blackwell, with recent memories of the prisoner indolently perusing a book in his cell and the reaction to van Raale's plea was, predictably, negative, but Blackwell must have seen Dr Murray's confirmation of an improvement in Stinie's attitude. 'He is at present employed as a tailor and has recently conducted himself rationally. He still maintains his innocence of the crime . . .'

Stinie's enthusiasm for the Allied cause may not have extended to conversations with his fellow-prisoners. 'When . . . the prison chaplain read out the news . . . his face lit up with glee at the list of ships sunk by German submarines—for he had come to hate the country with a terrible hatred.'[1]

However that may be, the many petitions Stinie vainly submitted in the war years contain all manner of offers to serve: 'Willing to join the army as manual labourer' (1915); 'I am sure that I would be ever so much more useful to Great Britain as a volunteer in the Army or Navy' (May 1916); 'I could be ever so much more useful on board a mine-sweeper if only you would kindly give me the chance' (November 1916); 'I am . . . just the build for the heavy artillery' (1917). All fell on a particularly deaf pair of ears at the Home Office.

One event seems to have brought Stinie unalloyed joy, whatever his true convictions about the war. The Zeppelin raid of 23/24 September 1916 gave London a foretaste of the Blitz. Seven airships made the perilous North Sea crossing and two were shot down, their crews burned alive. Thirty-eight men, women and children, ordinary members of the public with one notable exception, were killed, and scores injured in the bombing. The exception was Chief Detective-Inspector Alfred Ward, whose death was a sufficiently important occurrence to influence the censor, who ordered that newspaper reports of Ward's death should not reveal that it was a result of enemy action. *The Times* blithely suggested that 'many of the men whom he had tracked to justice looked upon him in after years as one of their greatest benefactors'.[2] Not so Stinie. He is said to have wept tears of delight on hearing the news, declaring his belief in Providence at last.

The war did not completely suppress the campaign for Stinie's release, but publicity was rare. A brief passage in the *Daily Herald* late in 1916 spoke of a 'man in khaki' who had called at Lumley's office.[3] But it was not until 1919, the year of the Versailles Peace Conference, that coverage was given to a resumed and rather muted effort by Lumley, Abinger and a handful of other well-wishers. In February of that year an arcane reference was made to 'fresh evidence' in the United States, and in August there were reports that a man in the Indian army might prove to be a vital missing witness, but it all fizzled out before the end of the year.

On 7 June 1920, Stinie petitioned for his release for the thirtieth and last time. In contrast with many of his earlier submissions, the tone is respectful, even resigned. Later that year he wrote to a London contact, possibly Lumley, asking him to 'redouble' his efforts towards release.[4]

But the will to go on was failing. By the end of 1920, Stinie was approaching his eleventh year of continuous imprisonment. So long a period in jail must quell even the most rebellious spirit. Over the years, to be sure, the authorities, mindful of Stinie's earlier conduct, had shown some tact, and his work regimen was regularly changed and diet varied, 'judicial treatment' in the words of Dr Murray. On 26 November 1920, though, he was taken into the prison hospital, very depressed and unsettled. Stinie was now sleeping only for some three or four hours and would spend the rest of the night moodily pacing about his cell. He complained bitterly to Murray that other 'lifers' had been released, while no such hope had been extended to him. He also spoke of persecution by some of the prison staff and threatened, morosely, to do 'something to myself'. That was enough for Murray, and the transfer to a hospital cell was duly effected, but Stinie's response was progressively to reduce the quantity of food he ate. This was not, then, strictly a hunger strike, which would have enabled the authorities, from the outset, to practise forcible feeding with a stomach tube, the grotesque and painful treatment then regularly meted out in such cases.

In contrast, Stinie played a little game with the Medical Officer, saying that he could take more bread with his milk and butter if he had jam. Jam was provided, but Stinie changed tack and started drinking nothing but tea, two pints a day of it, in which, in bizarre fashion, he would put his jam and a 'very small piece of pudding'. As a result, he started to lose weight rapidly and the prospect of forcible feeding arose; according to

Murray, however, examination revealed that Stinie was suffering from a heart complaint, later found to involve an advanced deterioration of the aortic valve and the heart muscle itself. Murray afterwards said that he had decided in those circumstances not to use the stomach tube but instead an invalid's feeding-cup. He did not add that the latter course must have involved the use of some physical restraint, such as a strait-jacket. In mid-January 1921, Stinie was told that his life would be in danger if he persisted in eating so little, but when he was told about the proposed use of the feeding-cup he angrily threatened to cut his throat. This caused Murray to order Stinie's immediate removal to a padded cell where, in restraint, he was subject to 'fairly forcible feeding', as reported by Murray's deputy, Dr Craig. Stinie, whose strength was ebbing daily, none the less had enough vigour left to resist the treatment and it is clear that a contingent of warders ensured, by their combined efforts, that the prescribed refreshment ('milk, egg, brandy and Benger's food') was taken twice daily.

On 24 January, Murray penned a memorandum to the Home Office warning that Morrison's condition was 'not satisfactory. His strength is considerably reduced.' The doctor had, in fact, spoken to Stinie at about midday for some five or ten minutes, warning him again about the possible consequences, but Murray did not think that there was then any immediate danger to life.

The official account of Stinie's death was given by Dr Craig at the inquest. At about 2.15 p.m. he had gone to Morrison's cell, armed with the hated feeding-cup (and, though unsaid, a retinue of prison orderlies). He saw at once that Stinie had suffered a heart attack and he administered an injection of strychnine—a stimulant in small doses—which rallied the prisoner sufficiently for him to be given a little brandy from a spoon. He was given more brandy after being moved on his cell mattress into a ward, where hot-water bottles were placed around him. Two hours later, Stinie had a second, fatal attack, from which he died at about 4.30 p.m.

Rumour has persisted over the years that Stinie did not die naturally. One account[5] suggests that he was strangled by a heavy-handed warder named Stirling: not unnaturally, there is nothing in the official sources to confirm such an allegation, but there is a real possibility that rough treatment during those 'fairly forcible' feeding sessions may have resulted in undue pressure on the branch of the vagus nerve which passes near the carotid artery at the left side of the neck. This nerve, which controls the mechanism of breathing, may become 'inhibited' by pressure, causing rapid unconsciousness and, if the interference is prolonged, death. Stinie's heart condition was an additional adverse factor, which could well have hampered any subsequent attempt at revival.

A darker possibility is that the hospital orderlies were well aware of the ease with which vagal inhibition can occur, either from their work in the prison hospital or from grim experience in the Great War, in which some of them had very likely served. Stinie, though less dangerous than legend would have it (at least in recent years), was ever deeply antagonistic to authority and must have made enemies among prison staff, some of whom may have been minded to pay off old scores while their victim was disadvantaged by physical weakness and the bonds of a strait-jacket. Gone were the days when Stinie's strength was enough to burst open such a restraint.

Had Stinie been truly strangled, however, there would have been obvious indications on his body, marks about the neck, protrusion of the tongue and 'petechiae': tell-tale spots of red or purple dotted about a suffused face. No doctor, whatever his commitment to the prison personnel, could have ignored those signs, but vagal inhibition can be accomplished without leaving any external evidence.

Dr Craig's story of the events of 24 January does not make clear whether the orderlies had already been preparing a reluctant Stinie for his forcible feed before the doctor had walked into the cell and found the prisoner in a state of collapse. Indeed, the report of the inquest,[6] held the day after Stinie's death, reads unconvincingly as an attempt to get at the truth, with a marked absence of evidence (or questioning) about the use of restraints such as the strait-jacket or the exact method of forcible feeding and the number of warders required to carry it out. It is significant that only one warder witness from the hospital wing was called to give evidence and he merely dealt with uncontroversial background information and appears not to have been present during Stinie's last moments.

The inquest jury, headed by a local councillor, was in no mood to be sympathetic. The coroner had canvassed the prospect that the 'wholesome verdict of suicide' might be recorded if Stinie's death had been caused by lack of food, but Dr Murray took the view that Stinie's object in acting as he did was to 'bring pressure to bear as to his possible release, apart from any desire to die'.

Taking his cue, the foreman pronounced solemn judgment. 'I think the prison authorities have done everything possible to save the deceased,' he said, adding that the prisoner was 'very stubborn'. His fellow jury members agreed, and the report records a wholehearted 'hear, hear' from those respectable folk obliged to share a small island with a large prison. In the end, the verdict was that Stinie Morrison had 'died from aortic disease, aggravated by voluntary abstention from food'.

Three days later, Stinie was buried in Carisbrooke cemetery. A bleak procession had trundled its way from the gates of Parkhurst to the graveside, some two miles off, through the raw drizzle of a January afternoon. The plain elm coffin, painted black, bore a simple plate, 'Stinie Morrison. Died January 24th 1921. Aged 39 years.' Two horses drew the hearse, which was accompanied by a chief warder proudly displaying his wartime medals, but reporters noted that 'not a single flower or other little mark of esteem was placed on the coffin of the convict'. There were no mourners, no Florrie, no Baroness, no Brodsky girls to say goodbye. Some twenty inquisitive locals had gathered round to hear the Vicar of Carisbrooke, the Reverend T. Story Busher, resplendent in cloak and biretta, read out the burial service from the Book of Common Prayer.

'Morrison,' wrote the *Evening Standard*, 'was, in spite of all reports to the contrary, a Protestant, not a Jew,'[7] a fine example at the very last of Stinie's exceptionally wayward character.

34

> The mystery of Stinie Morrison remains, hovering like a black shadow athwart the crucified [sic] Justice which, from the top of the Old Bailey, peers blindly across the housetops of London.

Thus the *Daily Herald* in melodramatic vein marked Stinie's death.[1] *The Times* got its facts wrong: Stinie had 'lured Beron in a taxicab' to Clapham Common and, moreover, it had been 'proved that Morrison after the murder . . . had had in his possession Beron's watch and this evidence was mainly responsible for his conviction'.[2] Most newspapers were content to refer more briefly to a 'sensational trial'; much water had flowed under the bridges of Marne and Somme since 1911. But the tabloids, freed from the constraints of libel as far as Stinie, at any rate, was concerned, made a bigger splash, and Florrie Dellow seems to have been handsomely rewarded for her memoirs which appeared, duly garbled, in the *World's Pictorial News* during the early months of the year.[3]

Throughout the twenties, newspaper articles spasmodically raked over the embers of the Clapham Common case. Sir Basil Thomson's revelation in the *Sunday News*[4] that Beron had been a fence was quickly followed up by another piece in the same paper,[5] penned by an anonymous author who seems to have had some access to official sources, putting forward the received police theory that Hugo Pool (unnamed, but clearly discernible) was the second man.

In weightier prose, Fletcher Moulton's edition in the Notable British Trials series, published in January 1922 and still a classic source, was the precursor of many attempts to 'solve' the Clapham crime, in which authors, learned or otherwise, advanced theories ranging from the probable to the most ethereal flights of fancy.

In real life, Stinie's ten years of incarceration had been matched by the hapless Solomon Beron who, ever since his attempt to 'make an application' to Mr Justice Darling in March 1911, had been closely confined in Colney Hatch asylum, repository of not a few characters in the Morrison story. There he died just two months after Stinie, the man he had always believed to be the murderer of his brother. Max Beron, paterfamilias of this strange family, too frail to give evidence at Stinie's trial, none the less outlived Stinie and at least two of his sons, dying at the age of eighty-three in the Wandsworth Home for Aged Jews in June 1922.

Muir, mellowed by the loss of his only son, who had succumbed to the terrible 'Spanish flu' just a week before the Armistice, lived on until 1924. Abinger survived him by just five years: their respective professional success can be gauged from their wills. Muir left over £36,000, while Abinger is recorded as leaving a mere £1,647.10s.

Ernley Blackwell, knighted in 1916, remained unshakably convinced of Stinie's guilt to the end. Just before his retirement in 1933, he received startling information that must have come as music to the official ear. At a dinner-party early in January, Blackwell met R.M. Tabuteau, the Deputy Governor at Parkhurst in Stinie's day. Not surprisingly, the Morrison case surfaced among the well-mannered chatter. Tabuteau recalled that Stinie had always protested his innocence, but Blackwell's rebuke was stern. 'Morrison's guilt was clearly established in 1913 by the statement of Mrs Hugo Pool,' he told Tabuteau, now Governor of Pentonville. Tabuteau said that one of his current prisoners was a man called Frank, but everybody agreed that Frank the receiver was probably dead by then, twenty-two years on from the Clapham murder.

But Tabuteau's curiosity was aroused and the next day he took advantage of a request by his inmate to visit him in a hospital cell. Some unspecified favour was granted before Tabuteau asked his now compliant prisoner if he had once had a shop in Lambeth Road. The man, who was indeed Max Frank, said that he had and became 'very pleased but amazed' and 'very communicative', in the language of Tabuteau's memorandum.

Unfortunately, Tabuteau's account of proceedings goes on to describe the posing of two, very 'leading', questions addressed to his sick and compliant subject. 'I asked him,' wrote Tabuteau, 'if he remembered that big gold watch. Was not there an unusually big one he bought? He said, "Yes, I got that from Stenie [sic] Morrison." "And a thick bit of sovereigns, too," I added. "Yes," he said, "he wanted them changed into notes as they were easier carried."' Frank added that he could explain 'the cause of Morrison going to him in Lambeth was because he kept a girl on the top floor of the house.' Intriguingly, Max went on to speak of 'knowing Leon Beron', but the governor could not recall any point he made about him.

The day of that interview, and surely not as a coincidence, Blackwell was to be found lunching at Pentonville with the governor, who told his eager listener what had taken place. A delighted Blackwell minuted that it was 'most interesting that ... this conclusive piece of evidence has come to light ... especially so because in the meantime many attempts have been made by writers of the ... Fletcher Moulton type to induce the public to believe that Stinie Morrison was an innocent victim of British justice.' This slighting reference to Fletcher Moulton, who had in fact remarked 'how strong the case for the prosecution really was,' was followed by some equally crabby observations. Blackwell admitted that 'the case for the prosecution had broken down on various points. I do not attribute blame to anyone for this. The witnesses were mostly foreign Jews and awful liars.' Stinie had been 'badly defended and, I think, badly tried by Darling J., who being short-sighted himself could not understand the cabmen's evidence of identification'.

Blackwell's criticism of Darling was obviously for Home Office eyes alone and the old judge was gratified to read of the latest development, minus Blackwell's gloss on the conduct of the trial. 'I never had the slightest doubt of his guilt,' Darling replied, 'but I gave him a very good chance in my summing-up.'

Several years later, in 1939, Blackwell sent Roland Oliver, a very junior defence counsel at Stinie's trial but now a High Court judge, a copy of his minute of the 1933 disclosures. 'I have always had searchings at heart at Morrison's conviction,' wrote Oliver, adding, 'as you say, this information puts the matter beyond doubt.'

But does it? It can hardly have mattered to Frank, ill and twenty years older, with Morrison long in the grave, that he should take vicarious responsibility for receiving Beron's watch, surely not the only large gold watch to have passed through those dishonest hands. Furthermore, if he had known Beron, which is quite probable, he would surely have been aware, jeweller and receiver as he was, of the prized timepiece. Had Morrison brought that item in for sale on New Year's morning, Frank would have put two and two together at once, making a nonsense of the claim of Goodwillie's 'very reliable informant'. At that stage of his life, in 1933, Frank would have been anxious to have told so important a figure as his prison governor anything he thought Tabuteau wanted to hear. Bearing in mind the way in which the subject was raised, and the questions put, this episode ranks no higher than Ethel Pool's declarations of 1913. To describe it as 'conclusive', in the absence at the very least of more detailed inquiry, was as unjust as it was absurd.

Ernley Blackwell died, full of years and public honours, on 21 September 1941.

Envoi

(1)

What was the real defence of Stinie Morrison, the hidden truth never revealed at the trial or during those long bitter years of imprisonment? It was certainly not a defence involving the Holloway fraud of November 1910, which Stinie had alluded to in his final desperate words before sentence of death was passed upon him. He had given some detail about the fraud to Abinger shortly after the trial, claiming that he was solely responsible. This was easily disproved by Ward, who reported to the Home Office on 10 April 1911: 'It is possible,' he concluded, 'that the prisoner was concerned in the forgery and that his share of the proceeds might have been anything from £50 to £100, but having regard to his gambling propensities, love of fine dress and the company of loose women it is quite possible for him to have squandered the whole of it in a few days.'

Nevertheless, contrary to Muir's assertions at the trial, Stinie may well have been able to support himself, after a fashion, in December. Burglary was his real game and Ethel Pool had told police that Stinie was committing burglaries at that time with 'Shonkey'. The fatal temptation for Stinie was to move into a higher division of crime, which might more easily support his extravagant lifestyle.

The West End of London, home of fashion and wealth, was the draw and it may have been the elaborate process of changing moneys from the Holloway fraud that brought Stinie into the streets around Piccadilly and Mayfair, searching out the West End branches of Cook's and other bureaux de change. It is certain that the idea of a big West End job, ruthlessly planned and executed, crossed Stinie's mind. Perhaps some underworld contact told Stinie of a suitable site: a fortune in gold and jewellery lying in steel safes amid a large office complex at 49 Old Bond Street, not far from Piccadilly and outrageously near Vine Street Police Station. Stinie would have been grimly amused to recall how hard he had worked in the bakery so near that other police station in Lavender Hill. The rewards from 'working' in Old Bond Street would be immeasurably greater and enormous satisfaction lay in doing the job under the very noses of the police.

'Shonkey' was one of Stinie's closest associates and it would have been with him that the scheme was first discussed. Both men were aware that such an enterprise would need a good deal of planning: reconnaissances to be made, equipment obtained to gain entry as well as to open the safes, and sources of finance—major crime comes expensive. Above all, the ultimate receivers had to be carefully chosen. Stinie would already have had Frank and Rotto on his list, but a really big job would involve several receivers, each capable of 'placing' the items within a widening circle of dishonest outlets, making the task of tracing back any goods recovered all the more difficult. There was another factor: Frank and Rotto both had convictions for receiving and it would be very useful to have at least one other major receiver with a clean record who might attract less attention in the early days after the crime. Such a man was Leon Beron who, for good measure, was known to be willing to put up money to finance criminal operations.

A team had to be organized. Late in November 1910, a young Polish Jew, Adolph Mondshine,[1] walked into a restaurant in Commercial Road. He had arrived in England from Lodz only two months before, had not found work and was very hungry. He must have known something about Stinie Morrison because he went straight up to his table and said he wanted something to eat. Stinie obligingly treated him to a meal, but the gesture was not altruistic. Stinie, in his turn, knew his man, although the West End job had not yet been thought up. Two days later, Mondshine saw Stinie at the corner of Plummer's Row and Whitechapel Row, having his boots cleaned. As they left the bootblack's stand, Stinie told him, in Yiddish, about the Holloway fraud.

The two men did not meet again for a week, by which time the scheme had crystallized. To ensure privacy, Stinie took the young man to his new lodgings in Newark Street, telling him that the job would be in the West End and that he wanted help in opening the street door to the premises, mooting that Mondshine should rent residential accommodation in the building. Stinie produced the Browning revolver and, as if to test Mondshine's reaction, declared, 'If anybody comes, I'll shoot them.' Morrison would give no further detail of the scheme without a firm commitment but, in the event, Mondshine quickly developed cold feet and was shown the door.

The acquisition of the revolver and cartridges by Stinie is of considerable significance. As has been seen, firearms played no part in Beron's murder: he was bludgeoned to death, then stabbed. The gun must have been obtained for a different purpose, for use, if only as a 'frightener', in a burglary scheduled to take place so near a police station.

Leon Beron had lived in Whitechapel for sixteen years, knowing the area and its shadier characters better than Stinie, whose freedom to explore had been interrupted by lengthy spells of imprisonment. Leon would have developed a host of underworld connections useful to the success of Stinie's ambitious enterprise. It was natural that the two men should be drawn together, however inexplicable this may have seemed to some of the Warsaw's customers. But discussion about the Old Bond Street raid was not the only reason for intimacy. Leon may also have been fencing the property that Stinie had been stealing in domestic burglaries throughout December. There is also evidence[2] hinting that Stinie may have fronted for Leon in dealings with other receivers. A close working-relationship, thoroughly dishonest, grew up between the two men, whose association did not go unnoticed elsewhere in the underworld.

Late in December, Stinie called at an estate agent's office in Commercial Road and, as 'George Williams', tried to rent a small house in Key Street, Whitechapel. When the clerk asked for references, Stinie became distinctly cagey, then rather stupidly gave Rotto's address in Charlotte Street. The house may have been intended as short-term storage for property taken in the West End job. If so, using Rotto as a referee was risky indeed and Stinie seems to have thought better of the idea and did not return.[3]

The identity of the other conspirators is not easy to establish. There may have been a fair-haired Russian and clues to other personnel may lie in a strange declaration which Stinie wrote to the Home Office in 1912, shortly before his breakdown, and contrary to his usual rule of not naming names. Among those who 'could prove my innocens if they chose' was 'Rube Mickles . . . well known to the E. End police as a byer.' Reuben Michaels, as he was known to police records, not unnaturally declined to help when seen about the matter by Wensley, but he appears to have been a major fence, operating from the Three Tuns in Aldgate, often dealing with Leon Beron.[4]

Stinie's arrest on 8 January 1911 may not have put a stopper on so elaborately planned, so potentially lucrative an adventure. Three days later, the day that Lord Gort was fined £2 for speeding at 'over 28½ miles an hour', early morning cleaners, arriving to char the office block at Old Bond Street, found that three floors had been systematically ransacked in 'as daring a burglary as has been carried out successfully in London for some time'.[5] After ripping off a heavy padlock on the entrance gates, the thieves had opened an inner glass door with a skeleton key and moved in heavy safe-breaking equipment to the job. The third-floor office took the brunt when the backs of two safes, one of which weighed half a ton, were prized off. The largest jemmy ever yet seen by the Metropolitan Police was found among the debris. Other safes elsewhere in the building were forced, the entire process taking place only yards from a regular point-duty policeman. Official chagrin at this impudent break-in, so close to Vine Street Police Station, was mollified by the ironic discovery that only about £100 worth of property was missing, a ludicrously poor reward for so much effort.

By mid-January, police must have been aware of significant pointers to Stinie's involvement in a major burglary conspiracy, if not also to the West End job itself, which seems to have occupied a unique position in the 1911 calendar of crime. Yet Stinie was never taxed about the matter, never asked about his conversations with Mondshine nor interviewed about his possession of the revolver and cartridges. For the authorities, the problem was that Stinie had already been charged with Beron's murder. They were happy enough to use evidence about the gun in Stinie's trial in order to brand him as a dangerous criminal, but officialdom had nailed its colours to the mast of murder and proof that Stinie's relationship with Leon had been on an entirely different footing would plainly have put the prospect of a capital conviction in jeopardy. So matters were left where they were, even though in the end there was sufficient doubt about the case to prompt a reprieve. But the witness statements of Mondshine and others were kept under wraps and certainly not disclosed to Stinie's defending lawyers, still less to the public at large.

On the other side of the equation lay Stinie himself. He could have come clean. After all, his neck was at risk. But from the outset of proceedings, he thought he would be acquitted of murder. Abinger's histrionics buoyed him up and he was, after all, a gambling man. After the verdict, taking a calculated risk, he brought in the Holloway fraud, which was to prove an ineffective ploy. The West End job was a very different consideration, not only because it was likely to attract a longer sentence for Stinie's part in the conspiracy, but because a firearm was involved, which introduced the issue of violence and the real prospect of a second flogging.

When Jane Brodsky visited him in Wandsworth Prison, with execution still in prospect, Stinie referred to an unspecified crime which he would rather die than reveal and it may have been the probable penalty that was gnawing at his mind. He could never forget his dose of the cat, that judicial thrashing he had received sometime between 1906 and 1910, during his second 'five year stretch'. Blackwell confirmed this dread when he recalled in 1913 how Stinie had been 'terribly afraid of being flogged upon his reception at Dartmoor' two years before. This secret fear probably accompanied him throughout the remainder of his sentence, his very lifetime. Just as he thought he would escape a conviction for murder, so he hoped to be released, despite periods of intense despair. Even after the hecatomb of the Great War, he had never been wholly abandoned and would have known, though he was never allowed to see them, that Lumley and Abinger were still agitating for his freedom. Better to serve his time, to confine his outbursts to other matters, than risk the possibility of yet another lengthy sentence and, above all else, a repetition of that cruel and humiliating punishment. Thus Stinie Morrison and the authorities collaborated in a conspiracy of silence.

(2)

Who murdered Leon Beron—and why? For any solution to these macabre conundrums reference must first be made to Beron's character, so far as it can be known nearly three-quarters of a century after his death. Important clues can be found in the attitude of the police and, in particular, the reactions of Wensley. When asked about Beron during the trial, Wensley said that he had known him for four or five years, possibly longer, but he did not say in what circumstances and he evaded further probing by referring to Beron's reputation for wealth, which could be seen as rendering him a likely target for robbery. The jury, the public and, it would seem, the Home Office were misled: in the statement, referred to earlier in this chapter, written by Stinie in 1912, various allegations, which may have been true, were made about Leon's criminal activities between 1901 and 1910. Wensley's response was awkwardly phrased. 'Apart from the allegations made by Morrison that Leon Beron planned burglaries, received stolen property and knowingly associated with foreign criminals, for which I can find no substantial ground, he was certainly eccentric and miserly in his habits, but he bore the reputation of being a respectable man.' Wensley and Ward had adopted this view of Beron the 'respectable man', both in public and privately to the Home Office, from the outset of the investigation.

Apart from a few oblique references in the press, as when the *People* described Beron as a man with 'queer ethical standards' whose business 'flourished under cover of darkness',[6] the public would be given little indication of the truth about Leon until shortly after Morrison's death when the *World's Pictorial News* published a lurid series entitled 'Secret Life History of Stinie Morrison,' which hinted that Beron had criminal connections.[7] In May 1925, Sir Basil Thomson, former Assistant Head of the CID, wrote an article for the *Sunday News*, in which he noted that at the time of the investigation,

It does not appear to have occurred to anybody that the murdered man might have had an occupation which he preferred to keep to himself, and that that occupation was the receiving of stolen property.[8]

Although Thomson was not directly concerned with the case, he must have known that the police had reason to believe all along that Leon was a receiver. And in comparison with those private submissions to the Home Office, a passage from Wensley's autobiography, published in 1931, makes astonishing reading:

> I was able to give Ward [on 1 January 1911] a few points about him and his friends and associates ... He was believed to be fond of the society of women, and there was an impression that he was not unwilling, under favourable conditions, sometimes to dabble in stolen property. All of this was roughly registered on my memory, but, of course, up to then I had never had reason to test its accuracy. It was, in fact, largely gossip that had come to my ears.

The language is guarded, but it describes someone far removed from the 'respectable man' laid before the Home Office and is in marked contrast to what was publicly being said about Beron during 1911 and throughout the remaining years of Morrison's life. Moreover, if the information possessed by Wensley were as flimsily-based as suggested by his last sentence, there was no reason to include the matter in his book as a relevant factor in the course of the inquiry. All the indications point to a suppression of aspects of Beron's character which the authorities thought better not revealed while Morrison was still alive.

Beron was a fence[9] and a source of finance for crime. He was able to support his indolently promiscuous lifestyle on the proceeds of dishonesty, perhaps also gaining revenue from prostitutes living in his slum properties at Russell Court. But it was another hidden aspect of character that was ultimately to cause his doom. Leon's freedom from arrest, his apparent luck in avoiding detection, the very reticence of the police themselves, suggest that he was a very useful informer. The police have always jealously guarded their sources of information and to this day no officer can be compelled to reveal the identity of his informants in court. There is also reason to believe that from time to time the criminal activities of informants themselves may be overlooked if bigger fish can be landed. So there were complications if the truth emerged. Quite simply, it was not convenient for authority to reveal what it knew about Leon's background and so it was not revealed, at any rate, not until after Stinie's death which rendered an official re-opening of the case unlikely.

Those S-shaped mutilations were not mere random slashings. That there was a ritualistic element about the death is beyond doubt, despite the valiant efforts of police, prosecution, judge and the then Home Office personnel, all attempting to rob the case of any arcane significance. The signs which had been carved on bodies during the Polish uprising of the 1860s, markings which Dr Friedrich Ave-Lallement had described in a German forensic textbook,[10] were typical of a terrifying technique, emanating from eastern Europe and Russia, in which the patterned incisions made it plain to others that they, too, would pay with their lives if they co-operated with the authorities. The way in which Leon's body had been arranged, the mutilated face framed by a black silk handkerchief, which was not Leon's and could not be traced to Stinie, confirm an awful warning broadcast to the underworld.

Abinger has been criticized for trying to establish a link between Leon Beron and the Houndsditch gang. In terms of the defence case at the trial, it was a gross tactical blunder: Abinger was trying to make bricks without straw. Recent research,[11] however, suggests that there may have been a connection, but one quite different from Abinger's clumsy speculations. Depositions made to Australian police by a man called Ernest Dreger, his brother and a girl, Sarah Ligum, concern the involvement of a man nicknamed 'Yahnit' in both the Houndsditch and Clapham Common affairs. 'Yahnit' was said to have claimed that Beron's murder was a 'Leesma' operation, carried out not because Beron had given information, but because someone thought that he was *about* to inform the police.

And there is another possible lead to the killers of Beron. If Stinie was right, Leon's criminal career showed a cross-

Channel dimension. On 25 May 1901, a pawnbroker's shop in Bristol was broken into by East London burglars in what police described as a 'well planned robbery'. The team, which may have been seven strong, 'brock through the roof and cut open safes', Stinie's words, but three were arrested the next day and some property recovered. Harry Benjamin, alias Kruger, escaped to France 'carrying away with him a lot of veliable jewells' which he sold to Leon Beron and a man named Lazare, or Lazarus, 'who keeps a restaurant at No. 50 Rue Sidane. A turning off the Bollevard Voltare, Paris'. Wensley would not confirm Beron's involvement, but it is possible that he made return trips to France after 1894.[12] Leon's sister was still living in Paris, carrying on a drapery business, which might have provided respectable cover for dishonest activities.

Stinie also alleges that, six years before the murder, two Frenchmen tried to kill Beron and that in 1909 or 1910, he had been attacked in the street by two assailants, also French, using a motor spanner. Wensley wrote, disparagingly, 'I have been unable to obtain the slightest confirmation ... as to any attempt being made upon the life of Leon Beron, neither have I been able to obtain any information regarding the allegation that two Frenchmen had made an attack on that person at Jubilee Street.' This was another instance of Wensley being less than frank. In fact, Stinie's words were 'somewhere near or in Jubilee Street' and it is curious that Wensley did not refer to the proven attack on Beron in Watney Street, ostensibly a robbery of his watch and chain, during which he had been knocked down. Watney Street is not far from Jubilee Street. Leon's sister, Mrs Josephson, recalled the incident clearly enough in January 1911, telling reporters that it had taken place 'two or three years ago',[13] reasonably in accord with Stinie's chronology. Stinie may have derived the material for his allegations from what he had read shortly after Leon's murder, but it is extraordinary that Wensley should have ignored the Watney Street incident in his report to the Home Office.

Wensley also omitted to mention an early line of police inquiry into the Clapham Common crime. Press reports made in January[14] indicate that police were searching for 'two

Frenchmen', one of whom was about forty, acquaintances of Beron, who had been seen in his company. Police, it was said, were of opinion that Beron had made enemies in life. This early approach is significant, because it occurred before the police had completed their interviews with the Warsaw personnel and seems to have been a separate line of investigation. Indeed nothing in the statements made by the restaurant witnesses suggests that they thought of Stinie (or Pool, for that matter) as being French. Ward, as reported in the *Morning Post*,[15] probably the best-informed newspaper, was drawing a distinction at this early stage between the search for the Frenchmen and that for an unnamed man, who was clearly Stinie Morrison. When the spotlight began to shine on Stinie the other two suspects quickly disappeared from the police inquiry, a disturbing feature in view of the unsatisfactory case later presented against Morrison by the Crown. The information upon which the police were acting must have come from somewhere and, for a while at least, that trail was being taken seriously.

There was scope, then, for a whole crop of murderous intentions to have grown up about the person of Leon Beron. If there was a French connection (and conversation heard by Mrs Rider on board the Paris tram must not be overlooked), it may have involved French-speaking Russian criminals, aware of the betrayer's mark, the sign of S, and not necessarily unconnected with the Leesma organization, whose ranks included crooks as well as idealists.

Leon had not always been in Stinie's company during the three weeks of their brief acquaintanceship and must have had a wide circle of contacts beyond the Warsaw, men he met late at night in the brothels, shebeens and spielers. Stinie's West End scheme may not have been the only underworld proposition to tempt the wily receiver, but, on that New Year's morning, there was a hidden snag for Leon—a contract out on his life, the pickings of robbery forming the assassins' reward.

It would have been well known in Leon's usual haunts that he was inclined to drink too much as the night wore on, an unusual weakness in the normally sober Jewish community.[16] No difficult task, then, to persuade the inebriated Beron to journey away from Whitechapel, but why Clapham Common? Leon had never visited his father in the Home for Aged Jews nearby, but he knew about this large open space. Perhaps he went along with Solomon and David, on better terms with their father, and, if the trip had been made on a summer week-end, sat beside the bandstand, eyeing any passing girls until his brothers returned from their visit.

Well away from Whitechapel, Clapham Common offered the prospect of uninterrupted and unobserved discussion of a criminal enterprise, or, possibly, the attraction of a discreet brothel, more up-market than the East End could boast, set among the respectable villas; but it is unlikely that Leon was persuaded to travel by the opportunity of examining goods recently stolen: receivers usually prefer property to be brought to them.

Stinie, as we know, had never made any secret to criminal intimates of his six weeks' honest labour at the bakery so close to the Common and, if Leon had been kept under observation by those with murder in mind late in December, his association with Morrison (who was, it must be said, not without enemies himself) would have been plain to see, rendering Stinie an easy subject to put in a frame. The choice of Clapham Common for a rendezvous, the use of a man of similar build and appearance to Stinie as Leon's companion and the filtering of 'information' to the police could complete the process.

Whatever may be the truth about Leon Beron's mysterious death, a tangle of circumstance was to trap Stinie as surely and as finally as a fly in amber.

Notes

Introduction
1 *The Trial of Steinie Morrison*, Notable British Trials, ed. H. Fletcher Moulton (1923).

Chapter One
1 W.H. Reed, *Elgar*.
2 Noel Coward, *Present Indicative*.
3 *Evening News*, 3 January 1911.
4 *Clapham Observer*, 6 January 1911.

Chapter Two
1 *The Times*, 4 January 1911.
2 *East London Observer*, 7 January 1911.
3 *The Times*, 21 December 1910.
4 *The Times*, 19 December 1910.
5 *South-Western Star*, 6 January 1911.

Chapter Three
1 *Morning Post*, 6 January 1911.
2 *Daily Chronicle*, 7 January 1911.
3 B. Leeson, *Lost London*.
4 D. Rumbelow, *The Siege of Sidney Street*.
5 F.P. Wensley, *Detective Days*: Introduction by George Dilnot.
6 F.P. Wensley, op. cit.
7 F.P. Wensley, op. cit.
8 Solomon Beron: depositions at Inquest, 5 January 1911 and Committal, 17 January 1911: CCC papers.
9 *Daily Chronicle*, 9 January 1911.
10 *Morning Post*, 6 January 1911.

Chapter Four
1 Petition to Home Secretary, July 1909, quoted in trial.
2 *The Times*, 7 February 1906.
3 B. Thomson, *The Criminal*.
4 'Warden', *His Majesty's Guests*.
5 *World's Pictorial News*, 28 May 1921.
6 Trial: 11 March 1911.
7 *The Times*, 18 February 1911.
8 *South-Western Star*, 13 January 1911.

Chapter Five

1 The details are reconstructed from Home Office papers and Morrison's evidence at the trial; also from E. Abinger, *Forty Years at the Bar*.
2 *Morning Post*, 3 January 1911.
3 *John Bull*, 16 May 1914.
4 *Daily News*, 3 January 1911.

Chapter Seven

1 See *Sunday Express*, 5 June 1932 and R. Samuel, *East End Underworld*, for a different story of Morrison's movements that morning.
2 Home Office papers.
3 C. Bermant, *Point of Arrival*.
4 Home Office papers.
5 Sometimes given as Rapport: Home Office papers.
6 Declarations of Sidney Pitt, Jack Bouvier, William Yockney and Lawrence Rappolt, June 1912, Home Office papers.

Chapter Eight

1 Randolph S. Churchill, *Winston S. Churchill*, Vol. II.
2 Ibid.
3 *Morning Post*, 7 January 1911.
4 *East London Observer*, 14 January 1911.
5 *Morning Leader*, 12 January 1911.
6 *The Times*, 1 February 1911.
7 *Morning Post*, 5 January 1911.
8 *Daily Chronicle*, 7 January 1911.
9 *The Times*, 7 January 1911.

Chapter Nine

1 CCC papers.
2 'There was reason to suspect him, but not a scrap of evidence to connect him with the murdered man . . .': F.P. Wensley, op. cit.
3 The *Pall Mall Gazette* for the same day carried a similar story.

Chapter Ten

1 *Daily Graphic*, 9 January 1911.
2 *Daily News*, 9 January 1911.
3 *Morning Leader*, 9 January 1911.
4 *World's Pictorial News*, 5 February 1921.
5 H. Fletcher Moulton, op. cit.
6 *South-Western Star*, 13 January 1911.

Chapter Eleven

1 S. Felstead, *Sir Richard Muir*.
2 E. Lustgarten, *The Murder and the Trial*.
3 Richard du Cann, *The Art of the Advocate*.
4 S. Felstead, op. cit.
5 E. Abinger, op. cit.

Chapter Twelve

1 *South-Western Star*, 3 and 10 February 1911.
2 *South-Western Star*, 27 January 1911.
3 *Daily Chronicle*, 9 February 1911.
4 *Morning Post*, 31 January 1911.
5 Muir attended the adjourned inquest, not as prosecuting counsel, but instructed by the Treasury Solicitor, an 'interested party'.

Chapter Thirteen

1 *Morning Post*, 13 February 1911.
2 CCC Sessions paper, February/March 1911: Trial of Rappolt and others.
3 *The Times*, 28 February 1911; *Daily Chronicle*, 28 February 1911; *Daily News*, 28 February 1911.
4 *Daily News*, 4 March 1911.
5 J.P. Eddy, *Scarlet and Ermine*.

Chapter Fourteen

1 D. Rumbelow, op. cit.
2 Seymour Hicks' account of the Morrison trial, *Not Guilty, M'Lord*.
3 *The Times*, 26 October 1897.
4 Derek Walker-Smith, *The Life of Lord Darling*.
5 Ibid.
6 Randolph S. Churchill, op. cit.
7 D. Walker-Smith, op. cit.
8 CCC Court Book, 1911.
9 S. Felstead, op. cit.
10 Ibid.
11 *Evening News*, 6 March 1911.

Chapter Fifteen

1 *Daily Mail*, 7 March 1911.
2 *South-Western Star*, 6 January 1911.

Chapter Sixteen

1 I.H. Oddie, *Inquest*.
2 *Daily Graphic*, 8 March 1911.
3 Produced before Court of Criminal Appeal, 27 March 1911.
4 F.P. Wensley, op. cit.
5 J.P. Eddy, op. cit.
6 E. Abinger, op. cit.

Chapter Seventeen

1 Ibid.
2 *Daily Telegraph*, 9 March 1911.
3 *Daily News*, 2 January 1911, refers to 'certain well-defined footprints in the soft ground'.

Chapter Eighteen
1 *Daily Graphic*, 10 March 1911.

Chapter Nineteen
1 S. Hicks, op. cit.
2 Sir Chartres Biron, *Without Prejudice*.

Chapter Twenty
1 Home Office papers.
2 S. Felstead, op. cit.
3 *The Times*, 16 March 1911; *Evening News*, 16 March 1911; *Penny Illustrated Paper*, 15 April 1911.

Chapter Twenty-Two
1 E. Abinger, op. cit.
2 Home Office papers.

Chapter Twenty-Three
1 *Daily Graphic*, 16 March 1911.

Chapter Twenty-Four
1 *The Times*, 16 March, 1911.
2 *Evening News*, 16 March 1911.
3 *Pall Mall Gazette*, 16 March 1911.
4 *East London Observer*, 25 March 1911.
5 Copy in Home Office papers.
6 E. Abinger, op. cit.
7 *People*, 2 April 1911; *Reynolds*, 26 March 1911; *Lloyds Weekly News*, 19 March 1911.
8 Brian Inglis, *Roger Casement*.

Chapter Twenty-Five
1 E. Abinger, op. cit.
2 *Star*, 27 March 1911.
3 *Daily Mail*, 29 March 1911.
4 Letter to author from Mrs Betty Maisner (Becky Snelwar), 13 December 1980.
5 Sir Hall Caine writing in the *Daily Graphic*, 28 January 1921.

Chapter Twenty-Six
1 E. Abinger, op. cit.
2 *Hansard*, 4 April 1911.
3 *Evening Standard*, 13 April 1911.
4 *Morning Post*, 13 April 1911.
5 *Daily News*, 11 April 1911.
6 *Evening Standard*, 12 April 1911.
7 *Star*, 30 March 1911.
8 *Daily Mail*, 13 April 1911.

Chapter Twenty-Seven
 1 Rider & Co., publishers of occult subject matter.

Chapter Twenty-Eight
 1 *Thomson's Weekly News*, 25 July 1925.

Chapter Twenty-Nine
 1 J. Timewell, *The Prison Life of Stinie Morrison*.
 2 Ibid.
 3 See the *Daily Sketch*, 4 March 1914. She was said to be half Danish and half Irish. Her father 'was created a baron in Austria'.
 4 A lawsuit eventually took place; see, inter alia, *Daily Telegraph*, 4 and 5 March 1914.

Chapter Thirty-One
 1 *The Times*, 23 and 24 June, 12 July 1912.

Chapter Thirty-Two
 1 Earl Russell, *My Life and Adventures*, 1923, quoted in R. Samuel, *East End Underworld*.

Chapter Thirty-Three
 1 E.T. Woodhall, *Detective and Secret Service Days*.
 2 *The Times*, 26 September 1916.
 3 See the *Daily Herald*, 19 November 1916, 22 and 23 August 1919; *Daily Express*, 12 February 1919; *Evening Standard*, 12 February 1919; *Daily News*, 20 and 21 November 1919.
 4 Home Office papers.
 5 R. Samuel, op. cit.
 6 *Isle of Wight County Press*, 29 January 1921.
 7 *Evening Standard*, 26 January 1921.

Chapter Thirty-Four
 1 *Daily Herald*, 26 January 1921.
 2 *The Times*, 26 January 1921.
 3 *World's Pictorial News*, 29 January, 5, 12, 19, 26 February, 5, 12, 19 March, 28 May 1921.
 4 *Sunday News*, 31 May 1925.
 5 *Sunday News*, 12 July 1925.

Envoi
 1 Statement of Adolph Mondshine to police, 9 January 1911: Home Office papers. See also *Morning Post*, 5 January 1911. Mondshine did not give evidence in any of the legal proceedings involving Morrison.
 2 Statement of Louis Optiz to police: Home Office papers.
 3 Statement of William Read to police, 12 January 1911.
 4 R. Samuel, op. cit.
 5 *Evening Standard*, 11 January 1911.
 6 *People*, 19 March 1911.

7 *World's Pictorial News*, see Chapter Thirty-Four, note 3.
8 *Sunday News*, 31 May 1925.
9 See also R. Samuel, op. cit.
10 Dr F. Ave-Lallement published numerous books on forensic subjects between 1861 and 1888.
11 F.G. Clarke, *Will-o'-the-wisp*.
12 Though Solomon Beron denied this in his deposition at Committal proceedings, 17 January 1911: CCC papers.
13 *Daily Telegraph*, 3 January 1911.
14 See, inter alia, *Daily News*, 5 January 1911.
15 *Morning Post*, 4 January 1911.
16 *Morning Post*, 6 January 1911. Solomon Beron was reported as saying, 'I knew he [Leon] was fond of liquor.'

Select Bibliography

ABINGER, Edward, *Forty Years at the Bar* (Hutchinson, 1930)
ARTHUR, Herbert, *All the Sinners* (John Long, 1931)
BERMANT, Chaim, *Point of Arrival* (Eyre Methuen, 1975)
BIRON, Sir Chartres, *Without Prejudice* (Faber, 1936)
CLARKE, F.G., *Will-o'-the-wisp.* (Oxford University Press, 1984)
EDDY, J.P., *Scarlet and Ermine* (William Kimber, 1960)
FELSTEAD, Sidney, *Sir Richard Muir* (Bodley Head, 1927)
HOLROYD, James Edward, *The Gaslight Murders* (George Allen & Unwin, 1960)
KINGSTON, Charles, *A Gallery of Rogues* (Stanley Paul, 1924)
LEESON, Benjamin, *Lost London* (Stanley Paul, 1934)
LINKLATER, Eric, *The Corpse on Clapham Common* (Macmillan, 1971)
LOGAN, Guy, *Wilful Murder* (Eldon Press, 1935)
LUSTGARTEN, Edgar, *The Murder and the Trial* (Odhams, 1960)
MACNAGHTEN, Sir Melville, *Days of My Years* (Edward Arnold, 1914)
MOULTON, H. Fletcher, *The Trial of Steinie Morrison* Notable British Trials series (Wm Hodge, 1922)
ODDIE, H. Ingleby, *Inquest* (Hutchinson, 1941)
RUMBELOW, Donald, *The Siege of Sidney Street* (St Martin's Press, 1973)
SAMUEL, Raphael, *East End Underworld* (Routledge, 1981)
STEPHENS, C.L. McCluer, *Famous Crimes and Criminals* (Stanley Paul, 1924)
SYMONS Julian, *A Reasonable Doubt* (Cresset Press, 1960)
THOMSON, Sir Basil, *The Criminal* (Hodder & Stoughton, 1925)
TIMEWELL, James, *Is Stinie Morrison Innocent?* (James Timewell, 1914)
TIMEWELL, James, *The Prison Life of Stinie Morrison* (James Timewell, 1914)
WALKER-SMITH, Derek, *The Life of Lord Darling* (Cassell, 1936)
'WARDEN', *His Majesty's Guests* (Jarrolds, 1929)
WENSLEY, Frederick Porter, *Detective Days* (Cassell, 1931)
WOODHALL, Edwin T., *Detective and Secret Service Days* (Jarrolds, 1929)

Documentary Sources

1   Home Office files 1905–1948. HO 45/22261–22263/127263;PRI COM.8/
    101/17035 (including full shorthand transcripts of the trial and appeal).
    Closed to general public access until 1990.
2   Central Criminal Court records: see Public Record Office CRIM 1/119
    a) Depositions of committal proceedings and inquest
    b) Some original and copy exhibits
    c) Central Criminal Court Book 1911
    d) Calendar of Prisoners 1911
    e) Central Criminal Court Sessions Papers 1911
3   Letter to author from Mrs Betty Maisner (Becky Snelwar) 13 December
    1980

Newspapers and Periodicals

The Times
Morning Post
Daily Chronicle
Daily Graphic
Daily Mail
Daily Mail (Continental Edition)
Daily Mirror
Daily News
Daily Telegraph
Morning Leader
Pall Mall Gazette
Evening News
Evening Standard
The Star
East London Observer
South-Western Star

Clapham Observer
Isle of Wight County Press
News of the World
Lloyds Weekly News
Reynolds News
John Bull
Penny Illustrated Paper ('P.I.P.')
Weekly Times

1921 and after

Daily Herald
Sunday Express
Sunday News
World's Pictorial News

Acknowledgments

The extract from a letter written on behalf of His late Majesty King George V is here reproduced by the gracious permission of Her Majesty the Queen and was originally published in *Winston S. Churchill*, Volume II, by Randolph S. Churchill (Heinemann 1967).

Acknowledgment is also due to Oxford University Press for permission to use material from *Will-o'-the-Wisp* by F. G. Clarke (1984). I have been unable to trace holders of copyright in *Detective Days* by Frederick Porter Wensley (Cassell 1931) and in two pamphlets, *Is Stinie Morrison Innocent?* and *The Prison Life of Stinie Morrison*, both published by James Timewell in 1914. These and other sources are acknowledged elsewhere in this work.

The author has been allowed to examine Home Office papers held at the Public Record Office. The Home Office cannot however be held responsible for the accuracy of any part of the book.

My particular thanks are due to the following: the Right Honourable Leon Brittan QC MP, Home Secretary, who kindly gave me permission, when he was Minister of State at the Home Office, to examine the Home Office files on Stinie Morrison; the Departmental Record Officer, Home Office, and his ever-helpful staff; the Courts Administrator, Central Criminal Court; the Librarian, Museum of London; Mrs Betty Maisner (Becky Snelwar) for her written recollections and Mr M. Goldbart and Mr R. Dent for their personal memories of the period; Richard du Cann QC and other members of chambers offered useful advice; Donald Rumbelow spoke to me at length, especially on aspects of the Sidney Street siege; Dr Frank Clarke of Macquarrie University, New South Wales, Australia wrote to me about matters later published in his book; Richard Whittington-Egan was a mine of information and a great encouragement; and, not least, James Todd, without whose professional expertise and long-suffering attention this book could not have been written.

Thanks are also due to the following holders of copyright photographic material: the British Library, plates 5–11; the Public Records Office, plates 4 and 12. Plates 2 and 3 appeared in H. Fletcher Moulton: *The Trial of Steinie Morrison* (1922).

Index

217

FOR THE BEST IN PAPERBACKS, LOOK FOR THE

In every corner of the world, on every subject under the sun, Penguin represents quality and variety – the very best in publishing today.

For complete information about books available from Penguin – including Pelicans, Puffins, Peregrines and Penguin Classics – and how to order them, write to us at the appropriate address below. Please note that for copyright reasons the selection of books varies from country to country.

In the United Kingdom: Please write to *Dept E.P., Penguin Books Ltd, Harmondsworth, Middlesex, UB7 0DA*

In the United States: Please write to *Dept BA, Penguin, 299 Murray Hill Parkway, East Rutherford, New Jersey 07073*

In Canada: Please write to *Penguin Books Canada Ltd, 2801 John Street, Markham, Ontario L3R 1B4*

In Australia: Please write to the *Marketing Department, Penguin Books Australia Ltd, P.O. Box 257, Ringwood, Victoria 3134*

In New Zealand: Please write to the *Marketing Department, Penguin Books (NZ) Ltd, Private Bag, Takapuna, Auckland 9*

In India: Please write to *Penguin Overseas Ltd, 706 Eros Apartments, 56 Nehru Place, New Delhi, 110019*

In Holland: Please write to *Penguin Books Nederland B.V., Postbus 195, NL–1380AD Weesp, Netherlands*

In Germany: Please write to *Penguin Books Ltd, Friedrichstrasse 10–12, D–6000 Frankfurt Main 1, Federal Republic of Germany*

In Spain: Please write to *Longman Penguin España, Calle San Nicolas 15, E–28013 Madrid, Spain*

In France: Please write to *Penguin Books Ltd, 39 Rue de Montmorency, F-75003, Paris, France*

In Japan: Please write to *Longman Penguin Japan Co Ltd, Yamaguchi Building, 2–12–9 Kanda Jimbocho, Chiyoda-Ku, Tokyo 101, Japan*

PENGUIN TRUE CRIME

Titles published and forthcoming:

Who Killed Hanratty?   Paul Foot

An investigation into the notorious A6 murder.

Norman Birkett   H. Montgomery Hyde

The biography of one of Britain's most humane and respected judges.

The Complete Jack the Ripper   Donald Rumbelow

An investigation into the identity of the most elusive murderer of all time

The Riddle of Birdhurst Rise   R. Whittington-Egan

The Croydon Poisoning Mystery of 1928–9.

Suddenly at the Priory   John Williams

Who poisoned the Victorian barrister Charles Bravo?

Stinie: Murder on the Common   Andrew Rose

The truth behind the Clapham Common murder.

The Poisoned Life of Mrs Maybrick   Bernard Ryan

Mr Maybrick died of arsenic poisoning – how?

The Gatton Mystery   J. and D. Gibney

The great unsolved Australian triple murder.

Earth to Earth   John Cornwell

Who killed the Luxtons in their remote mid-Devon farmhouse?

The Ordeal of Philip Yale Drew   R. Whittington-Egan

A real life murder melodrama in three acts.

FOR THE BEST IN PAPERBACKS, LOOK FOR THE

CRIME AND MYSTERY IN PENGUINS

Call for the Dead   John Le Carré

The classic work of espionage which introduced the world to George Smiley. 'Brilliant . . . highly intelligent, realistic. Constant suspense. Excellent writing' – *Observer*

Swag   Elmore Leonard

From the bestselling author of *Stick* and *La Brava* comes this wallbanger of a book in which 100,000 dollars' worth of nicely spendable swag sets off a slick, fast-moving chain of events. 'Brilliant' – *The New York Times*

Beast in View   Margaret Millar

'On one level, *Beast in View* is a dazzling conjuring trick. On another it offers a glimpse of bright-eyed madness as disquieting as a shriek in the night. In the whole of Crime Fiction's distinguished sisterhood there is no one quite like Margaret Millar' – *Guardian*

The Julian Symons Omnibus

The Man Who Killed Himself, The Man Whose Dreams Came True, The Man Who Lost His Wife: three novels of cynical humour and cliff-hanging suspense from a master of his craft. 'Exciting and compulsively readable' – *Observer*

Love in Amsterdam   Nicolas Freeling

Inspector Van der Valk's first case involves him in an elaborate cat-and-mouse game with a very wily suspect. 'Has the sinister, spellbinding perfection of a cobra uncoiling. It is a masterpiece of the genre' – Stanley Ellis

Maigret's Pipe   Georges Simenon

Eighteen intriguing cases of mystery and murder to which the pipe-smoking Maigret applies his wit and intuition, his genius for detection and a certain *je ne sais quoi* . . .

FOR THE BEST IN PAPERBACKS, LOOK FOR THE

PENGUIN CLASSIC CRIME

The Big Knockover and Other Stories   Dashiell Hammett

With these sharp, spare, laconic stories, Hammett invented a new folk hero – the private eye. 'Dashiell Hammett gave murder back to the kind of people that commit it for reasons, not just to provide a corpse; and with the means at hand, not with handwrought duelling pistols, curare, and tropical fish' – Raymond Chandler

Death of a Ghost   Margery Allingham

A picture painted by a dead artist leads to murder . . . and Albert Campion has to face his dearest enemy. With the skill we have come to expect from one of the great crime writers of all time, Margery Allingham weaves an enthralling web of murder, intrigue and suspense.

Fen Country   Edmund Crispin

Dandelions and hearing aids, a bloodstained cat, a Leonardo drawing, a corpse with an alibi, a truly poisonous letter . . . these are just some of the unusual clues that Oxford don/detective Gervase Fen is confronted with in this sparkling collection of short mystery stories by one of the great masters of detective fiction. 'The mystery fan's ideal bedside book' – *Kirkus Reviews*

The Wisdom of Father Brown   G. K. Chesterton

Twelve delightful stories featuring the world's most beloved amateur sleuth. Here Father Brown's adventures take him from London to Cornwall, from Italy to France. He becomes involved with bandits, treason, murder, curses, and an American crime-detection machine.

Five Roundabouts to Heaven   John Bingham

At the heart of this novel is a conflict of human relationships ending in death. Centred around crime, the book is remarkable for its humanity, irony and insight into the motives and weaknesses of men and women, as well as for a tensely exciting plot with a surprise ending. One of the characters, considering reasons for killing, wonders whether the steps of his argument are *Five Roundabouts to Heaven*. Or do they lead to Hell? . . .'

PENGUIN CLASSIC CRIME

Ride the Pink Horse   Dorothy B. Hughes

The tense, taut story of fear and revenge south of the border. It's fiesta time in Mexico but Sailor has his mind on other things – like revenge. Among the gaudy crowd, the twanging guitars and the tawdry carnival lights are three desperate men fighting over a dark and bloody secret.

The Narrowing Circle   Julian Symons

The editor's job at Gross Enterprises' new crime magazine is 'in the bag' for Dave Nelson. Or so he thinks, until the surprising appointment of Willie Strayte. When Strayte is found dead Nelson must struggle to prove his innocence and solve the elaborate puzzle. 'One of our most ingenious and stylish home-grown crime novelists' – *Spectator*

Maigret at the Crossroads   Georges Simenon

Someone has shot Goldberg at the Three Widows Crossroads and Maigret is carrying out a thorough investigation, getting to know the lives of the small community at Three Widows. Although he is suspicious of everyone, he has a hunch about the murder – and that means the case is as good as wrapped up.

The Mind Readers   Margery Allingham

When rumours of a mind-reading device first came out of Godley's research station, Albert Campion found it difficult to take them seriously. Especially as the secret seemed to rest exclusively with two small boys, who were irritatingly stubborn about disclosing their sources . . .

The Daughter of Time   Josephine Tey

Josephine Tey's brilliant reconstruction of the life of Richard III, now known to us as a monster and murderer, is one of the most original pieces of historical fiction ever written, casting new light on one of history's most enduring myths.

A CHOICE OF PENGUIN FICTION

The Dearest and the Best Leslie Thomas

In the spring of 1940 the spectre of war turned into grim reality – and for all the inhabitants of the historic villages of the New Forest it was the beginning of the most bizarre, funny and tragic episode of their lives. 'Excellent' – *Sunday Times*

Only Children Alison Lurie

When the Hubbards and the Zimmerns go to visit Anna on her idyllic farm, it becomes increasingly difficult to tell which are the adults, and which the children. 'It demands to be read' – *Financial Times* 'There quite simply is no better living writer' – John Braine

My Family and Other Animals Gerald Durrell

Gerald Durrell's wonderfully comic account of his childhood years on Corfu and his development as a naturalist and zoologist is a true delight. Soaked in Greek sunshine, it is a 'bewitching book' – *Sunday Times*

Getting it Right Elizabeth Jane Howard

A hairdresser in the West End, Gavin is sensitive, shy, into the arts, prone to spots and, at thirty-one, a virgin. He's a classic late developer – and maybe it's getting too late to develop at all? 'Crammed with incidental pleasures . . . sometimes sad but more frequently hilarious . . . *Getting it Right* gets it, comically, right' – Paul Bailey in the *London Standard*

The Vivisector Patrick White

In this prodigious novel about the life and death of a great painter, Patrick White, winner of the Nobel Prize for Literature, illuminates creative experience with unique truthfulness. 'One of the most interesting and absorbing novelists writing English today' – Angus Wilson in the *Observer*

The Echoing Grove Rosamund Lehmann

'No English writer has told of the pains of women in love more truly or more movingly than Rosamund Lehmann' – Marghanita Laski. 'She uses words with the enjoyment and mastery with which Renoir used paint' – Rebecca West in the *Sunday Times* 'A magnificent achievement' – John Connell in the *Evening News*

A CHOICE OF PENGUIN FICTION

A Fanatic Heart   Edna O'Brien

'A selection of twenty-nine stories (including four new ones) full of wit and feeling and savagery that prove that Edna O'Brien is one of the subtlest and most lavishly gifted writers we have' – A. Alvarez in the *Observer*

Charade   John Mortimer

'Wonderful comedy . . . an almost Firbankian melancholy . . . John Mortimer's hero is helplessly English' – *Punch*. 'What is *Charade*? Comedy? Tragedy? Mystery? It is all three and more' – *Daily Express*

Casualties   Lynne Reid Banks

'The plot grips; the prose is fast-moving and elegant; above all, the characters are wincingly, winningly human . . . if literary prizes were awarded for craftsmanship and emotional directness, *Casualties* would head the field' – *Daily Telegraph*

The Anatomy Lesson   Philip Roth

The hilarious story of Nathan Zuckerman, the famous forty-year-old writer who decides to give it all up and become a doctor – and a pornographer – instead. 'The finest, boldest and funniest piece of fiction that Philip Roth has yet produced' – *Spectator*

Gabriel's Lament   Paul Bailey

Shortlisted for the 1986 Booker Prize
'The best novel yet by one of the most careful fiction craftsmen of his generation' – *Guardian*. 'A magnificent novel, moving, eccentric and unforgettable. He has a rare feeling for language and an understanding of character which few can rival' – *Daily Telegraph*

Small Changes   Marge Piercy

In the Sixties the world seemed to be making big changes – but for many women it was the small changes that were the hardest and the most profound. *Small Changes* is Marge Piercy's explosive new novel about women fighting to make their way in a man's world.

Is That It? Bob Geldof with Paul Vallely

The autobiography of one of today's most controversial figures. 'He has become a folk hero whom politicians cannot afford to ignore. And he has shown that simple moral outrage can be a force for good' – *Daily Telegraph*. 'It's terrific . . . everyone over thirteen should read it' – *Standard*

Niccolò Rising Dorothy Dunnett

The first of a new series of historical novels by the author of the world-famous *Lymond* series. Adventure, high romance and the dangerous glitter of fifteenth-century Europe abound in this magnificent story of the House of Charetty and the disarming, mysterious genius who exploits all its members.

The World, the Flesh and the Devil Reay Tannahill

'A bewitching blend of history and passion. A MUST' – *Daily Mail*. A superb novel in a great tradition. 'Excellent' – *The Times*

Perfume: The Story of a Murderer Patrick Süskind

It was after his first murder that Grenouille knew he was a genius. He was to become the greatest perfumer of all time, for he possessed the power to distil the very essence of love itself. 'Witty, stylish and ferociously absorbing . . . menace conveyed with all the power of the writer's elegant unease' – *Observer*

The Old Devils Kingsley Amis

Winner of the 1986 Booker Prize
'Vintage Kingsley Amis, 50 per cent pure alcohol with splashes of sad savagery' – *The Times*. The highly comic novel about Alun Weaver and his wife's return to their Celtic roots. 'Crackling with marvellous Taff comedy . . . this is probably Mr Amis's best book since *Lucky Jim*' – *Guardian*

FOR THE BEST IN PAPERBACKS, LOOK FOR THE

PENGUIN BESTSELLERS

Goodbye Soldier   Spike Milligan

The final volume of his war memoirs in which we find Spike in Italy, in civvies and in love with a beautiful ballerina. 'Desperately funny, vivid, vulgar' – *Sunday Times*

A Dark-Adapted Eye   Barbara Vine

Writing as Barbara Vine, Ruth Rendell has created a labyrinthine journey into the heart of the Hillyard family, living in the respectable middle-class countryside after the Second World War. 'Barbara Vine has the kind of near-Victorian narrative drive that compels a reader to go on turning the pages' – Julian Symons in the *Sunday Times*

Rainbow Drive   Roderick Thorp

If Mike Gallagher (acting head of the Homicide Squad, Los Angeles Police Department) hadn't been enjoying himself in the bed of a married German movie producer, he wouldn't have heard the footsteps and seen the Police Department helicopter . . . 'Quite exceptional . . . powerful, gripping and impressive' – *Time Out*

Memoirs of an Invisible Man   H. F. Saint

'Part thriller, part comedy, part science fiction . . . a compelling, often frightening novel. H. F. Saint makes the bizarre condition of his hero believable' – *Listener*

Pale Kings and Princes   Robert B. Parker

Eric Valdez, a reporter on the *Central Argus* has been killed in Wheaton. His chief, Kingsley, suspects he was involved in the local pastime – cocaine smuggling. But, knowing Valdez's penchant for the ladies, it could be sexual jealousy. Spenser is about to find out. 'The thinking man's private eye' – *The Times*

Pearls   Celia Brayfield

The Bourton sisters were beautiful. They were rich. They were famous. They were powerful. Then one morning they wake up to find a priceless pearl hidden under their pillows. Why? . . . 'Readers will devour it' – *Independent*

BIOGRAPHY AND AUTOBIOGRAPHY IN PENGUIN

Jackdaw Cake   Norman Lewis

From Carmarthen to Cuba, from Enfield to Algeria, Norman Lewis brilliantly recounts his transformation from stammering schoolboy to the man Auberon Waugh called 'the greatest travel writer alive, if not the greatest since Marco Polo'.

Catherine   Maureen Dunbar

Catherine is the tragic story of a young woman who died of anorexia nervosa. Told by her mother, it includes extracts from Catherine's diary and conveys both the physical and psychological traumas suffered by anorexics.

Isak Dinesen, the Life of Karen Blixen   Judith Thurman

Myth-spinner and storyteller famous far beyond her native Denmark, Karen Blixen lived much of the Gothic strangeness of her tales. This remarkable biography paints Karen Blixen in all her sybiline beauty and magnetism, conveying the delight and terror she inspired, and the pain she suffered.

The Silent Twins   Marjorie Wallace

June and Jennifer Gibbons are twenty-three year old identical twins, who from childhood have been locked together in a strange secret bondage which made them reject the outside world. *The Silent Twins* is a real-life psychological thriller about the most fundamental question – what makes a separate, individual human being?

Backcloth   Dirk Bogarde

The final volume of Dirk Bogarde's autobiography is not about his acting years but about Dirk Bogarde the man and the people and events that have shaped his life and character. All are remembered with affection, nostalgia and characteristic perception and eloquence.